The Complete Book of

WOMEN'S WISDOM

Other books by the author:
Aura Reading
Complete Guide to Divination
Complete Guide to Fairies and Magical Beings
Complete Guide to Magic and Ritual
Encyclopedia of Magic and Ancient Wisdom
Magical Guide to Love and Sex
Piatkus Guide to Pendulum Dowsing
Piatkus Guide to Psychic Awareness
Piatkus Guide to Tarot

CASSANDRA EASON

The Complete Book of

WOMEN'S WISDOM

PIATKUS

Copyright © 2001 by Cassandra Eason

First published in 2001 by
Judy Piatkus (Publishers) Limited
5 Windmill Street
London W1T 2JA
e-mail: info@piatkus.co.uk

The moral right of the author has been asserted

A catalogue record for this book is available from the British Library

ISBN 0 7499 2209 5

Text design by Paul Saunders
Edited by Krystyna Mayer
Illustrations by Sarah Young and Rodney Paull

This book has been printed on paper manufactured with respect for the environment
using wood from managed sustainable resources

Typeset by Phoenix Photosetting, Chatham, Kent
Printed and bound in Great Britain by
Mackays of Chatham, Chatham, Kent

CONTENTS

CONTENTS

INTRODUCTION

❧

'I AM THE LAST of the roots and soon they will plant me.' So said an old lady I met in a coastal church in Brittany as we both lit candles before the shrine of the Madonna. I am not a Catholic or particularly religious in the conventional sense, but the Virgin Mary surrounded by candlelight in the early evening gloom as mist came in from the sea, awoke in me a desire for connection with an all-wise, all-embracing Divine Feminine power. For at the age of fifty-two I had more questions than answers, and although I am a mother and a wife, an author and a broadcaster, I felt that I had lost connection with my own roots in the very different world of industrialised Birmingham. The excited child that I had once been, who could float downstairs at will and know what was going to happen minutes or even hours before an event occurred, who saw fairies in the scrubby bushes of the backyard and angels perched on top of the factory chimney, had become buried beneath work, bills and family worries. Time, too, was passing so swiftly that my eldest daughter Jade, who it seems only yesterday was digging sandcastles on sunlit Breton beaches on holidays that lasted forever, now owned her own home. My own mother had died more than thirty years ago.

Around Mary's altar were bunches of flowers, some with scribbled notes of thanks for blessings received; others were entreaties from women who were ill or were praying for a baby of their own. Incense mingled with the fragrance of the roses and Madonna lilies, and I thought of the austere church on top of the windy hill that I had visited earlier in the day, with its stone floors and unadorned niches, built on the site where once Druidessses had their healing grove. Now the Divine Feminine was consigned to a dark corner; there was only cold stone to kneel upon before the broken statue of the Virgin in this church, the spire of which pointed to the empty skies. For this stark place of worship was the realm of the Sky Gods in their remote heavens, a place intended, declared the guide book, to inspire awe and dread. It was not a place that welcomed women except as penitent sinners.

But my homely Madonna, bathed in light, held open her arms. She could easily have been the Egyptian Mother Goddess Isis, for the statue was covered in stars to indicate that she was Stella Maris, Star of the Sea, the name also given to Isis in seagoing communities.

The old lady, Marie, a devout Catholic, was lighting her candle for much the same reason that I was, to stretch across the millennia to someone who

would hold and reassure her, who would not offer promises of a heaven hereafter for obeying all the rules, but who gave comfort now, as mother to mother, or mother to daughter. For this Mary was also the haggard Mater Dolorosa, Mother of Sorrows, whose statues I had seen in other shrines, lovingly cradling her adult son as though he were an infant.

Marie had been coming to the church all her life. She had buried her husband in the churchyard, the silent fisherman who had been away for much of the year for much of their life together. Her only daughter lived in Paris; her grandchildren were strangers. The legends of old Brittany were being forgotten as people whose families had lived for generations in the same house and in the same town were moving away. The land of the Mother, as she called it, was dying.

Marie held my hand although we were strangers and the female energy of Mother Mary moved through us and in us. I was aware that we were joined with all women in all places and times: those who worshipped the Earth Mother within inner caves illuminated by tiny tallow torches; the dancing Lady of the Sun; the Mistress of the Moon; the Wild Huntress; the Sea Woman who might bring fertility or death; the Bone Goddess who stripped bare illusion and reformed life anew; and the Maiden, who as the first snows melted, lay with the king as representative of the Goddess in order to renew the sacred bargain with the land and to make the crops grow. All these were part of the starry Madonna, or Isis, a goddess said to have ten thousand names, and each one represented an aspect or strength of the Great Goddess herself. They were a part of me too, and a part of the old lady who was going home alone with her memories.

What the Book is About

This book is about the connection with female power that women, and in earlier times men, have called the Goddess. She is manifest in your grandmother, mother and daughter, in the lonely old lady across the sea, in powerful executive women, in those who stay at home with children or elderly relatives or who choose to write or paint or grow beautiful sunflowers rather than to pursue financial gain, in women who share deep love with a partner and in those who mourn one they have lost, in women who suffer mental and physical abuse or betrayal by individuals or political systems, and in those who choose to go home at night alone and shut the doors on their sanctuaries.

Women have always laughed with their mothers, sisters, daughters, grandmothers and best friends, with total strangers on a bus or train, in a hospital waiting room or at a protest meeting to save trees or to stop a children's playground from being vandalised. They have cried too, tears that course down the centuries in roaring torrents of pain and grief. Linked in understanding, sympathy and friendship, women share feelings that originate deep in the heart's cavern, warm, joyous, joyful feelings, but agonising too, since shared pain is not halved, but doubled and tripled as it is relived in the telling. For that is the nature of true caring whether it is manifested in goddess, priestess or woman in the everyday world.

Over the millennia, around the dying embers of firesides when the work was done and the men slept, and now on emails written in those restless hours between midnight and dawn, women tell jokes, spill secrets, and spit out resentments that they cannot express to those who hurt them and yet who they love. Above all, women share their dreams, and when these are broken, they laugh and cry and then laugh a bit more, then settle down to the painstaking task of picking out the shattered shards of glass from the cuts to the soul and putting the dreams together again in a totally original, if sometimes rather lop-sided pattern.

This book is about that female wisdom, its mythological roots, its healing powers, and its connection with the earth beneath our feet and the sky above our heads. It is not about the remote, closed heavens for which you need a clean spiritual bill of absolution, signed by a priest, to enter. Rather, it is about the light of the sun goddesses who put on their best summer dresses and brushed their golden hair to come to Earth to make sure that the crops were growing and to guide lost travellers to their homes. It is about the kindly crone goddesses who cared for animals in the winter and broke the ice so that they might drink, rewarding richly those by whose fires they sheltered on cold nights in the Scottish Highlands or the wild Welsh mountains, and it is about the creator goddess of the Australian Aboriginals who, like a celestial market gardener, planted food and medicinal herbs with her digging stick.

The book also touches on the millennia of myths and rituals that mark the passage of the seasons and the years, the dances around the ancient stone circles, the screams of women burned alive or hanged – almost a quarter of a million of them between the fifteenth and seventeenth centuries – because they were midwives dedicated to relieving pain or wise women herbalists and seers to whom time was not a line stretching away, unknowable and

unalterable, but a cycle that could be interpreted though divination and intuitive awareness.

The book begins beyond magic or mythology in the conventional sense. It explores the meanings behind women's myths and some of those ten thousand goddess names. It examines female spirituality in different ages and cultures, from the female mystics of mediaeval times who, when women were powerless, challenged corrupt popes and kings because of the certainty of their visions, to the women of the Vikings who wove magical spells of power and protection into their loved one's clothes with their crystal spindles. The stories and the meanings of the entwined lives of these goddesses, priestesses and ordinary women form an important part of the book, as do the many rituals, chants, exercises and divinatory methods that I have suggested. These are ways of unfolding your spiritual nature, of pushing back the limitations of linear time and space, and of connecting with the natural cycles of the moon and the seasons. Above all, however, they are ways of transforming the negative messages of many centuries of patriarchal reworking of myth to reclaim the well of power locked in the demonisation and downgrading of the women who refused to comply with a world view that was not their own.

This book, then, is written for every woman, young and old, who hears the call of the birds, the rush of the wind or the sound of the sea and instinctively kicks off her shoes to dance in spirals and cry out with joy.

I know only too well that spiritual development may have to be fitted into precious moments borrowed from the demands of the world; so the book is structured in such a way that it can be referred to in a spare five minutes as well as for more concentrated work. You may wish to read straight through the book or there may be areas with which you feel a resonance that you prefer to study first. For a woman already far on her spiritual path, the book may suggest interconnections and perhaps alternative perspectives on earlier work that can be adapted or discarded.

Methods of Exploration

You may find it helpful to keep a journal recording the connections you make between different areas of study. When you have read more of the book, you can go back and adapt the early rituals in the light of your increasing knowledge. I have suggested books that will provide additional

information, and organisations that can help you develop areas that may be of special interest to you.

The World Wide Web has many images of goddesses that may be downloaded and can help to evoke your own imagery of specific qualities; these may reinforce or bring to the fore facets of your personality and aspects of your life. You may decide to dedicate an area of your home or part of a room as a special place where you can keep your candles, crystals, statues, oils, herbs and incense; where you can read, carry out rituals or sit quietly by candle light or moon light and connect with the still centre of your being. As you work in this place, it will accumulate positive power and can recharge or calm you if life becomes overwhelming or if you want to reconnect with the goddess woman within.

PART ONE

WOMEN
AND
CREATION
MYTHS

∾

*Tapping the generative
goddess energies*

THIS PART OF THE book looks at the most ancient and central goddess forms in mythology that are at the core of modern spirituality.

Encountering the Goddesses

Imagine going into a great exhibition hall and finding around the walls prototypes of the myriad nature of goddess forms, expressed in masks, garments, weapons and sacred animals that symbolise powers which filter through into the personalities of ordinary women. Each archetypal form or template has myths attached to it, labels that illustrate how these inanimate forms were infused with life and light and went into the world as the Wise Mother, the Guardian and Keeper of Mysteries and the Avenging Warrior Woman who nurtures the weak, but is ruthless towards those who hurt her loved ones or who usurp her right to freedom and respect. You will notice the male visitors scurrying away like chastened schoolboys or weaving fantasies about how they would teach her a thing or two.

Move out now into the city. Within a single, modern metropolis, the descendants of Ancient Egyptians, African nations, Native North Americans, Hebrews, Eastern Europeans, Celts, Mediterranean peoples, Scandinavians, Hindus, and those of countless other nations meet daily on buses and in apartment blocks, workplaces, gymnasiums and delicatessens. They carry within them miniature blueprints of the templates we saw in the hall. Some of these may be developed at different stages of life, and through marriage and the migration of ancestors, many women draw on several traditions in their genetic heritage.

Themes Behind the Myths

Running even deeper than the individual's ancestral inheritance is the universal cultural heritage that cuts across history and geographical boundaries, where the Goddess name is secondary to the function. The goddesses and spirits of the sacred wells and rivers, for example, are

found in every culture and serve the same purpose: to guard the entrance to the womb of the Great Mother from whom all sacred waters flow. The seasonal goddesses likewise mirror the deep inner tides of women throughout the world and in different ages, who at this deepest level feel the stirring of sexuality and the desire for new beginnings in the spring.

But let us return to the archetypes that make us shiver and prompt men to reach for their Viagra or security blankets. It is hard to take on the waiting mantle of demoness every time we challenge the status quo. Nowhere is this more true than with the serpent goddesses, leaving aside the apparent usurpation of the phallic symbol. The Greek Medusa with her serpent tresses could turn a man to stone with a single shrewish glance.

But peel back the labels on these exhibits to read the fading, more female-friendly labels. For Medusa was once the lovely Libyan Triple Serpent Goddess of Wisdom, whose ability to look into the human soul made men turn away. What did she do to lose her immortality, and beauty and wisdom? She had sex with Poseidon, the Sea God, who (of course) was entirely blameless and unblamed.

Even gentle old Mother Earth Gaia, who seems to bear without complaint the pollution and squandering of her resources and offers healing from her herbs and other plants to all who ask, initiated the castration of her husband Uranus because he imprisoned her children within her womb so that they might not usurp his powers. Over the millennia, she has raised winds, created floods, whipped up storms, and manifested her power as an erupting volcano; in recent years, she may have been creating crop circles in fields of grain as a means of spelling out a warning to her careless children that her patience is not infinite or her larder bottomless.

Women's magical and spiritual powers are hidden in symbolism in stories and images, and need to be unravelled, interpreted and worked with, initially in the exercises I suggest in this section.

The more connections you make, the more the jigsaw will take shape. You can draw on the strengths of your inner magic in the supermarket, on the train or in the office as easily as in some dimly lit ancient temple. Our lives today are the mythology of tomorrow.

GAIA AND THE CREATOR GODDESSES

ᕂ

SINCE PALAEOLITHIC TIMES, humankind has revered the Earth and regarded her as the Mother and Creatrix, the source of life, womb and tomb, who receives her children in death and restores them to life again in an unending cycle. The *Venus of Willendorf*, the earliest fertility figurine, dates from around 24,000–22,000 BC (see Fertility Symbols, page 269).

Through the ages, people have also called the moon their mother, bringer of fertility and controller of the tides and plant growth. Sometimes the roles of Earth and Moon Mother were combined. The Sun Mother too, is bringer of life, light and warmth to crops, animals and humans, and in Slavonic lands she is said to come down from the sky in her best summer dress to check that the corn is growing.

Many indigenous peoples who can trace an unbroken path to earlier patterns of living have kept their myths of female creators who used earth, mud, corn, and clay to fashion people, animals and plants. In Mayan myth, for example, Xmucani, the grandmother creator, is still said to grind the yellow and white maize to make the flesh and strength of humans, and to form the arms and legs of people from maize dough.

We can learn something about the early creating earth mothers of Europe by looking at the myths of the older surviving cultures.

Australian Aboriginal Creation

In Australian Aboriginal culture, the Mother Creator was sometimes depicted as the Rainbow Snake (see Serpent Goddesses, page 31). Australian Aboriginal Creation, known as the Dreamtime, or Alecheringa, is not within linear time, but is ever-present, a dimension and state of consciousness that can still be reached by both ordinary people and shamans in dreams and through sacred song and the retelling of the myths. Central to Aboriginal spirituality is the interconnectedness of all life, so that if a tree is cut down, both the man or woman who cut it down and the Creator share its pain. The Land is regarded as a living entity. Uluru (Ayers Rock), the vast mass of red rock in the Northern Territory that is the largest monolith in the

Minoan painted terracotta 'snake goddess' or 'snake priestess'.

ABOVE: Syrian mosaic showing Gaia, Earth Mother, in the centre. On the left is Xanthikos, the personification of the month of April and on the right is a hunter holding a hare.

BELOW: Detail of a Roman floor mosaic with the head of Medusa shown in the centre. The mosaic was found in the frigidarium of the thermal spring at Dar Smala in Tunisia.

Egyptian painting on wood of Nut, goddess of the sky.

Two Amazons in combat with a Greek soldier.

Gold figurine of one of the 'Virgins of the Sun' or Mamaconas who
were the concubines of the Inca emperors.

world, is called the navel of the Earth, the place where the Fertility Mothers first gave birth.

Fertility Mothers

Giving birth to life is not easy. In Australian Aboriginal myth, the Rainbow Serpent, Mother of All, who existed in the Dreamtime before any other form of life, sacrificed herself to bring forth life. She asked the Kingfishers, one of the first tribes to come forth, to shoot an arrow at her head to allow the rest of creation to be freed. The Rainbow Serpent is still actively present in her creation; for as her rainbow scales flew into the air to become the colourful Lorikeet tribe, the reflection of the colours became the rainbow in the sky, which acts as a continuing reminder that all life has a common source.

In a similar myth, another form of the Australian Aboriginal Creating Mother is Eingana, whose sacred animal is the kangaroo, and who is also described as a snake. Eingana's children grew inside her, but though she swelled, she had no means of giving birth to them until the God Barraiya pitied her pain and threw a spear at her, enabling life to pour forth. She survived the birth and still exists in the Dreamtime, continuing to give birth to new species. Eingana also brings death to her children: she holds a sinew of life that is joined to each creature and person; when she lets this fall they die. If she herself died, all existence would come to an end.

Another myth tells how the creator woman Warramurrungundjui emerged from the sea and gave birth to the first people; she is an amazingly practical creator, for she carried a digging stick and a bag of food plants, medicinal plants and flowers. Having planted them, she went on to dig the essential water-holes and then, leaving her children to enjoy the fruits of her work, she turned herself into a rock. Her energy is active in all Australian Aboriginal women – when the Aboriginals were able to roam freely, at least half their food came from plants and it was collected almost entirely by women who were also skilled healers.

Grandmother Spider Woman

Throughout the myths of many Native North American nations runs the symbol of Grandmother Spider Woman, the female creative principle who

wove the web of the world, taught wisdom and various crafts to her people and protected them from bad dreams with her Dreamcatchers. Although in Hopi myth she shared the creating power with the Sun, she was more powerful than he was, mainly because she remained closely involved in the lives of the people and taught them practical skills, reflecting the importance of women as teachers and healers in the Native North American world (see also Native American Healing Wisdom, page 241).

Grandmother Spider Woman and Tawa, the Sun deity, created the Earth between them. From the thoughts and images in Tawa's mind, Grandmother Spider Women fashioned clay animals, birds, and finally man and woman. Men and women were given life as Grandmother Spider Woman cradled them in her arms and Tawa blew his warm breath over them. Grandmother Spider Woman divided the people into different nations and led them from the Underworld to the land that Tawa had created by drying the waters with his fire.

Grandmother Spider Woman chose the women to be her representatives as the home-makers, and ordered that family names and property should descend through them to avoid quarrels. After the creation, the Sun remained in the sky, but Grandmother Spider Woman has returned to the Earth many times to teach and guide her children. She has done this in many guises: as the Navajo White Shell, or Changing Woman, who controlled the seasons; as Selu, the Cherokee Corn Woman who allowed herself to be dragged along the ground to fertilise the soil with corn; and as Lakota White Buffalo Calf Woman, who taught the people ceremonies of healing and promised that after a period of suffering their wisdom would be spread to many nations.

Earth Mother Against Supreme Sky Father

In monotheistic patriarchal religions, there is only one, very definitely male creator/designer of the universe, whether he be the God of the Judaic and Christian religions, or Allah in the Islamic faith. Even in pagan mythology, the Classical Supreme Father God Zeus, who lived high on Mount Olympus, swallowed Metis, whose name means wisdom, and produced their daughter Athena out of his head. When the power went from the Earth to the Sky and the gods moved to the heavens, or like Zeus to a mountain-top, the natural power of the Mother was downgraded. No longer was it present in all creation with Mother Earth; instead, it was

handed down from on high by a Supreme God who kept himself apart from the world and talked only though priests.

Sometimes where a patriarchal, warlike god takes over from a mother goddess, the legends may be altered so that the bringing forth of the world may result in her slaughter, rather than in her natural transformation into her creation. Take Tiamat, the Sumero-Babylonian Goddess Mother, whose formless body, or sometimes her shape as a great dragon, serpent or crocodile, birthed the universe from her menstrual blood, which flowed continuously for three years and three months. Whereas earlier Sumerian myths recall how she willingly offered her body, the Babylonians claimed that their supreme God, who was her son Marduk, split open his mother in fury because she preferred her younger son Kingu, thus creating the upper and lower firmaments. In effect, Marduk became the Creator and Shaper and she was reduced to the role of Chaos or inactive Primal Matter.

Covered all in Stars

Nut, the Ancient Egyptian Sky Creator Goddess, is perhaps one of the most beautiful and powerful images of the creating woman; in common with other women creators, she continued to actively protect her creation. By contrast, for male deities creation tends to be a once and for all extravaganza, following which they retreat to the heavens to act as divine judges and hurlers of thunderbolts if there is dissent below. Called the mother of the gods and of all living things, Nut was invoked in life and death by humans for protection. A prayer to Nut from the pyramid of Pepi 1 in Siggara, dated to around 2260 BC, says: 'The Sky Goddess, your mother, spreads herself above you. She hides you from all evil. The Sky Goddess protects you from all evil.' Nut's body was arched over the Earth to protect it, with her fingertips and toes touching it.

There are many representations of Nut's body showing her covered with stars, and this image was painted on tomb lids. Kings and Pharoahs claimed her as either mother or consort, and it was also said that every women was a miniature Nut. In other images she was a primal cow, whose udder produced the Milky Way. Her husband Seb was very definitely beneath her, his erect penis extending upwards depicted as an obelisk. But though she was the mother of Ra, the Sun God, by the time of the later Egyptian dynasties Ra claimed to have been born of himself and to have created every living thing from his essence.

Earth Mother Who Would Not Go Away

In almost every society, the Earth Mother continued to be venerated as the primal divinity long after she has been supplanted or absorbed into the mother/wife/consort figure of the supreme Father God. In Ancient Greek myths, the deities, including Zeus, swore oaths in the name of the Greek Earth Mother Gaia (Gaea, or Ge). The Romans, who called her Tellus Mater, swore oaths on her body by touching the ground and then their hearts with the points of their swords. Even today, the Motherland, or homeland, may form a focus for national loyalty.

Gaia

Gaia is the most famous of the earth mothers, who has given her name to modern Green spirituality. She is called variously 'the deep-breasted one', 'she from whom everything comes', and 'the first and the last', since she was the daughter of Chaos or swirling darkness. She created every living thing, plants, animals, hills, mountains, and the waters. She did this by embracing Uranus, the other primordial being that was part of her (Ur means to envelop). Gaia then separated herself from Uranus by birthing him and mated with him as goddess to god, so that they produced the Titans and the Cyclopes. It was Uranus, her son/consort, who became the first of the supreme Father Gods who were ultimately to subjugate her daughters.

Uranus hated his children so much that he imprisoned them within Gaia's body, causing her untold agony and bringing conflict into the world by attempting to halt the natural creative and progressive cycle. When Gaia pleaded with her children for help, the Titan Cronus (Saturn) castrated his father and assumed sovereignty, later mating with his sister Rhea, who became Goddess of the Earth (although she was less important than Gaia). Some of Uranus's blood fell on Gaia, and from the blood were born the avenging Furies and the Giants. The genitals of Uranus were cast into the sea, and from the foam was created the positive balance, Aphrodite (also called Urania), Goddess of Love. Gaia remained as the primal Goddess. It was said that she loved all her children the same, the beautiful and the hideous, the cruel and the benign. Like the Chinese female yin principle, Gaia is seen as the perfect mother, who embraces all creation without distinction.

The usurpation of the old order by the new, instigated by the Earth Mother, was an early motif in which the old god/king was replaced by force by a new and younger god, and is akin to a young, powerful stag in the herd killing the old leader. Such usurpations may be discerned in the mythology of many lands.

The Gaia Principle

Gaia has given her name to the modern ecological concept that perceives the Earth as a living entity. This idea dates back to the beginning of human consciousness and has continued among indigenous peoples, such as the Native North Americans and Australian Aboriginals, long after the Age of Reason and industrialisation encouraged urban humankind to regard the Earth as a larder and fuel store that could be raided and need never be replenished or kept clean. For example, in traditional Native American folk-lore, the Earth is sometimes depicted as Mother Turtle, upon whose back the weight of the world is carried. The Wichita nations relate how the 'first woman lay on her back naked in the sun. Slowly she sank into the earth and her nipples turned dark with mud. Before long her body was absorbed, and the earth became fertile' with trees, plants and creatures of all kinds, including humans.

It is only in the last thirty years that such a concept has become acceptable scientifically as well as mythologically, and this acceptance has coincided with and given power to Green spirituality. This environmental movement takes many forms, including the annual Earth Day, which had its thirtieth anniversary on 22 April 2000. On this day, millions of people gathered worldwide to address ecological issues. The principle of the movement is perhaps encapsulated in the Malaysian proverb 'we have not inherited the Earth from our forebears but borrowed it from our descendants'.

The Gaia Hypothesis was first proposed in the 1970s by James Lovelock, a British biologist, and by Lynne Margulis, a microbiologist. While working for the Jet Propulsion Laboratory of the National Aeronautics and Space Administration in Pasadena, California, Lovelock came to the conclusion that the Earth was a biological self-regulating mechanism. He stated that:

> '. . . as life regulates the physical and chemical environment of the planet so as to maintain suitable planetary conditions for the good of life itself, the planet can be thought of as a single, integrated, living entity with self-regulating abilities. It is unlikely that chance alone accounts for the fact that temperature, pH and the presence of compounds of nutrient elements have been, for immense periods, just those optimal for surface life. Rather . . . energy is expended by the biota (earth) to actively maintain these optima.'
>
> LOVELOCK AND MARGULIS 1974

From this it can be concluded that the Earth has provided and continues to provide resources for those who are part of her and connected because they are microcosmic reproductions of the Earth herself. Moreover, she provides healing for all ills of the mind, body and psyche from the plants and minerals on her surface and within her womb. So if people harm the Earth either physically or spiritually, this damages their own life-support system and that of their descendants.

Crop Circles

It has recently been suggested by some psychic researchers that the phenomena of the crop circles which appear, apparently spontaneously, in fields of grain may be a direct warning by Gaia that humankind should cease pollution, deforestation and destruction. One explanation for the corn formations is that that they are a deliberate communication from Earth entities, or devas, powerful guardian nature spirits. Alternatively, it may be that energy vortexes from within the Earth, both spiritual and physical, create the sacred geometrical patterns and ancient magical symbols, such as spirals and helixes, which appear consistently in crop circles and are also found in early cave markings. Crop circles tend to reappear over a period of years on the same sites near sacred centres, for example at Stonehenge, Avebury, and the nearby Silbury Hill, Wiltshire. These places are known for their powerful Earth energies, which are measurable scientifically as well as detectable by psychic means.

Creating With Dough

One of the earliest principles of magic involved the absorption of energies through food. Thus in a pre-Christian tradition, hot-cross buns were marked with the astrological sign for the Earth, making them sacred to the Earth Mother (see also Seasonal Goddesses, page 18).

❧ Make a dough or pastry, either with the basic ingredients or from a prepared mixture if you are in a hurry.

❧ The important thing is to mix the ingredients thoroughly with your hands to endow them with any strengths or creative qualities that you need in your life right now – courage, initiative, concentration, or fertility, whether physical or in bringing a project into being.

❧ Recite a chant or mantra over and over again as you work: it can be something as simple as 'Creating Mother, may courage empower me.' As you work, see the dough or pastry filled with light.

❧ When you are ready, create a featureless Earth Mother out of the dough or pastry, seeing concentrated in it the power to overcome any obstacles in bringing plans to fruition or making dreams a reality.

❧ Form the psychic dough or pastry into biscuits or cakes and bake it. While it is still warm, eat it and absorb its energies. You can make empowered biscuits or cakes to take with you to work if you are facing a challenge in your workplace.

SEASONAL GODDESSES

Tapping into the Energies of the Changing Year

SEASONAL RITUALS ARE among the oldest in existence: because of the connection between the Earth Mother, the land, the animals and the people, it was once considered important to carry out magical rituals that would bring the rain or cause the crops to grow. We can look at the customs of indigenous cultures to see how this connection worked.

Australian Aboriginal Earth Mother Rites

One of the most important rituals in the Aboriginal ceremonial year was the annual sacred sex ceremony of Kunapipi, the Earth Mother, and Jarapiri, the male form of the Rainbow Snake in northern Australia. He still slumbers in sacred water-holes, under waterfalls or in caves, and manifests himself in the ritual through the dance, ceremony and lovemaking by the individual Aboriginal male.

Kunapipi is the symbol of the reproductive qualities of the Earth, the eternal replenisher of humans, animals and plants. She is represented in the rites by the female Aboriginal; together male and female re-enact the sacred marriage with the Earth to ensure the fertility of the land and people, and to bring the rains. This ceremony was held just before the monsoons were due to begin and the male's ejaculation imitated and was believed to stimulate the falling rain.

Triple Goddess

The Triple Goddess was pictured in many cultures as the Maiden, Mother and Crone aspects of existence. Their progression mirrored the cycles of the moon (see page 187), but the Triple Goddess also reflected the passage of the Earth Mother through the seasons.

Among the Native American Navajo people, it was believed that Changing Woman, or White Shell Woman, came from the first Medicine corn bundle, which was held up by the First Man. In this ritual action, Sky and Earth, White Shell Woman's parents, came together in her creation.

Each year, she mirrors the seasons, growing older from spring and onwards through the year. In summer, Changing Woman is the fertile Corn Mother. By mid-winter, she has grown old and wise and enters the altar room within her shining home. She undergoes rebirth, and is once more a beautiful young maiden when spring arrives. Changing Woman ensures that the seasons revolve, controls the weather and grants abundant harvests if her people remain in harmony.

Seasonal Cycles and Women

It may be that our very early ancestors made love mainly in the late spring and early summer, when the energies of the Earth were rising and the days getting longer and warmer. In this way, the newly pregnant mother could benefit from an abundance of fresh food in summer and autumn, and give birth at a time when she would naturally be resting more, the long, cold nights of winter making work in the fields impossible. She would also be able to spend time with the infant before returning to the fields in spring. This pattern is reflected in the old Celtic myths, which tell of the Virgin Goddess becoming pregnant at the Spring Equinox and giving birth to the new Sun/Sun God on the Mid-winter Solstice, which became Christianised as Christmas. In AD 320, the Christian Church placed the date of the birth of Christ as 25 December to overwrite the pagan births of the earlier Sun Gods at the Mid-winter Solstice.

Wheel of the Year

Earth and corn, humans and animals were in earlier times reputed to be in harmony, not only physically but also spiritually, and the bodily ebbs and flows of the woman/goddess represented the cycles of the seasons.

These cycles are celebrated as the 'Eightfold Wheel', a magical and spiritual division of the year that may date back to the first agricultural societies, although it was formalised by the Celts. The Wheel of the Year co-exists with wider seasonal divisions and incorporates the four solar festivals that fall on the Solstices and the Equinoxes, the astronomical marker points of the highs and lows and stable points of Cosmic and Earth energies. Between each of these Solar festivals is one of the four annual Great Fire Festivals, which are major rites in the Wiccan and neo-pagan calendar, as they were to the Celts.

In the Southern hemisphere, many practitioners reverse the magical associations so that the Mid-winter Solstice will fall in mid-June, the natural height of winter, rather than in December, so that the energies flow more easily. However, some places do not have four seasons. Parts of Australia and other lands in the Southern hemisphere have only a wet and a dry season, and others six or three seasons. In parts of the US too, variations in the seasons are not well defined, while in northern areas of Scandinavia, America and Canada, it may still be snowing and icy on May Day. Thus the Swedes, for example, have the equivalent of the May maypole dancing/Flower Goddess celebrations around their Midsummer tree.

The Wheel of the Year nonetheless forms an important motif for cyclical growth, decay and rebirth. Each culture has its own seasonal goddesses, who rule each of the segments of the Wheel and form aspects of the Earth Goddess, who is herself the lifeforce of the Wheel.

In the annual celebrations, women, or in earlier times priestesses, would represent the Goddess, for it was believed that she was present in spirit and might be seen leading the processions by those with clairvoyant sight, children or virgins. The Celtic Solar and Lunar Goddess Aine was, for instance, seen at the Summer Solstice Eve festival on her sacred hill by maidens who looked through a ring at the moon.

I have begun the descriptions of the cycle below with the early spring festival, as this seems most natural to modern Western society, although the Celtic New Year actually began on what we now call Halloween, which is celebrated at the end of October.

Oimelc: the Return of Light

This runs from sunset on 31 January to sunset on 2 February.

Although this is the time of the Maiden, two other aspects of the Goddess overshadow her. One is the newly delivered mother of the Sun King, whose milk is mirrored by the milk of the ewes that gave this festival its name of Oimelc (it is also known as Imbolc, or Brigantia). Also present is the Crone of Winter, whom the god/tribal chief embraced, and who was transformed into the Maiden Goddess of Spring.

In Roman times, the love and fertility festival Lupercalia was held on 15 February. The festival was dedicated to Lupa, the Goddess She-wolf who suckled Romulus and Remus, the twins who founded Rome (see also Virgin Goddesses, page 118). Love and sex rites by young, unmarried girls and

men were performed in the Grotto of the She-wolf to bring fertility to animals, land and people.

The Goddess Brighid/St Bridget is discussed in the section on Fire Goddesses (see page 152), but she was also central to the Celtic and post-Celtic agricultural year as a fertility/corn goddess. She is patroness of dairy animals and dairy workers, both as goddess and saint, and statues show her with a cow and crook.

On Bride's Eve, 31 January, a Bride Bed was made from a sheaf of corn, which was sometimes preserved from the last corn cut down at the first harvest at Lughnassadh/ Lammas (at the end of July). It would be decorated with ribbons in honour of the Earth Goddess, and adorned with any early spring flowers.

The Bride Bed was made in front of the fire of the tribal hall, or later the main farmhouse in the area. At dusk the inhabitants would shout: 'Bride (Bridget), come in, your bed is ready.' The symbolic Bride Maiden would leave her cows and a cauldron at the door, and bring in peace, fertility and plenty. (From this we get the term 'bride' for a woman who is about to be married.) Milk and honey were poured over the Bride Bed by the women of the household. The menfolk were summoned and, having paid a coin, a flower posy, or a kiss, would enter the circle of firelight and ask for help with their craft or agriculture and make a wish on the Bride Bed. Bridget crosses, none of whose three or four arms are parallel, were woven from straw or wheat and hung around the house for protection. They are still a feature in Irish homes today (see Saints for their origin, page 246).

Ostara: the Vernal or Spring Equinox

This runs from sunset on around 21 March for three days, according to the astronomical calendar.

It is now that the Mother Goddess conceives a child, which is to be born at the next Winter Solstice. This links with the Christian Annunciation of the Blessed Virgin Mary on 25 March, the day on which the Angel Gabriel told Mary that she was to bear a son. It is also close to the UK Mothering Sunday.

Ostara was the Viking Goddess of the Moon and Spring, the maiden aspect of Frigga, the Mother Goddess; she was named Eostar and Eostre in the Anglo-Saxon tradition, giving us the modern names for Easter and oestrogen. The first eggs laid in the lighter days of spring were painted and placed on the shrines of Ostara and later dedicated to the Virgin Mary. In

Poland, it is said that Mary painted eggs in bright colours to delight her infant, and Polish women continue this custom to this day.

In Classical Greek art, Kore, or Persephone, is portrayed rising out of the earth as the personification of the young grain sprouting in the spring. As the Corn Maiden, she comes back from the Underworld; her mother Demeter, Goddess of the Grain and a form of the Earth Mother, rejoices and the land can be fertile once more.

Beltane: May Time

This runs from sunset on 30 April to sunset on 2 May.

Beltane, Beltaine or Beltain is named after the Irish Bealtaine, meaning 'Bel-fire', the fire of the Celtic God of Light known as Bel, Beli or Belinus. Also known as May Eve, May Day, and Walpurgis Night, Beltane celebrates the coming of the summer in the Celtic calendar and the flowering of life. The Goddess is manifested as the May Queen Maia, the Greek Goddess of Spring, who gives her name to the month, and Flora, Goddess of Flowers, whose love and fertility festival was celebrated in Ancient Rome as Floralia from sunset on 28 April until May Day. On 1 May, young people would collect baskets of flowers while children constructed tiny Flora images out of flowers.

In Germany, the Goddess of this festival, Walpurgis, or Walpurga, was Christianised as St Walpurga, sister of St Willibald and St Wunnibald. The three sisters were reputed to have travelled as missionaries from England to Germany in the eight century (see also Saints, page 246).

The chief feature of Beltane was the custom of young couples going into the woods and fields to make love and bring back the first May or hawthorn blossoms to decorate homes and barns, thus linking human fertility with that of the land. This custom dates back to the first farming communities and finds echoes worldwide. Beltane marks the marriage of the Sun God and the Earth Mother, though in modern May celebrations the bridegroom, in his form as Jack o'Green or Robin Hood, is absent from the throne and is leading the processions, or Morris dancing, dressed in foliage, bearing horns or darkened with soot.

Litha: the Summer Solstice

This runs from sunset on around 21 June for three days.

Just as, with the spread of Christianity, the Mid-winter Solstice became

Christmas, so the Summer Solstice was linked with the feast of St John the Baptist on 24 June. In the early Christian Celtic tradition, John was connected to the dark brother of the solar deity who would, after the longest day, rule the waning year (but see also Autumn Equinox, page 24). On the Eve of St John, 23 June, women who wanted to become pregnant would walk naked in a garden at midnight and pick St John's Wort, the golden herb of midsummer.

In all areas where the Solar Goddess was recognised, this was a time of rejoicing. In the Basque region of northern Spain, the sun is still revered in folk custom as Grandmother Sun. Her worship has been transferred to the Virgin Mary, who is associated with Mother Mari, the Storm Goddess in whose wise bosom Grandmother Sun sleeps at night.

Until recently, sun vigils were held on Midsummer Eve to see the Sun Goddess touch the mountain tops and dance at dawn. The watchers would then bathe in the magical Midsummer waters of streams that are still believed to have healing and empowering properties.

In the Celtic tradition, the Goddess shared her power with the Sun King, who was at his full height on this day; they sat together side by side on their thrones. Because she loved him, bonfires were lit and sun wheels thrown down the hillsides to delay the moment when his power must wane and he must leave her in death.

Lughnassadh/Lammas

This runs from sunset on 31 July until sunset on 2 August.

Lugh is the Celtic Sun God who gives his name to this festival. It was also the special time of the Celtic Sun and Water Goddess Sulis, who was Romanised as Sulis Minerva. She was worshipped on hill-tops, especially at the man-made Neolithic Silbury Hill near Avebury, Wiltshire, which was built in about 2600 BC. On the Full or Harvest Moon in July, when the sun set as the moon rose, the light would be reflected in the moat then surrounding Silbury Hill. It was said that milk was pouring from the Great Mother's breast into the water, and that it was time for harvesting to begin. On Lughnassadh, processions were held at the top of Silbury Hill to honour Sulis.

On Lughnassadh in the Irish tradition, Lugh rededicated his vows to serve the Celtic goddess Eire, or Eriu, the Irish Earth and Sovereign Goddess, and transferred to her what was left of his solar strength, which had been poured into the crops during the summer months. In one of the

magical transformations from Maiden to Mother to Crone, Eriu was portrayed in ceremonies held all over Ireland – with their Druidic representations acting the part – as a hag who was made lovely by the golden light of the sun. These ceremonies took place when the last sheaf of corn was cut down. This sheaf of corn was said to be the body of the Sun/Corn God, and from it was fashioned a Corn Mother.

In the Classical world, the festival of bread was dedicated to corn goddesses such as the Greek Demeter, the Roman Ceres, and Juno, the Roman Mother Goddess. In the Christian tradition, a loaf of bread made from the last sheaf of corn is offered on the altar on 1 August at Lammas, or Loafmass.

Mabon: the Autumn Equinox

This runs from sunset on around 22 September for three days.

Mabon is the celebration of the Green Mother as the last of the corn and the fruits and vegetables are gathered. The Goddess is now alone. In traditional celebrations, a priestess and later a woman representing the Goddess would carry a wheat sheaf, fruits and vegetables, and distribute them to the people. A priest or man representing the slain God, given the name of John Barleycorn, would offer them ale made from the fermented barley cut down at Luhgnassadh. In Ancient Greece, the rites of the Greater Eleusinian mysteries took place at this time in honour of Kore/Persephone and her mother Demeter.

The harvest supper pre-dates Christianity, and on the day when equal night and day heralded winter, the feast formed a sympathetic magical gesture to ensure that there would be enough food during the winter. In later times, when it seemed inconceivable that a woman could rule alone, the Goddess was said to mate with the Dark Twin of the God of Light Goronwy, to produce his child at the next Summer Solstice.

Samhain

This runs from sunset on 31 October until sunset on 2 November.

Samhain means summer's end. This festival marked the beginning of the Celtic New Year. The Celts believed that at the festival – and especially on the evening that we now celebrate as Halloween – the family dead could be welcomed back. It was also a time for looking into the future, especially in regard to matters of love.

The three days of no time when the dimensions parted, and ghosts, witches and fairies roamed free, represented the period when the Goddess descended into the Underworld to be with her husband or – in later myths – married the Dark Lord so that he could take charge of the world.

The Cailleach, the Crone Goddess of the Celtic World (see Crone Goddesses, page 125), is also goddess of this festival. She is the winter sun that shines from All Hallows to Beltane Eve; Grainne, or Dia Greine, the Celtic Sun Goddess, rules the rest of the year. They are mother and daughter in a revolving cycle.

Yule: the Mid-winter Solstice

This runs from sunset on around 21 December for three days.

As mentioned at the beginning of this section, in many traditions the Mid-winter Solstice was the time when the Goddess gave birth to the Sun. Earlier myths from Ancient Egypt identified this as the time when the Sky Goddess Nut gave birth to the Sun God Ra, father of every Pharaoh through impregnating the wife of the existing monarch.

The Egyptian Mother Goddess Isis also gave birth to Horus, the young Sky God, on this night. She did this secretly in a cave, and Horus had to be hidden because the reigning King, his uncle Set, would have killed him. Representations of Isis holding the infant are believed to have been the inspiration for many Black Madonna images (see The Black Madonna, page 224).

The Anglo-Saxons named 25 December the Day of the Infant, and Christmas Eve was 'The Night of the Mothers', or Modraniht, after the shadowy guardians of the hearth and home, the midwife goddesses who protected both women in childbirth and their infants. But most of all it was given its name to recall all mothers, living and deceased, who contributed to the collective energies of this period.

The most famous midwife goddess of Christmas was St Bridget; according to myth, immediately after Christ was born she placed three drops of water on his head, in accordance with Celtic birth custom.

BEE GODDESSES
The Creative Power of the Great Mother

∾

Bees in Mythology

FROM EARLY TIMES, the bee was used as an image to represent the Mother Goddess, while the hive was likened to the womb of the Great Mother. The most famous icon, depicting the Goddess with the head of a bee and the feet of a bird, was found in a cave painting in southern Spain dating from Neolithic times.

It is known that bees existed in their present form long before humankind. In many cultures they were a symbol of immortality; in an ancient Hindu tradition that has survived until today, for example, a father will feed a child honey while asking Parvati, the gentle Mother Goddess, that the child might live to see a hundred autumns.

Bees, like butterflies, another early Mother Goddess representation, are often etched or painted on protective amulets made specially for children, babies, pregnant women, mothers, or very old or sick people, and to guard against loss, rejection, loneliness and grief.

The power and ferocity of the bee should not be underestimated. The potency resides in the queen bee and the female virgin worker bees who gather the pollen. The Queen Bee in myth symbolised the Goddess or her High Priestess, and the worker bees her priestesses. Priests would become eunuchs to serve the bee goddesses: this happened, for example, at the Ancient Greek temple of Artemis, the Greek Huntress and Moon Goddess at Ephesus, whose statues were adorned with bees. The priests were called *essenes*, which means drones, the name given to male bees. It is said that a virgin can walk through a swarm of bees and not be stung (however, I would not recommend trying this!).

Bees were adopted as the icon of Rhea, the Greek Earth Mother; Demeter, the Grain Mother; Cybele, originally an Anatolian Earth and Mountain Goddess, whose worship spread throughout the Ancient Greek world and the Roman Empire, and Artemis and her Roman counterpart Diana. In Celtic myth, bees were regarded as sources of great wisdom and messengers between the dimensions; in Christianity, they were said to be emissaries of the Virgin Mary. For this reason, they were kept informed of any major changes in their owners' lives, as it was thought that they would

otherwise leave the hive. It is still considered unlucky to kill a bee that goes into a house as she is bringing blessings to the home.

The Goddess was also perhaps depicted as a Queen Bee in Minoan Crete, and this image may have been tied to early bull worship that was perhaps originally dedicated to the Mother Goddess (see also Labyrinths, page 279 and Totems, page 73). Similar beliefs were common in other European cultures, and were recorded in mediaeval times in England. In Ancient Greece, the dead were embalmed with honey and placed in the foetal position in huge urns, waiting for their restoration to a future life.

Melissae

Aphrodite, the Greek Goddess of Love, was worshipped at a honeycomb-shaped shrine on Mount Eryx. Her High Priestess was called *melissa* (meaning bee) and the other virgin priestesses *melissae*. By virgin this meant that they belonged to no man, but practised a form of sacred prostitution which celebrated the fertility aspect of Aphrodite, the Queen Bee, and the sacred marriage between Earth and Sky. The hexagonal shape of the honeycomb (six was believed to be the number of Aphrodite and later Venus) was the sacred geometric shape of harmony. Bees, who were considered in Ancient Greece to be the souls of dead priestesses, were creators of this perfect form and thus greatly revered. Indeed, the mathematician Pythagoras believed that the honeycomb form suggested a symmetry that was reflected in the cosmos itself.

Magic of Honey

Because honey was, apart from salt, the main preservative, for thousands of years it was treated as a magical substance and used in folk rituals. It is placed in the south of a circle in magic (see Honey Ritual, page 29).

Honey in the form of ambrosia was the food of the Olympian deities, and Hera, Greek Mother Goddess and wife of Zeus, gave honey to the other gods and goddesses to keep them young. In Celtic practices, honey was placed on the straw Bride Bed of the maiden Goddess Brighid at her festival, Imbolc, which was held at the beginning of February. The bed was created near the hearth in farmsteads, and workers would come from the fields to ask the Goddess in the form of the virgin representing her to bless their

craft. This custom persisted at least until the Industrial Revolution. The honey represented fertility and abundance; in Celtic times the chief of the tribe would mate with a maiden representative of Brighid on the Bride Bed in order to renew the sacred marriage with the land. Fertility is still one of the magical meanings of honey.

Both the Egyptian Papyrus Ebers, which was written in about 1500 BC, and the Jewish Talmud cite honey as a healer for many external and internal illnesses. In an African tradition, the Yoruba Mother Goddess Oshun heals humankind with her sacred honey, which is administered by her medicine men and women.

Bees and Prophecy

Because bees were thought to be divine messengers, honey made into sacred mead – wine created from fermented honey – has traditionally endowed prophetic powers on the favoured. The Ancient Greek *Thriae*, three maiden seers at Delphi, were the daughters of Zeus and they demanded payment in honey for their services. They drank mead brewed to a secret formula from the nectar of sacred bees that lived in the grove. The recipe was handed down to their successors, who continued to prophesy at Delphi. The High Priestess, the Oracle of Delphi herself, assumed the name Queen Bee, and the bee symbol was engraved on coins at Delphi. When the Oracle was taken over by Apollo, the priestesses retained the title *melissae*.

The most famous mead was that brewed by the Viking giantess Gonlod, who is called the mother of poetry. She owned the cauldron of inspiration, which was stolen from her by the Father God Odin so that he might possess the gift of inspired utterance (see also Cauldron Goddesses, page 237). Interestingly, the name of one of the few Old Testament prophetesses, Deborah, means bee.

Virgin Mary

Bees are symbols of the Virgin Mary throughout the Western world, but especially in Eastern Europe. In Slavonic folk tradition, the bee is linked with the Immaculate Conception; 26 July, the feast of St Anna, Mother of Mary whose birth (like that of Jesus) resulted from an immaculate conception, is the time when beekeepers pray for the conception of new, healthy

bees. In the Ukraine, bees are the 'tears of our Lady', and the Queen Bee of any hive is called Queen Tsarina, a name associated with Mary, Queen of Heaven. Throughout Eastern Europe, Mary is regarded as the protectress of bees and beekeepers, and consecrated honey is offered on altars at the Feast of the Assumption of the Virgin Mary on 15 August, the date linked with her ascension into heaven.

Honey Ritual to Bring Abundance and Fertility of all Kinds into Your Life

The following ritual is adapted from folk magic; it uses the fruits and grains of the Earth Mother to represent her abundance.

- Outdoors, create a circle of yellow, brown or gold flowers or leaves, beginning in the north (you can use a compass or an approximation). As you do so, visualise the circle radiated with light.

- Make the circle large enough to walk around. You can either work alone, or with friends, family or a partner if you have a joint project or area of your life in which you need to increase abundance or fertility.

- In the centre, on a small, round table, place a beeswax candle. (I have seen such candles for sale with small wax bees adorning them.)

- To the north of the candle, within the flower circle, set a small, round loaf of bread to represent the element of earth and the winter.

- To the east, place a dish of seeds to represent the element of air and the spring.

- To the south, place a dish of honey in a pottery jar with a spoon to represent the element of fire and the abundance of the summer.

- Finally, to the west, place a small jug of milk to represent the element of water and the autumn.

- Light the candle and say:

  'Melissa, Lady, Mother Bee, ever shine your light on me.'

⚬ Take the bread and hold it high above the candle, saying:

'Wake from thy winter sleep. Mother of the grain, nourish in me the stirrings of new life.'

⚬ Crumble a little of the bread into a small pottery tribute dish, which you can place in front of the candle, saying:

'Accept Mother Earth, Mother Bee, this my/our tribute.'

⚬ Then eat a little bread yourself, saying:

'Life giver, bringer of healing and protection, I/we give thanks.'

⚬ Take the dish of seeds and hold it high over the candle, saying:

'Take seed new life that you may be fertilised by the sun and the rain and grow strong and tall.'

⚬ Drop a few seeds into the tribute dish, saying:

'Nurture Mother Earth, Mother Bee, this my/our tribute.'

⚬ Eat some seeds, saying:

'Womb of new growth, bringer of energy, vitality and hope I/we give thanks.'

⚬ Hold the honey over the candle, saying:

'Let the warm sun bring forth flowers for the bees, grass for the cattle and sheep and fertility in this endeavour.'

⚬ Spoon a little honey into the tribute dish, saying:

'Melissa, Mother Bee, take your own as tribute.'

⚬ Eat a little honey, saying:

'Gift of the bees, your priestesses, for this sacred ambrosia that promises abundance, I/we give thanks.'

⚬ Finally, hold the jug of milk over the candle, saying:

'Milk of the Mother, in richness and sweetness flowing free, I/we give thanks for your nourishment and nurturing.'

§ Pour enough milk into the tribute dish to dissolve the honey and stir it clockwise, saying:

'Melissa, milk to your honey, mingled in tribute to you.'

§ Drink a little milk, saying:

'We have eaten and drunk of your bounty; why should we fear you will not grant our dearest wishes; for all your gifts I/we give thanks.'

§ Sit in the circle and eat and drink the bread, honey, seeds and milk. When you have finished, walk anti-clockwise around the circle, beginning just to the west of your starting point and ending where you began, saying:

'May the circle of the Mother Bee, the sacred hoop of life, be uncast, but never broken.'

§ Leave the dish of offerings in front of the candle within the circle of flowers. When the candle has burned through, either cast the contents of the tribute dish into flowing water or bury them in earth (you may have seedlings by spring).

SERPENT GODDESSES

NOWHERE IS THE contrast in mythology greater between the creative and destructive aspects of the Goddess than in the symbolism of the serpent. This is partly because of the biblical connotations of the serpent: according to the Book of Genesis, the serpent is condemned to crawl forever on its belly for tempting Eve to eat the fruit of the Tree of Knowledge (woman and knowledge being incompatible in patriarchal religions and societies). The snake image also touched on deep-seated patriarchal fears because this most ancient of symbols associated with the Great Mother was a phallic symbol. The idea of a powerful goddess wreathed with snakes was quite frightening to societies struggling to marry off the 'inferior' Earth Goddesses to the 'superior' Sky Gods (see also Eve, page 274).

31

Serpent as the Great Mother

The spiral that often appears as a coiled snake is one of the earliest and most widespread of Goddess motifs, being found in the art of the Native North Americans and Australian Aboriginals, and in Asian and European cultures. It is also the basic form of the labyrinth (see also Labyrinths, page 279).

The images of Palaeolithic goddess figures often include spirals in the form of coiled hair. By Neolithic times, the Goddess was pictured with snakes entwining or close to her body, an image that continued to appear in Classical times, although it was progressively demonised. The Etruscan snake goddess Vanth, for example, who was depicted with coiled serpents around her arms, lived in the Underworld and eased the passage of those who were dying, visiting them on their sickbeds. The Romans, however, regarded her as demonic and feared her as a harbinger of death, rather than welcoming her as the Great Mother who took her children back into the earth for healing and restoration.

In early and indigenous cultures that have survived into recent times, the snake was regarded not primarily as phallic, but as the umbilical cord connecting the Goddess to her creation. Alternatively, she herself was described as the primal serpent containing all life within her. In a number of African and Australian Aboriginal myths, the Rainbow Snake Mother gave birth to animals, plants, birds and humans. Indeed, among many Australian Aboriginals, in the ritual death enacted during a shaman's initiation she or he is believed to be swallowed by the great Mother Serpent at a water-hole (in almost every culture, wells are regarded as entrances to the womb of the Goddess). The shaman is then reborn and regenerated from the womb of the Earth Mother. In other Australian Aboriginal tales, however, Jarapiri is the phallic rainbow snake sent by Balame the All Father, although this snake creates the landscape rather than the people, and it is Balame who endows the new shaman with power.

Serpents as Wise Goddesses

The wise aspect of the serpent is frequently linked with virgin goddesses — meaning that the Goddess answered to no man, rather than being a physical virgin. The cobra, a sacred but potentially death-bringing snake, was associated with the Ancient Egyptian Goddess Uadjet, who was portrayed as a winged and crowned cobra and was a goddess of the Underworld, justice

and truth. Wings were protective images among the goddesses of Ancient Egypt. Uadjet is sometimes shown as a snake with a human face. She guarded the infant Horus in the reeds while his mother Isis was looking for the body of her husband, and she was called the Lady of Heaven because she was associated with the heat of the sun. Like Vanth, she was both protector and destroyer, spitting poison at anyone who would do the Pharaoh harm, but also administering the death sting to him when his appointed time on Earth was over. In her role as Bone Goddess, she guided souls through the snares of the spirit serpents on their progress through the Underworld.

The power of the wise snake did partially survive in Ancient Greece. There were sacred snakes in Athena's temple at Athens, and a serpent image of Medusa was depicted on Athena's shield. But the patriarchy was winning. The most famous oracular site in the ancient world was at Delphi in Greece; its name comes from *delphys,* meaning the womb. As the Womb, or Creation, the Mother Goddess in her form of Delphyne was worshipped here with her son/consort Python, the Great Lightning serpent, who was said to have descended into the womb to fertilise the Mother Goddess. In this tradition, Python was the oldest god, and he was later called the Dark Sun – Apollo's alter ego who lived in the regions of night.

The chief prophetess at the shrine at Delphi was called the Pythia. It was said that Apollo killed Python and took over the shrine, so ending the Mother Goddess's power and the acknowledged reliance on her wisdom. In practice, however, the prophetesses continued to prophesy in exactly the same way (as in so many other, similar cases), although they were now officially servants of the patriarchs (see also Bee Goddesses, page 26). The priestesses continued to seek their answers at the oracular cave, but now Apollo took the credit. It was left to the Crone Goddess Hecate, who was linked to death and the Underworld, still to be adorned with serpents, and it is said that she was the last of the true independent goddesses.

The serpent goddess may also have been important in the Minoan culture of Crete, perhaps as early as 3000 BC and possibly to at least 1600 BC. In Greek myth, Ariadne was originally a powerful goddess of fertility and rebirth, bare-breasted, with snakes coiled around her or holding twin snakes, like the healing caduceus or rod of Hermes, the Greek messenger. She was later downgraded to maiden daughter of King Minos and sister of the fabled Minotaur, who was half-bull, half-man (see Labyrinths, page 279). In patriarchal myth, Ariadne assisted the hero Theseus by giving him a thread to guide him out of the labyrinth once he had killed the Minotaur.

Serpents as Temptresses

According to Rabbinical lore, the serpent that tempted Eve was Lilith, Adam's first wife, who was motivated by jealousy (see also Lilith, page 64). Lamia is the name given to the daughters of Lilith, or in Greek legend to a serpent-like seductress/vampire who stole small children. The Lamiae could assume lovely mortal form, but would drain their lover of his life force. John Keats wrote the poem *Lamia*, in which the young and innocent Lycius was seduced by the beautiful Lamia. She was unmasked at the wedding feast by the penetrating stare of his old teacher Apollonius, because as a snake-woman she had no eyelids and so could not turn away.

> "*F*ool! Fool!" repeated he,
> "From every ill
> "Of life have I preserv'd thee to this day,
> "And shall I see thee made a serpent's prey?"
> – Then with a frightful scream she vanished:
> And Lycius' arms were empty of delight,
> As were his limbs of life, from that same night.

Similar seducing serpents are found in the folklore of the New Hebrides Islands; here they are called the Mae and assume many forms, including those of local village maidens, wreathed in flowers.

The Mae are connected to a powerful Freudian male fantasy of the man being drained of his life force, or sexual essence, by the vampiric female, a belief that is echoed in Oriental sacred sexuality, where the male retains his yang essence by not ejaculating during sex. The theme of the sexually insatiable female serpent and the (for once) helpless male is one that recurs in many forms throughout patriarchal mythology, philosophy and religious writing.

Avenging Serpent

When the legends of evil serpent women are examined, it can be seen that there is often good reason for their avenging nature. In Greek legend, the vampiric Lamia was originally a Libyan Goddess/Queen; she was seduced

by Zeus and turned into a serpent by his wife Hera, who also killed the children Lamia had borne to Zeus. A similar sad tale is told of Medusa, eldest of the Gorgons, who was originally the triple serpent Goddess of Wisdom of the Libyan Amazons, An–Ath. According to myth, Medusa was originally quite beautiful and was on occasions allowed to take mortal form, but she was seduced by or seduced Poseidon in the temple of Artemis. As a result, Artemis made her permanently mortal and changed her then still-lovely hair into snakes. Because she was mortal, Perseus the hero could cut off her head. Medusa, however, appears on the shield of Athene, who was said to be her daughter and is sometimes called the Avenging Goddess in recognition of her wise goddess persona.

Another persistent theme is the wise/powerful goddess who is threatening. The gods are scared of her so one of them seduces her, then (poor innocent) shouts for help from another goddess. Sometimes it is the wife of the deity who turns the powerful, lovely goddess into an ugly and at times mortal form, so that she can be completely destroyed. Thus the Greek Scylla, who had twelve snake-like heads was, according to some legends, once a beautiful sea maiden, who was seduced by Poseidon. His wife filled Scylla's favourite pool with poisonous herbs, whereby Scylla became a monster. Who is to blame for such scenarios? The original goddess for encouraging the god, the nasty, jealous wife or the affronted goddess who found the couple copulating in her temple and who does the dirty work while the offending god goes back to his watery palaces or up to Mount Olympus to drink ambrosia and mark out his next quarry? It is a scenario that is still played out on the middle pages of tabloid newspapers and in the divorce courts every day.

Evil Serpent

One of the most fascinating appearances of the evil serpent can be found in folklore surrounding the early Christian saints St Patrick of Ireland and St Hilda of Whitby, north-east England, who both cast out snakes, a variation on the dragon-slaying myth (see also Totems, page 73 and Saints, page 246). Both dragons and serpents have been taken to symbolise the destruction of the indigenous goddess worship, specifically in Ireland in the fifth century. In Ireland, there was a serpent-worshipping cult called Crom Cruaic. A legend that describes St Patrick driving all the snakes into the sea with his wooden staff probably refers to this. St Hilda was also famed for

ridding the land both symbolically and actually of snakes (that is, goddess worshippers). In AD 657, St Hilda founded a double monastery for monks and nuns at Streaneshalch, near Whitby. The land was infested by snakes, which she turned into stone and cast over the cliff, so that they fell on Whitby beach as ammonites. Ammonites with painted snake heads are still sold in the area in remarkable numbers.

Of course, it may be that St Hilda had practical rather than religious reasons for her grandiose gesture. Celtic Christianity involved close connection with and respect for the natural world, and many of Hilda's nuns would have been former pagan priestesses. However, the Celtic saints were also very good at providing crowd satisfaction designed to win over a largely indifferent population.

Serpent Power

In Hindu myth, Brahma, the Hindu Creator God, and other gods, slept between incarnations on the coils of the world serpent goddess *shesha*, or Ananta, the Goddess of Infinite Time. She is identified with the Goddess Kundalini who, according to Eastern philosophy, is manifested as the psychic life force that resides coiled like a serpent at the base of the human spine. This area corresponds with the Root chakra, or lowest psychic energy point in the human body.

In Tantra, a Hindu system of spirituality at the core of which is sacred sex, sexual energy is used to ignite the Kundalini. This is associated with the female polarity of the Shakti, or Mother Goddess energy, that activates Shiva, the Father Sky creative force, which enters the body through the Crown chakra in the centre of the head (see also Kali, page 71). This Root Shakti can be raised in lovemaking by 'riding the wave of bliss' to merge with Shiva energy, in which a couple experience (through the build-up of controlled spiritual orgasms) a final cosmic rather than a physiological orgasm. It is said that at this moment their etheric or spirit selves leave their bodies and merge on the astral plane in an evolved spiritual awareness.

The Ancient Egyptian serpent goddess Mehan the Enveloper is also an energiser of male power. Each night, it was said that the Sun God Ra rested in the womb of Mehan, Goddess of the Underworld and Rebirth, who in the morning restored Ra to travel in his solar boat across the sky. This nightly descent into the Underworld represented the union of the Pharaoh with the Goddess in the person of his queen, thus renewing the sacred

marriage between the Earth and the ruler. Cleopatra, in common with other Egyptian queens, was called the Serpent of the Nile, and killed herself by placing an asp in her bosom, thus taking back into herself in death the power and wisdom of the serpent.

Shedding the Old

The power of the serpent to shed its skin led to the belief that snakes did not die, but were reborn each time their old skins fell off. This became a magical symbol for renewal. If there is something you wish to shed from your life – an old sorrow, a bad habit, a destructive relationship – the snake can form a good focus for your intentions.

- Go to a park or forest and find a stick or twig shaped like a snake. Each type of wood has its own power: ash = healing, willow = intuition, hazel = wisdom, holly = karma, oak = permanence, yew = immortality, hawthorn = magical powers, rowan = protection, apple = fertility, olive = peace, orange = love, pine = purification, birch = regeneration, elder = the ability to see devas and fairy folk.

- Hold the wooden 'snake' and as you touch the bark, name whatever it is you wish to shed (a run of bad luck, anxiety, family problems, loneliness, ill health). Then, with a chisel or plane, or with another stick, chip away all the loose bark from the snake, so that only smooth wood remains.

- Endow the smoothed snake with all the positive people and attributes that you have decided to carry forwards into the next stage of your life, for example good friends, an animal that you are very fond of, an interest or a career move that is proving fruitful, and all the strengths that will be helpful to you in the weeks ahead.

- Paint the snake in bright colours and decorate it with spirals: red stands for courage, green for love, yellow for happiness and clear communication, blue for wisdom and power, purple for psychic abilities and spirituality, brown for firm foundations and security, pink for peace and friendship, orange for fertility and self-esteem.

As you work, fill the snake with your positive intentions, naming each one as you work.

§ Finally, varnish the snake and place it where you can see it, perhaps in a special corner or on a table where you keep your treasures.

GODDESSES OF WELLS AND SACRED WATERS

FROM EARLY TIMES, the waters from sacred wells and streams were a focus of worship, offerings and petitions to the Earth Mother. A pure and flowing water source was regarded as a divine gift, without which a community could not survive. The deities of fountains, wells and streams were invariably female, localised aspects of the Goddess herself, from whose womb the waters were believed to flow.

In western and northern Europe, and in the Mediterranean lands, many wells survived a change of patronage as Christian saints (usually female) or the Virgin Mary became their official guardians. Moreover, the ceremonies and role of the earthly custodians of the wells, an office handed down from mother to daughter, remained in essence unaltered over hundreds of years. This was in spite of disapproval from the priesthood, which was deeply suspicious of the magical (and female-rooted) powers still attributed to these shrines in defiance of numerous papal orders to suppress water worship.

The Christianised wells of St Anne, or Anna, grandmother of Christ (see also the Virgin Mary, page 257), became known as grandmother wells and offered healing for childhood ailments, for infertility, for the medical problems of older women and to bring about easy childbirth. Especially associated with Celtic places, they were formerly dedicated to the Irish Mother Goddess Anu, or Danu, who also gave her name to the River Danube. Brittany abounds in Anne wells, including the well of St Anne-la-Palue, which was created, according to Breton folklore, by Christ when he visited Anne while she was living in Brittany. Other legends relate how her remains were brought to France by Mary Magdalene and Martha, the woman who tended Christ while her sister sat back and listened to his message, and who became famed as a dragon slayer. In one of her patronages, Anne became saint of miners and underground places.

Rivers

Throughout northern and Western Europe, the Mediterranean and Asia, rivers were dedicated to female goddesses. The Seine in France was under the guardianship of Sequana, and the Boyne in Ireland under that of Boanna, or Boanne. To Hindus, the Ganges in India, named after the Water Goddess Ganga, daughter of the Mountain God Himavan, or Himalaya, is the embodiment of the goddess Ganga Ma, or Mother Ganges herself. Daily offerings of fruits and flowers are cast into the river, and at dawn people face the east on her banks and pray to Mother Ganges. Bathing in the water is meant to wash away all sin, and those who have died are, where possible, cremated close to the river; their ashes, and even those of Hindus who have passed away in other lands, are scattered in the waters. For it is said that the Ganges offers the deceased safe passage to Pitriloka, the Place of the Ancestors. Every twelve years, a month-long festival called Purna Kumbha (Full Urn) is celebrated in Haridwar and Allahabad. The most recent festival took place in January 2001; this was particularly significant, because it was the twelfth in a cycle of festivals.

Fountains of Immortality

Brittany is especially famous for its magical fountains and I describe in the section on Celtic spirituality how the white-clad female fairies, the Corrigans, gathered around the fountains at night. Very close to Merlin's tomb in the forest of Broceliande near Rennes is La Fontaine de Jouvance, the fountain of youth (see also Grail Women, page 59), where even today healing is sought and offerings left around the natural pool that has formed just downstream from the bridge. According to one legend, the spot acquired its name from the fact that a census of the local tribes was once taken here each year on the Summer Solstice. All the children born in the past year were taken to the fountain on that night and, by the light of great fires to keep them warm, were officially entered in the census book, the *marith*. This ceremony was originally performed by the High Priestess, probably a senior Druidess, and was akin to a baptism ceremony, but by the

Middle Ages it was officiated by a priest. Those infants who were too young to be taken out at night were left at home and their names were entered in the book the following year, officially at zero, which meant that they immediately became a year younger; it was perhaps this practice that gave the fountain its name. Others, however, believed that the water had the power to restore youth and beauty, and that it was jealously guarded by fairy maidens.

It is said that at the Fountain of Barenton in the same forest, the appointed guardian could, by sprinkling water on the stone slab called the step of Merlin, conjure up storms. This was a power similar to that attributed to the Druidesses of Mont St Michel. The fountain was associated with the Lady of the Lake Vivien/Viviane. Merlin first encountered Vivien sitting on the step of the fountain (see Grail Women, page 59) and was subsequently enchanted by her. She was probably guardian of the fountain and a raiser of storms, and thus a fairy/goddess with power equal to Merlin's. Later Arthurian legends, however, give the fountain goddess/spirit an earthly male protector (in the form of a black knight), a definite downgrading of her magical powers. Laudine, Lady of the Fountain, was married to the black knight guardian, who demanded a duel to the death with anyone who came to the fountain bearing arms. Yvan, nephew of King Arthur, killed the black knight and then married Laudine.

Sacred Wells

Pilgrims to the Well of the Triple Goddess at Minster Abbey Gatehouse on the Isle of Sheppey, Kent, which has gained a reputation for bringing fertility to modern as well as to Celtic, Saxon and mediaeval women, have reported seeing a lady dressed all in white who disappears when approached. Christians interpret her presence as a vision of the Virgin Mary, while others call her the White Lady and regard her as the well spirit. A strong scent of flowers or perfume near the well has also been recorded by pilgrims. Similar occurrences have been observed near sacred waters in many parts of the world.

At another English fertility well, St Agnes Well at Whitestaunton, Somerset, Henrietta, wife of King Charles I, drank the waters and became pregnant soon afterwards. Barren woman would, in ceremonies that had been handed down through the ages, walk three times following the direction of the sun or clockwise around the fertility pools and wells that were once quite common in eastern and western Europe and the Mediterranean. They would wash their abdomens in the healing waters, while the keeper of the waters sang ancient magical chants as she splashed water over their wombs and breasts.

Divinatory and Magical Wells

As late as Victorian times, country girls would visit divinatory waters such as the Fairy's Pin Well in Selby, Yorkshire; this well was named after the custom of young women dropping bent pins (made of gold or silver if the suppliant was wealthy) into the well as offerings, and asking the well to bring a dream of a future bridegroom. They would drink the water, with sugar added, and sleep all night by the well; many a 'fairy pregnancy' as well as significant dreams were reputed to have resulted from this practice.

St Catherine, the fourth-century patron saint of young women, also inspired maidenly prayers for love and marriage. Especially on her feast day, 25 November, young spinsters would pray for a husband, not only in her chapels, but also at her sacred wells, like the one in the now ruined abbey grounds at Cerne Abbas, Dorset, above which the chapel of St Catherine formerly stood. Young girls would turn around clockwise three times and ask St Catherine for a husband, at the same time making the sign of the cross on their foreheads with the water.

Marian Springs

Various healing wells and springs are associated with apparitions of the Virgin Mary. At Lourdes on 25 February 1858, St Bernadette, watched by a crowd of about four-hundred people, began to dig with her hands on the instructions of the Lady. Muddy water surfaced, which she scooped up and three times threw away. At last Bernadette drank the water. The witnesses laughed because her face was covered with mud, but by late in the afternoon, on the spot where Bernadette had dug, the trickle had become flowing water that hollowed out its own channel in the topsoil. No chemically recognisable therapeutic properties have been found in the water, despite exhaustive testing; nonetheless, countless visitors to the grotto have claimed that they have been cured of illnesses, some of them life-threatening (see also The Black Madonna for other ancient Marian wells, pages 227).

Creating Your Own Sacred Water for Special Rituals

It is still possible to obtain water from holy wells, usually in return for a donation towards the upkeep of the well. You can drink it or add a few drops to your bath at any time you feel vulnerable, or rub it on your forehead if you have a headache, or on your pulse points when stressed. It is also soothing and protective for children and pets.

Some sacred water is now commercially available as bottled spring water. You can use one of these 'sacred' mineral waters as an ingredient in your own special healing water.

❧ Use a clear glass or crystal jug or decanter for storing the water. The kind with a stopper or lid used for wine is best.

❧ In the bottom of the jug, place a pure, clear, round quartz crystal. Wash the crystal first to remove any impurities introduced by the modern world.

❧ Pour in mineral water. Some practitioners, following the ancient Celtic tradition, boil two litres of water to which nine quartz crystals have been added. Allow to cool.

❧ Leave the jug of water in a circle of white flowers, where it will absorb the twenty- four-hour light-cycle. Place a lit white candle or night light behind the water if the moon is not visible at night because of clouds.

❧ Finally, using a twig from one of the protective trees – rowan, ash, palm, thorn or olive – pass over the jug nine times anti-clockwise to remove any lingering negativity, and then nine times clockwise to empower it. At the same time, say: 'Water of the Goddess, flowing from the Earth, filled with lingering moonbeams, healing bring to birth. Water filled with sunlight, crystal light empower, flowering life entering, blessings on us shower.'

Keep the water on a special shelf in a cupboard. When it is almost empty, pour what is left into a pond or lake and wash out the jug or decanter under running water.

PART TWO

THE POWER
OF THE
GODDESS

*The untapped potential
of the female psyche*

THIS PART OF the book examines the myths of female power. These involve the struggle both goddesses and powerful women had to retain autonomy as the patriarchal gods became supreme from the second millennium BC onwards. The choice was either to marry or to be vilified. The more obliging goddesses that were married off to the Sky Gods kept their golden tresses and a lesser festival or two. If, however, they objected to the Sky God's extra-marital explorations, they acquired a shrewish reputation, which of course further justified his wanderings. Argumentative women, however, became old and ugly overnight, at least according to the reworked legends. Assertiveness was terribly bad for the skin.

Politics and Myth Weaving

The downgrading of the Mother Goddess to wife and mother of the Supreme Father was not a peaceful affair in myth or in actuality. Perhaps the clearest example that sets the theme for this part of the book is Hera, wife of the Greek Sky God Zeus. Hera was one of the Mother Goddess names among the indigenous pre-Hellenic races of Greece, who were thought to have been matrilineal peoples. It is speculated that in around 2200 BC, the Hellenes invaded from the north, bringing with them the Sky Gods and the supreme Father Zeus. The two types of religion merged, with the invading faith being placed in top position.

Myth relates that the couple honeymooned for three hundred years. Hera was, however, not at all eager to become a bride. Zeus therefore shape-shifted into an injured cuckoo which Hera then placed next to her breast. Instantly, Zeus resumed his god-like form and raped her. By being dishonoured, she was forced into marriage – he, on the other hand, was feted for his ingenuity.

Hera's sphere was now primarily confined to patronage over marriage, childbirth and the home, and she was portrayed as a jealous, spiteful wife who objected to her husband's frequent infidelities and took revenge on various nymphs for allowing themselves to be seduced.

Transforming the Power

The power is still there in the myths for us to use if we can move beneath the surface to the true nature of the feisty goddess/women. Take Jewish Lilith, first wife of Adam, her lips red with the blood of the babies she devoured before breakfast. She seduces innocent males in their sleep, giving them erotic dreams not about their wives, but about raven-haired beauties with corpse-white skin. What was her original crime that led her to couple with demons? She refused to submit sexually to her husband. Lilith has a great deal to say to modern women about the need not to accept the role of either virgin or whore, not to take on guilt for other people's inadequacies, not to deny their own powerful emotional instincts in order to make a weaker man feel macho, and not to accept either sexual or intellectual bullying.

We can adopt the mask of the Amazonian warrior women who lived in peace with each other, and only fight to defend our territory when we are sold shoddy goods or are betrayed by a partner, or when our child is being bullied at school and the authorities refuse to take action.

We can refuse to be sidelined as the Celtic goddesses were when the Roman leader refused to negotiate with the Iceni Queen Boudicca, who was flogged and saw her young daughters raped without reason. She wiped out nearly the entire Roman army in southern Britain in retaliation, and in the end, when the tide went against her, she killed herself rather than allow herself to be taken. The goddesses too, were downgraded under the Romano-Celts to incubators for future hero kings but, like the powerful Mother Goddess Macha, they set a curse on those who broke the sacred promise to respect the women of the land.

Women are natural weavers and interpreters of myth, using these stories not only as allegories, but also as catalysts for new aspects of the inner self that can emerge and transform their daily as well as their spiritual world.

Amazons and Spartans

Women of War and State

I N THE ANCIENT GREEK world, Menander, an Athenian playwright (342–291 BC), was expressing popular opinion when he said: 'Teaching a woman to read and write? What a terrible thing to do! Like feeding a vile snake on more poison.' It is not surprising, then, that two societies in which women did have power were the subject of sensationalist Greek myths that veered from Amazonian women searing off their right breasts to better aim a bow, to licentious females in Sparta who, according to the Greek philosopher Aristotle (384–322 BC) 'live in every sort of intemperance and luxury, running wild while their menfolk were at war'.

The Amazonian warrior women, of whom some archaeological evidence is emerging, were, it would seem, a true matriarchal society (possibly surviving from the Bronze Age), which governed its own states in Asia Minor from about 1000 to 600 BC. These lands were originally thought by the Greeks to be located in the Black Sea area, and also in Libya and on the Eurasian Steppes.

In contrast, Spartan women lived in a patriarchal state but, unusually for the world and time, were allowed to own land and to govern when their husbands and sons were at war, and were taught how to defend themselves. This 'freedom' was perhaps cynically endowed because it was advantageous to have strong women who could prevent slave rebellion when the men were absent. Equally important was ensuring that the women were fit in every way to breed strong, brave sons for the war machine that was the focus of Spartan life. As Gorgo, Queen of Sparta, commented when she was asked by a woman from Attica why Spartan women were the only ones who could rule men: 'Because we are also the only ones who give birth to men.'

Amazons

According to Greek mythology, there were three nations of Amazonian women, all of whom lived in areas remote from Greece. It has been suggested that when the Greeks colonised the Black Sea area and did not find the legendary Amazons, they invented the account of how the ancient hero Heracules had destroyed the fighting women living in the area on his

quests, any survivors having escaped to distant parts (see page 49). This discovery may have coincided with the increase of Libyan Amazon legends and those of female warriors westwards in Mongolia. It may be that the legends of the Amazons had their roots in nomadic matriarchal tribes in southwest Asia – they were perhaps armed, displaced slave girls from goddess temples that were destroyed by invading Sky God worshippers. Or perhaps they were a folk memory that became entwined with the exploits of the Greek heroes. Certainly, the legends continued into the second and third centuries AD.

According to the myths, the Amazons were descended from Ares, the Greek god of war, and the nymph Harmonia. Their strength and skill in fighting made them worthy opponents of the Greeks, so their destruction served to emphasise how amazing the Greek heroes were, because women who fought must be half-supernatural beings. Legend tells us that the Amazons were the first to tame and ride horses into battle, bearing their ivy or crescent-headed shields, and *labrys*, their double-headed axes. They had two queens, one to lead them into battle and one to rule the land, for they were also famed for their agriculture. In Greek art, including sculpture, they were shown with two breasts, one bare, and they originally resembled Athena, Goddess of Wisdom. However, as time progressed they were portrayed more in the manner of Artemis, the huntress Goddess who was patroness of both the Amazonian and the Spartan women, but who was not as wise as Athena in the eyes of the Greeks.

Certainly, it was said that the Amazonian leader Hipp, or Hippo, whose name means horse, and who is said to have helped to create the towns of Ephesus, Smyrna, Cyrene, and Myrina, erected a wooden image of Artemis in Ephesus, around which ceremonial shield dances took place. This shrine was transferred to Diana, the Roman Artemis, and eventually to the Virgin Mary, whose worship at Ephesus overlapped with that of Diana for centuries.

So were the Amazons bloodthirsty women who kept men as slaves and used them for breeding and domestic duties, mutilating them to prevent rebellion and killing the boy children (perhaps keeping enough alive to serve the reproductive needs of the next generation)? More benign myths recount that the women had sex with the neighbouring Gargareans and returned any infant boys (whether dead, whole or mutilated depends on the misogyny of the chronicler).

Some of the Queens were said to chose heroes or worthy voyagers for procreation, wrestling them to the ground before lovemaking to test their

worthiness: fantasies guaranteed to excite the macho Greeks. The Amazonian Queen Thalestris is said to have unsuccessfully tried to impregnate herself by sleeping with Alexander the Great (356–323 BC) for thirteen nights in succession.

Certainly, the Greeks were in awe of these 'women who were not womanly'. Quintus Smyrnaeus wrote of them: 'Like Goddesses amidst earth born heroes the Amazons pursued their reeling foes, dashed them down, cut them apart, and, scoffing, tossed them through the air – till the Greek formations dissolved in consternation.'

Amazons in Libya

Diodorus Siculus, a Greek historian born in around 80 BC, described the Amazon women who had lived centuries earlier in the western part of Libya. He says that they remained virgins while they served in the army, and when they became mothers would concentrate on state, economic and agricultural business. But, it seems, the men were definitely subservient: 'The men, however, like our married women, spent their days about the house, carrying out the orders which were given to them by their wives; the babies were turned over to the men, who brought them up on milk.'

The most famous Libyan Queen was Myrine, who was claimed to have invaded and subdued Atlantis with an army of 3,000 women armed with bows and axes and wearing snake skins. Another Libyan Queen, Omphale, enslaved Heracles, forcing him to spin and weave until she grew tired of him, a fate worse than death according to the first-century Plutarch.

Eurasian Amazons

The historical Amazons may well have come from Eurasia. Fifty ancient burial mounds have recently been excavated near Pokrovka in Russia at a site close to the Kazakhstan border. Seven women's graves revealed a great deal of weaponry, as well as numerous artefacts which suggest that the women, rather than the men, were the dominant warlike members of society. One female skeleton had a battle injury, and another, of a teenage girl, indicates long periods spent on horseback. It is known that the nomadic Sauromatians buried their dead in this area in about 600 BC. The geographer Herodotus (485–425 BC) claimed that the Sauromatians were descended from the Amazons. Even if this were not so, other female nomadic warriors may well have existed on the Eurasian steppes, and tales

of their exploits could have been carried by explorers or traders from Greece.

Heracles and the Amazons

The most famous myth relating to the Amazons describes how the Amazonian women were finally overcome by the might of Heracles, as representative of the patriarchal powers. As the ninth of his tasks, part of his ongoing battle with Hera, wife of Zeus (and archetypal spiteful female), he was ordered to steal the golden girdle of the Amazonian Queen Hippolyta. This had been given to her by her father Ares as a sign of her sovereignty, so clearly it was time to take it back. Hippolyta, the most beautiful, and the strongest and most courageous of the Amazons 'fell in love' with Heracles (or perhaps regarded him as good breeding stock) and was willing, it is documented, to give him the golden girdle – which seems unlikely, since it was the symbol of her power. Hera, however, took the form of an Amazon 'out of spite', or perhaps because she was unwilling to let Hippolyta hand over her sovereignty to Heracles so easily. Hera told the warrior women that Heracles was abducting the Queen and her sacred girdle, so they attacked the hero and his army. With the help of the magical lion skin Heracles had taken when he killed the Nemaean lion, the first of his tasks, he was able to kill nine Amazonian warriors in single combat and destroy or maim many more. Hippolyta also died in the battle. Heracles took Antiope, her sister, back to Athens; there, he gave her as a wife to King Theseus. The remaining Amazonian women followed in pursuit, successfully fighting their way across Greece and at last entering Athens. Here, many of the women died, including Antiope.

Spartan Women

Sparta was a state dedicated to fighting. In 725 BC, the Spartans annexed all the fertile agricultural lands of the neighbouring Messenia, and turned the people living there into *helots*, or agricultural slaves, who tilled for Spartan benefit the land they formerly had owned. The Spartans became a military state of necessity, since the captured peoples outnumbered them ten to one. As a result of this situation, Spartan women needed to be educated. They even produced two female poets, Megalostrata and Cleitagora (Aristophanes). Indeed, it was estimated by Aristotle that through inheri-

tance two-fifths of the land was owned by women. The women's 'education', however, was physically very exacting; it included daily athletic events such as javelin and discus throwing, races and staged battles. The girls, like the boys, would train naked to build up their endurance so that they would become sufficiently strong to defend the homes should the *helots* revolt. Most importantly, their minds and bodies were prepared for peak fitness so that they might conceive quickly and give birth as efficiently as possible and with the minimum of fuss to many strong sons. One birth a year was the ideal. The boys were brought up in military training and lived in barracks from the age of seven. Until a man was thirty he remained in barracks and visited his wife only by night for sex (the wedding ceremony was basically an abduction).

So important was the regular production of children (a woman would sometimes have sex with more than one man if she was considered a good breeder) that it was said a Spartan might be honoured by name on a tombstone, through death either in battle or in childbirth.

Gorgo was the most famous Queen of Sparta, daughter of Kleomenes and wife of Leonidas. Interestingly, it was for her intuitive rather than her warlike qualities that she is remembered. In one incident among several quoted by Herodotus, when she was eight years old she warned her father not to trust Aristagoras who eventually led a revolt against the Spartans.

Spartan Mothers

By state decree, weak Spartan infants were left on a hillside to die, and the death of a son in battle was considered glorious, a cause for celebration, not mourning. According to Plutarch, the most famous saying of a Spartan mother as she bade farewell to her son when he left for battle the first time was: 'Son, (return) either with your shield or on it.' Indeed, one woman, Damatria, killed her son when he was branded a coward and was commended for her courageous action.

So were these Spartan women without feeling? Perhaps not. The same mothers were depicted on vases of the period weeping bitterly as the battalions bearing their sons departed.

THE FURIES

Anger and Vengeance in the Classical World

❧

IT IS PERHAPS significant that in Classical mythology the majority of fierce, avenging and ugly creatures are female. What is even more interesting is that a number were transformed into their hideous forms by malevolent deities and as a result have reason to feel real anger and a desire for revenge. Scylla, the lovely sea nymph, became a monster because either Circe or Amphyrite, Poseidon's wife, was jealous of Scylla's attentions towards her man (the male deities as usual escaped unscathed and blame-free). Scylla is covered in more detail in the chapter on Enchantresses (see page 95).

In earlier myths both the avenging Furies and the bird-women Harpies were beautiful; it seems that as the Sky Gods became more powerful, the role of the female deities was often downgraded to that of emotional/unstable wife like the Greek Hera (see page 44), or to the vengeful, ugly women-monsters of the kind that are discussed in this chapter. Hera was regarded as very spiteful and petty, while her husband Zeus's random acts of cruelty were looked upon as 'godlike'. The lower-status goddesses generally fulfilled the roles of pretty victim nymphs, while the more assertive goddesses were given negative attributes and depicted as ugly avengers in the cosmic drama.

Of course, it was not only in the Greek and Roman worlds that people needed hideous monsters to personify all their own nasty, vicious, murderous instincts. As described in the chapter on the sea goddesses in the next section, the perils and fierceness of the sea and the infidelities of sailors on long journeys were similarly blamed on goddesses and nymphs of the oceans and rivers.

Furies

The Furies, or Erinyes, were safe from the wrath of the unpredictable deities they served, for it was said that they could not be banished as long as sin remained in the world. The characteristics of the Furies, and indeed of the Harpies, overlap the avenging aspects of the goddesses of fate and justice.

The Furies were three sisters, Tisiphone, Megaera and Alecto. Like the Fates, they constituted a Triple formation of power; they were called 'those who walk in darkness', and were described by various myth-weavers as dripping tears of black blood and having hissing tresses of vipers.

The original 'night mare', the Furies were formed from the blood that spilled from the genitals of Uranus when he was castrated by his son Cronus (see page 14), and they were said to have been born out of anger and destructiveness. Of course looking at the situation from the Earth Mother Gaia's point of view, her consort Uranus had shut her children in her womb so that they would not take his power. This caused her immense agony, and arrested their development and the evolution of the natural order. Thus it might be said that the Furies were born out of Gaia's struggle for freedom. Uranus had to be sacrificed because that was the way a new order came about. Many centuries passed and many bloody wars were fought before the patriarchy was able to work out a civilised system of changing kings without such drastic measures.

In other cultures, the Furies were given the role of avenging angels; to avoid invoking their wrath, they were called euphemistically the Eumenides, or the Benign Ones.

The Furies were not indiscriminate in their destructiveness, for they often drove criminals and wrongdoers to their deaths, usually by suicide. They turned their attentions particularly to those who harmed their mothers, who were under their special protection. They also pursued those who ill-treated the elderly and violated hospitality. It was said that they made evil-doers long for their own deaths, and thus acted as an external conscience in what were very brutal times.

A temple to the Furies/Eumenides was built at Athens, the foundation of which went back to a time before their demonisation. Here, rites were performed only by women, and the goddesses were depicted not as monsters but as torch-bearing huntresses with serpents wreathed around their heads. In this role, they represented the Crone aspect of Demeter (see Seasonal Goddesses, page 25) and were thus icons of power.

Harpies

In early Greek mythology, the Harpies, like the Furies, were neither ugly nor evil. They had bodies of birds, and their heads and breasts were those of women; they were originally beautiful, long-haired winged goddesses of the

storm, with the ability to fly faster than the wind. Like the Valkyries, the swan maidens in Viking myth, they bore away the souls of the slain for healing. In time, however, they acquired the image of hideous old women with the bodies, wings, beaks and claws of birds, who seized mortals or semi-deities and carried them off to the Underworld, leaving in their wake a foul stench.

One of the most famous victims of the Harpies was the prophet Phineus, whom they tormented at the command of Zeus, either because he revealed the secret hiding place of the Sun's nightly resting place, or because he allowed the blinding of his own children at the behest of his second wife. However, Phineus's real crime was challenging the authority of Zeus and proving himself to be a more accurate seer, and it may have been Zeus himself who blinded him, leaving the Harpies as his celestial gaolers. But in an amazing about-turn, the winged sons of Boreas, the North Wind, Calais and Zetes, who were in league with the Argonauts, freed Phineus from his torment by the Harpies. He was given second sight according to the terms of a pact with Helios, the Sun God, to compensate for his blinding. The Harpies, on the other hand, were driven to the Whirling Isles, where for most of the year they were trapped in a vortex from which they were freed only when the islands came to rest for a short period. Indeed, they were only saved from total annihilation by their sister Iris, the Messenger Goddess of the Rainbow who appears as Temperance in some Tarot packs.

Eris

The deities of Ancient Greece and Rome had their own scapegoat goddess, who lived among their pantheon, but was excluded from their merry-making. Eris, or Discordia, was not originally superficially ugly, but with the passage of time sculptors, artists and writers gave her increasingly nega-tive features, such as fiery eyes, garlands of snakes around her neck, a shroud for robes, and speech that consisted of hisses and yelps. The other gods and goddesses plotted against each other, using heroes and nymphs as pawns in the celestial chess game, and projecting their baser instincts on the malevo-lent influence of Discordia: Eris was blamed for deceit, quarrels, rivalry, discontent, murder and wars.

Eris's brother was Ares, the Greek God of War, and along with her son Strife, she would ride in his chariot, stirring foe and friend alike into dis-

harmony. Her sisters were the Fates, who were also sometimes blamed for guiding both deities and humankind along destructive paths.

The most famous story told about Eris relates how she was excluded from the wedding feast of Cadmus and Harmony or, in other versions, Peleus and Thetis in Sparta. In revenge, she threw a golden apple into the midst of the revellers, on which were written the words: 'For the most Lovely Goddess'. Aphrodite, Hera and Athena each claimed the apple; Zeus sidestepped the decision, declaring that Paris, the young Trojan hero prince, should choose. Aphrodite promised Paris the most beautiful woman in the world if he selected her; unfortunately, that woman was Helen, identified with the Moon Goddess daughter of Hecate, who had been united with the Spartan King Menelaus in a sacred marriage that bound him to preserve the land and Helen with him. Her seduction/abduction by Paris, who took her back to Troy, led to the long and bloody Trojan Wars with the Greeks, for which the blame was placed not on the greed, vanity and lust of the deities, but on Discordia.

Destroying the Monster

Monsters do not have to be female. So you might like to create a mythical male or androgynous creature to represent those aspects of your life that you would like to remove, all the things and people that worry or bully you, as well as negative emotions and facets of yourself. This is very different from unconscious projection, and the power locked in negative thoughts and feelings can be released as positive energy into your everyday world.

§ First, create your monster, making it as hideous as you wish, either by drawing or painting it or by creating it on a computer screen.

§ Give the creature all the attributes that you dislike not only in yourself, but also in others, not forgetting people from your past whose words still have the power to hurt you. You can create symbols to represent these characteristics, for example sharp claws on furry paws for a colleague who appears sweet and helpless, but who is in fact often spiteful and manipulative at your expense.

§ Write words or phrases across the monster or make fire come out of its mouth. Allow yourself free expression, no matter how seemingly irrational or petty your outpourings, in order to get rid of all the anger and frustration. Begin either to delete, or to block out with a dark colour, the parts of your monster that trouble you the most.

§ As you do this, on a separate piece of paper or computer screen write or draw a symbol of something beautiful, such as a flower, a butterfly, a shell, a goddess or a fairy, to represent your transformed monster. Around it write or draw words or symbols of a corresponding strength or good quality. If, for example, you have been upset about being criticised for being extravagant, make your beautiful lady an icon of generosity, a giver of abundance surrounded by fruits and flowers, who is giving to those who appreciate it.

§ Repeat the exercise whenever negativity threatens to overwhelm you.

CELTIC SPIRITUALITY AND WOMEN

CELTIC CULTURE appeared in Britain in the second millennium BC, taking over and developing existing nature shrines, sacred wells and stone circles. From the fifth century AD, Celtic Christianity, with its belief that the creator was present in all life forms, including men and women equally, merged easily with the indigenous beliefs of the countries that the Celts invaded. The Celtic symbol for the sun and the Christian symbol of the cross together formed the Christianised Celtic cross. In parts of Brittany, menhirs (single standing stones) were engraved with the images of the Christian saints or left unharmed. This is why there are more of these megaliths remaining in Brittany than in any other part of the world. The Celtic women saints, who gradually replaced the goddesses as foci of worship, were strong and not in any way regarded as inferior. Indeed, in early Celtic Christianity, women such as the seventh-century St Hilda of Whitby (see also Serpent Goddesses, page 31) founded and controlled monasteries that accepted both male and female initiates.

Women and the Celtic World

Like the early Celtic goddesses and the later saints, Celtic women were powerful and respected, holding property, ruling tribes and being involved in law-making. Women warriors often trained boys to ensure that as men they would temper their strength with wisdom and compassion.

The root values of Celtic spirituality were those associated with women: the sanctity of life and thus reverence for the process of childbirth and for the fertility of the land and animals that were linked with the fecundity of the Goddess. All these came under the protection of the king/tribal leader, who was allowed to rule by the Goddess of Sovereignty. His power was renewed annually in the ritual mating at Oimelc/Brigantia, which took place at the beginning of February with the old Crone of Winter, who was transformed in his arms into the lovely Maiden Goddess (see also Seasonal Goddesses, page 18). This ritual represented the two opposing sides of life, birth and death, fertility and decay, in a never-ending cycle.

There was, however, a gradual movement away from reverence for the feminine as successive invasions by Romans, Vikings and Saxons, and the assimilation of the invading cultures, made war and conquest more valued than the peaceful cultivation of crops and wise counsel. The invading cultures were male-biased ones that worshipped the supreme Father Gods Jupiter of the Romans, Odin of the Vikings, and Woden and Thunor of the Anglo-Saxons. The Romans would not negotiate with female rulers, as shown by their brutal treatment of the Iceni Queen Boudicca, whom they flogged, and whose young daughters they raped. They regarded women as either meek child-bearers of strong sons, or evil hags if they attempted to retain power and independence. This devaluation of women in what had been at least partly a matrilineal society, and the evolution of the ideal man as warrior, farmer and ruler, like Jupiter himself, rather than as bard and priest, is reflected in later Celtic myths, in which strong goddesses are portrayed as bloodthirsty, destructive and sexually insatiable.

The once-transformative Cailleach, or crone form of the Goddess, whom the king had willingly embraced, was now locked into the form of the perpetually lovely but increasingly ineffectual maiden goddess, whom the king took sexually as his right. In the process, she lost her immortality, becoming the compliant wife, mother and housekeeper, who would suffer violence at the hands of her husband or lover, and who often died in child-birth after producing strong hero sons to continue the blood line. This change in tradition broke the cyclical view of existence, and the Heaven of

the Christians became increasingly the only escape from unending death. Christianity also became more patriarchal, as it gradually became influenced by contact with the Church of Rome, and God was very definitely set above his creation, with woman being regarded as the cause of man's fall from grace (see also Eve, page 274).

In Celtic myth, the watershed of this downgrading is best seen in the story of Macha, who with her sisters, Badb and Morrigon, was later demonised as the Morrigu, three sexually insatiable and bloodthirsty carrions of battle. Originally, myths and images of Macha depicted her as a beautiful solar mother goddess, patroness of creativity and the land, giver of life and sacred bringer of death. In battle, she and her sisters would protect the worthy and carry away the slain for healing and restoration in the Otherworld.

During the process of Macha's transformation from wise goddess to hideous crow, she was said to have married a rich older widower called Crunnchua mac Angnoman, and looked after his house (though this seems an unlikely willing choice for a powerful creatrix goddess). She became pregnant. At the Assembly of Ulstermen, her husband boasted that his wife could outrun the king's horses. Although Macha was in labour, she was forced to run with the horses. She won the race, but at the finishing-post gave birth to twins and died, cursing the men of Ulster that for nine generations they would be helpless in the face of danger, and in battle torn with agony like a woman in labour.

Because the king had failed to respect what had been set down as the sacred right of women to protection in childbirth, he and the other men were effectively deprived of their goddess-given right to rule and the whole land suffered (for similar cases see Grail Women, page 59 and Well Goddesses, page 38).

Druidesses

Druidesses originally had equal status with Druids, and seem to have formed separate colleges of teaching and healing in Celtic times. Druids and Druidesses were the high priests and priestesses who united the various Celtic tribes, preserving a common culture of religion, history, laws, scholarship, healing, magic and science between disparate tribes.

After the formal Druidic religion was wiped out in Wales by Suetonius Paulinus during his conquest of Britain, notably on Anglesey in AD 61, the

Druidic wisdom went underground. The knowledge was passed on to secret converts by male minstrels as they travelled around singing the old songs for entertainment. English Druidesses and Druids also fled to Ireland and Brittany, where their traditions survived for much longer.

Although in general the Druidic religion declined, a number of Druidesses survived in secrecy through the Middle Ages and beyond, certainly in remote parts of Brittany. This may be due to the important healing/herbal/midwifery work that they performed in the local community, which ensured their protection particularly in places far from the centres of power. In Brittany, the white fairies said to have been seen around fountains at night may have been Druidesses coming to fetch water and provisions that had been left for them. The stories of the lovely Corrigan maidens who turned into hideous hags by day may have been created to protect these Druidesses from attack.

However, the reputation of the wise Druidess did not survive intact. Throughout the Middle Ages Druidesses were depicted as sexual vampires or wicked witches, and these tales may be found today in the guide books of Brittany. Princess Dahut, who according to myth mated with the Devil and caused the drowning of the town of Ys, was almost certainly a Druidess who was resistant to conversion to Christianity (see also Women of the Sea, page 116).

According to legend, the Druidesses of Mont St Michel had magic darts which they threw at the waves to calm tempests. When the villagers wanted to ask favours of these priestesses, they chose a handsome young male virgin and sent him to the Druidesses. The young man was led to a cave in the rock, where he went through a series of voluptuous rites. After several days he went back to his village covered in cockle shells – for each time he had brought a Druidess to ecstasy she had sewn a cockle shell on to his clothes.

Other myths relate that Druidesses who lived on the islands of Brittany and Normandy would go to the mainland once a year, where they would break their vows of chastity for one day. Any boys that were born as a result would be sent to their fathers nine months later, while baby girls would be retained by the Druidesses. Other, less imaginative accounts recall priestess colleges that existed in the Middle Ages in Celtic lands, and it may be that pagan-orientated nobles or those who resented the power of the Church would send their daughters to the Druidesses rather than to Christian convents to be educated. Tales of the priestesses of Avalon (see also Grail Women, page 63) may have referred to one of these surviving Druidic colonies. Some may have gradually evolved into Christian convents and continued the old forms of worship and their role as healers and guardians of the land, while outwardly following the new forms of prayers and worship. We know that the Druidesses of the Ile de Sene, sometimes located on the Loire, but more usually off the Coast of Finistere in Brittany, did not come to the mainland to join a convent until 1700.

There were also Irish Druidesses. In one of his prayers, St Patrick asked for protection against their spells and incantations, and also from 'pythonesses', or female seers. The latter were probably the more oracular Druidesses who, like the Greek priestesses at Delphi, the original pythonesses (see page 33), drew inspiration from the Earth Mother in deep caves.

GRAIL WOMEN AND ARTHURIAN LEGEND

❧

I N THE CHRISTIAN tradition, the Grail is represented by the chalice that Christ used at the Last Supper. After the Crucifixion, Christ's blood was collected in the chalice, thus uniting the symbolic and actual blood that was offered as a willing sacrifice for the sins of humankind. There may have been two Grail cups, one belonging to Mary Magdalene, who is sometimes regarded as the wife of Jesus, continuing a long tradition of female guardians of sacred vessels (see also Cauldron Goddesses, page 237). She took the cup to France, which also has a strong Grail tradition. The other Grail cup is associated with Joseph of Arimathea, the wealthy merchant who cared for Christ's body after death. In the latter tradition, Joseph brought the cup to Glastonbury, and it was his descendants who became the male Keepers of the Grail. They were given the title Fisher King. There is no way of knowing which Grail was used in the Last Supper, but since both Mary and Joseph were at the Crucifixion, both cups may have caught Christ's blood.

In pagan times, the Grail icon was known as the Graal, the sacred cauldron of creation and nourishment that symbolised the womb of the Earth Mother. In the chapter on Cauldrons of Inspiration, this legend is described in detail (see page 239). Significantly, the guardians of the magic cauldron were nine maidens. Some mediaeval Grail stories feature a Grail maiden carrying the Grail and offering sustenance from it, maintaining links with this Celtic and perhaps even pre-Celtic older world. King Arthur (the fifth-century historical character) stole the cauldron from the Otherworld. In

doing so, he took by force a major source of female power; it would seem, however, from accounts of the disappearance of the Grail in mediaeval legend, that he was not allowed to keep his spoils – or the power.

In mediaeval times, the legend of the Christianised Grail, or sacred chalice, was transformed into a quest by King Arthur's Knights, who were altered from scruffy ancient Britons to represent the idealistic, courtly values of the Middle Ages. In mediaeval myths, the Otherworld Grail maidens, who were once aspects of the Goddess, became weak, faithless women such as Arthur's Queen Guinevere, who betrayed him with Lancelot, and Elaine, who tricked Lancelot into marrying her.

In these later chronicles, the sole purpose of the inclusion of the character of Elaine was to use her blood line from the male Grail guardians to produce Galahad, who was pure enough to succeed on the Grail Quest. The women who did seek to retain the original power of the female Grail goddesses were portrayed as evil and manipulative, as typified by the seductress Lady of the Lake Vivien/Nimue, or Morgan le Fey (see also Woman as Enchantress, page 95).

The original Arthur was an ancient British King of Celtic origin, who in the fifth century united parts of Britain against hostile forces following the collapse of the Roman Empire. Consequently, he was probably dependent on the ancient priestess/goddess tradition to sanctify and give authority to his claim as king over the many disparate Celtic and ancient British peoples who still followed the older matriarchal religions.

The importance of the Grail legends as a source of female wisdom exists in spite of rather than because of the portrayal of the woman themselves. However, the fascination with the Grail did ensure the transmission from pre-Celtic times to the twentieth century (and hopefully beyond) of knowledge of goddess worship through times when religion was dominated by patriarchal power. For in these Arthurian legends, beneath the characters of the Arthurian women can be found different aspects of the Goddess. In the mediaeval tales, all of the women acquired fairy blood or connections with the fairies, thus acknowledging, albeit as a downgrading from deity to fairy status, their otherworldly origins.

In the tales of King Arthur comes the first split in Celtic times between the religious and the secular that marked the beginning of the end of the power of the Goddess. So it was that King Arthur ritually married his half-sister Morgan as priestess of the old religion before he became king. However, his Christian marriage took place after he had become king, and Guinevere now became a downgraded representative of the sovereignty, or

the power of the land, which was endowed through sacred sex upon a new or would-be king to give him authority to rule. Arthur assumed the role of Sun/Sky God and was superior to his wife – and by inference now held the land by right not duty. It was Morgan who helped bring him down, using – perhaps for the last time – the waning power of the Goddess (compare this with the Macha legend, see page 57).

It is Arthur's ritual marriage with Morgan, his half-sister, that bears physical fruit in the person of Mordred, the seed of Arthur's destruction. The barren Guinevere is heavily Christianised, but in fact her betrayal of Arthur to the younger Lancelot reflects the Celtic myth of the triumph of the New Year over the Old, in ancient lore represented by the death of the old Sun God/King and the rebirth of the young Sun/Sun God to the Goddess at the Mid-winter Solstice on around 21 December. The Christian version of the myth could not allow this to happen: as Mordred was 'born in sin', so he too, died in the conflict with his father.

Origins of the Grail Women

Archaeological evidence for the female Grail guardians may be found at the well of the Celtic Triple Water Goddess Coventina, in Carrowbaugh, Northumberland. Here, a carving depicts Coventina on a water-lily, along with three women holding goblets or chalices.

The name of Vivien/Viviane, one of the designations given to the Breton Lady of the Lake, the chief priestess/goddess/fairy of the Grail guardians, may derive from Co-Vianna, a Celtic variation of the Romanised Coventina. The Roman name for Carrawburgh was Brocolitia, which bears a resemblance to Broceliande, the enchanted forest, one of the main locations of the Lady's lake.

The Breton *Graal,* one of the many mediaeval French accounts of the Grail story, continues this link in its account of the goddesses of the wells and springs of Logres (inner Britain, or Brittany), whose priestesses once gave hospitality and oracles to travellers. There were perhaps Druidess or priestess colleges, with a core of nine trained Druidesses, situated at sacred water shrines. King Amangons raped one or maybe more of these priestesses/water nymphs and stole the golden cup. (This may be a symbolic tale of more general attacks upon the Druidesses and oracular sites.) As a result, the priestesses gave no more sustenance or wisdom and, more importantly, would no longer perform the rituals of the sacred marriage that ensured the

fertility of the land. As in the case of the demise of the Celtic goddesses, once the male took by force the sacred sexuality that had previously been willingly given, the magic ceased to work. The country became a Waste Land and the magic Grail cup disappeared, as did the castle of the male Grail guardian, the Fisher King, who suffered a serious wound to his testicles but could not die until the Grail was restored by one of his descendants who had been untouched by sin. In some versions of the story, this sinless saviour was no less than Elaine's son Galahad, the grandson of Pelles, the Fisher King/Grail keeper and conveniently Elaine's father. The Fisher King is clearly associated either symbolically or actually with the raping king, and the whole land suffered as a result of his failure to protect the representatives of the Goddess of the Land from harm.

Thus in the mediaeval legends the Grail women became in effect, if not overtly, the protectors of the Sun King Arthur or, in the case of Morgan le Fey, the challenger of his worthiness to hold the throne if he failed to uphold the power of the Mother Goddess. Others were mothers/guides/lovers to the other men in the saga.

Lady/Ladies of the Lake

Several women, who are often blurred in the legends, carry the title of Lady of the Lake. Apart from Vivien, the most significant is Nimue, or Nineve. Vivien is in some accounts the aunt of Morgan le Fey and King Arthur, and Morgan, or Nimue, becomes her successor.

Nimue is linked with the Celtic Niame of the Golden Hair, who was the daughter of Manannan, the Manx God of the Sea and the Land of Youth; she was reputed to be an enchantress who took the mortal hero Oisin to her fairy home. Her name has also been associated with the Classical Mnemosyne, or Memory, mother of the Muses of Greek and Roman mythology. Nimue is interchangeable with Vivien as lover of Merlin.

According to the writings of the twelfth-century bishop of St Asaph, Geoffrey of Monmouth, Ynis Avallah, the Isle of Apples, which was synonymous with Avalon, was ruled by nine Lake women, the chief of whom was the enchantress Morgan le Fey. Avalon was frequently associated with the spiritual or magical isle of Glastonbury.

It has been suggested that the nine Lake women, the majority of whom have major roles in the Arthurian chronicles, formed a secret sisterhood, which was bound in a mystical sense, for in the tales they are often sworn

enemies. They came together united in love on Arthur's funeral barge to carry him to Avalon/the Otherworld for healing and to wait until the world calls him again. As well as Morgan and Vivien/Nimue, who gave Arthur Excalibur, the most significant of the Grail women who took their places on the barge were Arthur's mother Igraine, herself of fairy blood, who conceived Arthur by the hero king Uther Pendragon under magical enchantment, and Arthur's wife Guinevere. Most Christian versions of the legend send Guinevere to a nunnery to repent her sins after Arthur's death. Another of the women was Argante, a shadowy Queen of Elfland, who was said to know and guide the fate of the players in the drama. Argante has been identified with Morgan le Fey, and also with the Celtic goddess Arianrhod, who ruled the second realm Caer Feddwidd, the Fort of Carousal of the Celtic Otherworld. Here, a mystical fountain of wine offered eternal health and youth to those who chose to spend their immortality in the afterlife; perhaps it was the source of the Fountain of Youth in the Forest of Brociliande (see Goddesses of Wells, page 38).

The original Avalon may have been Tir na Mban, the Land of Women referred to in Celtic myth. There is a theory that the priestesses of Avalon may have predated the Celts, and that the memory and continuation of their centre on the sacred isle in Celtic times gave rise to the legends of the Land of Women. It may not, then, be fanciful to suggest that they were the original Grail women, who guarded ancient treasures and wisdom and were the makers and breakers of kings and tribal chiefs, and who were perhaps linked to other priestess enclaves such as that at Carrowbaugh. It could have been that these indigenous priestesses of a still matriarchal religion were instrumental in teaching the wisdom of the megaliths to the Druids.

We know that there were nine Druidesses living on the Ile de Sene, who were reputed to be great shapeshifters, or changers of form, and nine on Mont St Michel. In Druidry the Winter Solstice is called Alban Arthuran, the light of Arthur. As a training Druidess, I for one would like to think that Druidesses rather than the male priesthood were the true founders of Druidry.

Because of the vast amount of material that has accumulated on the Grail and Arthur over so many centuries, it is almost impossible to be objective when trying to analyse these stories, and this is an area where intuition may be the best guide. However, there is little doubt that speculation about the myths, and their reworking by future generations of women as well as men, will help to keep the Goddess tradition expressed in the Grail symbols a living one.

LILITH

Demoness or Icon of Female Power and Sexuality?

MANY FEMINIST researchers do not view Lilith, the first wife of Adam, as the demoness who forced virtuous men through the ages to leave the path of morality. Rather she is seen by them as a personification of repressed sexual desires, manifested as the erotic dreams of men whose conscious lives were bound by strict laws of morality.

Sexual desires were an issue in both the Jewish and the Christian faiths; the Apostle Paul declared that it was better for a man to marry than to burn with desire (see also Eve, page 274). Entirely normal nocturnal sexual fantasies were thus projected on to 'night hags', one name for Lilith and her demon daughters, the Lilim who 'forced' lascivious thoughts into the sleeping minds of respectable married men, or those sworn to celibacy. It was said that after a spending a night in his dreams with one of these dark-haired, beautiful creatures, a man would never again be satisfied with a mortal woman (and would thus be prone to commit adultery against his will on future occasions).

Mediaeval monks would sleep with a wooden cross held over their genitals to prevent visits by saccubae (or succubi), another name for the Lilim, while Jewish men were exhorted not to sleep in a house alone lest the Lilim came visiting.

Among people of the Jewish faith, amulets were, for many centuries, hung over marriage beds, for according to Kabbalistic (Jewish esoteric) literature written as late as the seventeenth century, Lilith could impregnate herself with semen stolen from nocturnal emissions. The demons created from this 'spilled seed' might, on their fathers' deaths, return to claim their inheritance, another emotive issue in patriarchal societies. If a man was visited by Lilith or her daughters, he would recite protective prayers as soon as he woke so that his seed would not produce demonic offspring.

Origins of Lilith

The biblical Lilith is conspicuous by her absence in the Bible, and her negative connotations as a seductress of innocent males and slayer of children were acquired mainly from Hebrew folklore, which was recorded during the

Middle Ages from an earlier oral tradition. The only direct biblical reference to Lilith is in Isaiah 34:14: 'The wild creatures of the desert shall meet with the jackals, the goat demon shall call to his fellow, the lilith shall also repose there and find for herself a place of rest.'

Lilith has been variously translated in this context as 'screech owl', 'night hag' or 'night-monster', an emphasis perhaps based on the Babylonian Goddess Lilitu, whose name has been translated as 'monster of the night', but that in fact comes from the early Semitic word meaning simply 'night'.

Of course, dark and night are often equated in mythology with the unconscious and hidden, and therefore with the Underworld and death. In Ancient Greece, Lilith was linked to Hecate, the Crone Goddess (see Crone Goddesses, page 128) and the Lilim were in some myths called Lamiae, Eripusae or daughters of Hecate.

A more female-friendly explanation would be that Lilith was a version of the ancient Earth Mother defeated by the Sky Father, Yahweh, and thus demonised. Over the last twenty years or so, a number of Jewish feminist researchers have suggested that Adam may have represented the nomadic herdsmen who invaded the matriarchal agricultural lands and met resistance. Cain was said to have been the son of Adam and Lilith, and Abel the offspring of Eve and Adam. Cain killed his half-brother Abel, and Lilith, according to rabbinical literature, drank Abel's blood, an early reference to Lilith as a vampire. According to oral Jewish folk tradition, which was written down in the Alphabet of Ben Sira between the sixth and the eleventh centuries, Lilith gave birth to a hundred children a day, originally with Adam and later with demons; this increases her link with the ancient fertility mother.

Lilith is also associated with the Queen of Sheba, who was dark-skinned, beautiful and wise. But although Sheba was as learned as Solomon, and coupled with him as a representation of the sacred marriage of the Earth Goddess with the sacred king, on her arrival at Solomon's palace she was tricked by Solomon, who created a floor of glass that appeared like water. Sheba lifted her skirts to wade across, thereby revealing her hairy and by implication primitive, animal-like legs. Unshaven female legs are still an emotive issue with some men who like their women tame, and one of the recurring motifs in legend is of the hidden demoness behind an outwardly beautiful woman who can lead even the wisest man astray.

First Eve

As in the case of Lilith, the Bible is scant on details of Eve. The later version of the Genesis creation story, although it appears first in the biblical texts, refers to God creating Man and Woman from the dust of the ground. Since Eve is described as coming from Adam's rib, the reference to Woman being created from dust or the earth would seem to apply to Adam's first wife, Lilith. This therefore implies that Adam and Lilith were created equal. Eve, being formed from the rib of Adam and so categorised as his inferior, was made as a 'help meet' (mate), which Lilith proved not to be.

Yalkut Re'uveni, a seventeenth-century collection of mainly Kabbalistic legends, states that Lilith was created from the 'filth and sediment' of the earth and was thus justifiably inferior. But it is the *Alphabet of Ben Sira* that initially associated with the first Woman both Lilith the temptress of virtuous men, and Lilith the slayer of infants. This and subsequent, often contradictory accounts of Lilith were recorded when the incidence of reported demonic sexual attacks was at a height. The Alphabet acknowledges Lilith, created from dust, as the first Eve, and sets in stone Lilith's real sin in the eyes of the rabbinical and, indeed, Christian communities. She refused to submit to Adam's will, we are told, specifically sexually by refusing to lie beneath him, and all manner of abominations were thereafter attributed to her. Lilith compounded her sin by speaking the 'Ineffable Name of the Creator', learned through feminine wiles against which even the Almighty was not immune. This empowered her to fly through the air, having been refused admission to the heavenly realms of the cherubim, one of the lower heavens. She fled to a cave (symbol of the womb of the Mother Goddess) near the Red Sea, where she thereafter 'coupled with demons'.

Three angels, Senoi, Sansenoi and Sammangel, were sent to force Lilith back to Adam. She was told that unless she obeyed them, a hundred of her offspring would die every day. Lilith responded with the counter-threat that she would slay a hundred of Adam's children every day. However, she promised that whenever she saw the names or images of the three Enforcer angels on an amulet or picture in a delivery room, or over a cradle in which there was an infant, she would not harm the human child. She also announced that she would only hold sway over boys until the eighth day after their births (when, under Jewish Law, they were circumcised) and over baby girls for twenty days after birth.

Thereafter, it was said that no pregnant or new mother would utter the name of Lilith for fear of conjuring her presence. Some might argue that

this sensationalised myth, which was perhaps created by the patriarchy, was a very drastic – if effective – way of preventing women from invoking the Mother Goddess, traditionally protector of childbirth, at a vulnerable time in their lives, and that the Enforcer angels were hardly gentle, child-loving figures.

In different versions of myth, Lilith's children were fathered by the Dark Angel Samael, sometimes associated with Satan, with whom Lilith in the form of a serpent supposedly tempted Eve out of jealousy for her rival. Lilith was thus also blamed for the Fall of Humankind. She herself only escaped mortality because she was created before the Fall.

The Christian Lilith is portrayed in the Sistine Chapel in Rome by Michelangelo as a half-woman, half-serpent. This serpent form may also be seen beneath the feet of the Madonna in various mediaeval and Renaissance paintings, for it was said that the Virgin Mary crushed the serpent, that is the darker, more sexual aspects of the Goddess (see also Serpent Goddesses, page 34). In other folk tales, Lilith was married to Asmodeus, the King of Demons. It has also been suggested that in spite of Lilith's apparent evil-doing, Adam put the blame firmly on Eve for his loss of Paradise, and that he unsuccessfully attempted a reconciliation with Lilith.

Lilith, Power Icon or Child Slayer?

Today, Lilith is regarded as a symbol of female power and defiance against an unfair patriarchal system, especially among some Jewish feminists. But what about her attacks on mothers and babies? For as well as harming infants she was also believed to cause miscarriages and disasters in childbirth, unless the mother and unborn child were protected by amulets.

This belief originated at a time when infant mortality was high, and when both mother and child frequently died in pregnancy or labour. God could not be blamed for the deaths of innocents, so who more likely to inflict such suffering than the jealous former wife of Adam? In patriarchal societies, was it not conceivable that a woman who defied her husband sexually was capable of anything?

The psychological legacy of Lilith has continued to some extent even until today, when males claim to be tempted by seductive enchantresses. Some women too, still rely on feminine wiles to manipulate willing men. The result may be that both partners experience an emotionally and spiritually arid relationship, or that the woman allows herself to become a sex

object or a 'trophy wife'. It is, however, encouraging that although there is a large number of Lilith pornographic sites on the World Wide Web, sites that focus on the spirituality of Lilith are also on the increase. For Lilith ultimately stands for the instinctive self, for the joy and power of female fecundity, and for sexuality and the unconscious, intuitive depths that, if acknowledged and used wisely, can bring freedom and fulfilment to both men and women.

KALI
and the Hindu Goddesses of Transformation

Great Goddess

ALTHOUGH THE FEMALE Hindu goddesses may all be regarded as aspects of the Great Goddess Mahadevi, each of these goddesses has her own distinct personality. In their earlier forms, the goddesses predate the gods to whom they became consorts.

Some texts describe Mahadevi as the creator of the universe, who oversees the main cosmic functions, creation, preservation and destruction. It is said that the three supreme gods of modern Hinduism, Brahma the Creator, Vishnu the Preserver and Shiva the Destroyer, assume these functions by her will. According to one myth, Ammavaru, the Goddess who existed before the beginning of time, laid an egg that hatched into Brahma, Vishnu and Shiva. However, other, more patriarchal writings attribute these cosmic functions as inherent to the male gods. Nonetheless, they still acknowledge the Goddess in the consort goddesses, some of whom are fierce and very independent, and who transmit the Shakti, the female active divine energy that empowers the gods, through sacred sexual union.

Some devotees of individual goddesses regard the particular deity they worship as the supreme Goddess. Others see the goddesses primarily as personifications of specific qualities of the Goddess form, for example the courage of the battle Goddess Durga, the cleansing powers of Kali or the Madonna-like gentleness and devotion to her family of Parvati.

Goddesses Role in Uniting Disparate Forces

Every Hindu goddess, though she may manifest mainly either nurturing and fertility, or destructive and protective strengths, carries within her the seeds of the other side of her nature. For example, the Mother Goddess form Aindri, who is popular in Western India, is both maternal and avenging, and is portrayed with a child on her knee and a thunderbolt in her hand. She was the wife of Indra, the first King of the Gods and the deity of Thunder. Manasa, the Snake Goddess, who is especially popular in Bihar and Bengal, inflicts snake bites on those who offend her, but guards her devotees against poisonous snakes. She is usually depicted with a child on her knee; the child is protected by the hood of the cobra (see also Serpent Goddesses, page 36).

The Mother Goddess is still important to ordinary people in the Hindu world, and in many villages in India the shrine to the local goddess forms the focus of personal prayers, offerings and entreaties particularly for women, as it has done for thousands of years. Household and local goddesses can evoke a personal relationship with their devotees akin to that of women with the Virgin Mary in the Western world.

The Eastern Indian goddess Anapura, or Annapurna, whose name means food-bringer, rules over the production and distribution of food; she is shown feeding a child from a full cooking pot and ladle. At her autumn festival a food mountain is created at her shrines, mirroring the harvest supper of the European Autumn Equinox celebrations (see Seasonal Goddesses, page 24). In the spring she is associated with the sprouting rice.

Major Hindu Goddesses

Even the most terrifying goddesses, such as the Dark Mother Kali, are considered by their devotees to be protective, and masks of Kali are placed in doors and windows in Nepal to guard the home and its occupants from harm.

Gentle Goddess Aspect

Many of these goddesses became consorts of the newer gods, although they were originally wise and powerful fertility goddesses in their own right.

Sarasvati

Sarasvati, deity of the Sarasvati River in Northwest India at the time when the Indo-Aryans were changing from a nomadic to an agricultural way of life, was originally the bringer of fecundity to the land and people. She was also Goddess of Medicine, Healing and Divine Knowledge, for her river was said to flow from the heavens to the earth. In later Hinduism, she became Goddess of Music, Poetry, Speech and Learning, and the wife or daughter of Brahma, the Creator God. In this tradition too, she owes her origin to Vishnu, from whose tongue she was created.

As Goddess of Learning, Sarasvati is sometimes shown with a book in her right hand representing sacred learning, and a vina, a stringed instrument. She also carries symbols that are a reminder of her fiercer other side, a noose of ignorance and a club to subdue evil, as well as a rosary as an emblem of meditation and inward learning. Sarasvati is patroness of school-children.

Parvati

Parvati is the beautiful young goddess and alter ego of Kali, who in some myths was formed from Parvati's skin. She is the reincarnation of Shiva's first wife Sati, and her name means 'she who comes from the mountains'. However, many of her devotees regard her as the incarnation of the Mahadevi, who was also pictured in her heavenly halls as a lovely young woman, Queen of the Heavens.

Parvati's purpose was, according to patriarchal literature, to give Shiva children. This function can be regarded either as a downgrading of her personal power, or as the catalyst and power source without which Shiva would be impotent. With her, Shiva is depicted as the ideal family man living in his sacred city Benares with their offspring Ganesh, the elephant-headed God of Wisdom and Prosperity, and Karttikeya/Skanda, God of War. Many statues depict the couple entwined, with Shiva touching her breast and Parvati holding the mirror of destiny.

The marriage of Shiva and Parvati is the model for humans; it is the union of the great god and his Shakti, or female essence, and the sacred marriage between Earth and Sky. They demonstrate the heights of sexual and spiritual ecstasy to be strived for by every married couple. These are momentarily experienced in tantric or sacred sexuality, in which the male delays or avoids ejaculation and he and his partner channel their sexual energies into creating a spiritual or cosmic orgasm, thus uniting human love

with that of the deities. The sacred marriage is celebrated annually in many places, the largest festival being held in Maduri, Southern India in April.

Fierce Goddesses

It is perhaps only to the Western mind, or one in which the monotheistic patriarchal deity holds sway, that there must be a good God and a bad Devil; that creation must be separate from destruction, and life separated from death which cannot be acknowledged for fear of attracting it and being cast into Hell if one is judged unworthy of Heaven. By contrast, in Hinduism the Dark Mother Kali and the Bone or Death Goddess Chamunda, with their necklaces of skulls, are perpetual reminders that death is as real as life, and that it is not the end, but rather part of an ongoing cycle.

Kali

Some say that Kali existed from the beginning of time as the Great Goddess herself, and that it was from her and by her that Vishnu, Brahma and Shiva were created. Vishnu calls her mother and grave. But in later accounts, Kali came into being when Shiva, whose body was covered by white ashes, taunted Parvati/Shakti for her dark skin. In fury she carried out magical rituals until her skin became golden inside. Parvati then shed her black outer skin like a snake. The skin, being full of her anger, formed the avenging-destroying persona of Kali, half-naked, with wild hair and protruding tongue, and covered in blood that signified her power over life and death.

Kali is beautiful yet at the same time terrifying. She is dressed in a tiger skin symbolising fierceness and courage, and around her neck are fifty human skulls, said to symbolise the fifty letters of the Sanskrit alphabet, and indicating that Kali is an alter-ego of Sarasvati, the Goddess of Learning. Kali has three eyes, so she can see into the past and future, as well as the present. Her third eye may also be regarded as the psychic eye associated with the Brow chakra, or psychic energy point on the human body. On her girdle are human arms, but though in one hand she carries a severed head, and in another the scythe of the reaper/severer of life, her remaining two hands make gestures that repel fear and promise spiritual enlightenment to those who worship her.

In another account, Kali came from the brow of Parvati in order to slay the demon Daruka. He was threatening the gods, but to shed a single drop of his blood would have caused millions more demons to spring to life. Kali therefore sucked the blood from the demon but, it was claimed, in saving the gods she developed a lust for blood and was no longer within their control (see also Lilith, page 64).

Kali is often pictured dancing on Shiva, whose body she trampled, destroyed and then danced on to restore him to life, thereby transforming Shava (Sanskrit for corpse) to Shiva (the living one). Kali cannot exist without the male principle as a vessel for her energy, and Shiva cannot activate his own power unless she kindles it. As she imbibes his seed by absorbing his penis into her vagina while devouring his entrails, they are not creating a child, but transforming Shiva as Lord of Life and Death and her as Lady of Death and Life, and rebirthing him in an endless cycle of creation and destruction. They are the Lord and Lady of the endless Cosmic Dance. The ocean of blood with which Kali is surrounded is, like the menstrual blood of the Sumero-Babylonian Creator Goddess Tiamet, who brought the world into being, both life-giving and maintaining, and destroying. This is the opposite of both the Oriental passive female yin and active male yang, and the Western view of the initiating male and receptive female.

Kali strips away illusion and what is stagnant and redundant. To her devotees, she brings mercy, bliss and the protection of the fierce Mother, but because she is so powerful she can only be invoked by those with the purest of heart and intent.

Durga

Durga is a slayer of demons and dragons and another consort of Shiva, although she is gentle and loving to all who worship her. She came into being when the Buffalo Demon could not be killed by any of the gods. They became so angry that their energies merged to form Durga; her head came from the energy of Shiva, her arms from Vishnu, her waist from Indra and her fiery eyes from Agni. She killed the Buffalo Demon, first seducing and then beheading him. Unlike Lilith, she is admired for these qualities. Durga rides on a lion or a tiger to emphasise her wild, independent nature.

The story of Durga's creation from the energies of the gods has been grafted on to earlier myths of her as a grain goddess. This independent role is still recalled in numerous villages, where her statue is placed on a mound of clay in which five types of grain have been planted. She was once also

linked to Sri, who is today primarily identified with Sri-Lakshmi, the goddess of good fortune and prosperity.

Chamunda

The Crone aspect, and in many ways the most fascinating Hindu goddess form, is Chamunda, an eight-armed goddess; she is portrayed as an old women with sunken eyes and a skull-like head, a Bone Goddess par excellence. She is associated with tantric (sacred sexuality) cults, much as the Cailleach was involved with the spring maiden transformation through the embrace of the god/chief in Celtic spirituality. Chamunda is a fearsome form of the Goddess. She was said to have been formed from the collective energies of the gods, although it is in fact more likely that she is a direct descendant of the Neolithic Bone Goddess. Like Durga, to whom she is closely related as the Crone form of the younger goddess, she defeated armies of demons and all their weapons and elephants and devoured them.

Chamunda holds a cap made of a skull in her left hand and wears a necklace of skulls, but she grants to those who can look her in the face rebirth in a new, more perfect form; to her devotees she gives protection and relief from suffering.

TOTEM ANIMALS

T HE CONCEPT OF totem (or power) animals is one that has existed in societies throughout the ages. Goddesses might assume the form of their totem creatures, or ride on or be accompanied by them. Macha, the Mother form of the Celtic Morrigu (see page 57), flew over battlefields as a huge crow or raven, accompanied by a flock of ravens, warning of the enemy's approach and spurring her chosen tribe to victory. Badb, the Morrigu's Death/Bone Goddess aspect, became a vulture, which conveyed the souls of the slain to the Otherworld for transformation and healing. She chose who should live and who should die.

Many Ancient Egyptian goddesses were identified with specific animals or birds, and their statues accordingly showed them with animal or bird symbols, or with the heads of their totems. The animals reflected the essential nature of the goddesses. Sekhmet, the Egyptian Solar Goddess of War,

was portrayed as a lioness, or in her goddess form with the head of a lion. She was a powerful magician and healer associated with fire and the hot desert wind, and was much loved by those whom she protected. She is still invoked as a lioness mother to give courage and to guard women who are in difficult situations. Bastet, the Egyptian maiden goddess who ruled women, the home, pregnancy and childbirth, pleasure, sexuality, dancing, music and happiness, took the form of a (usually black) cat, her sacred animal. Hera, the Mother Goddess of Greece, and Juno, her Roman counterpart, had their sacred peacock whose plumes held a natural amulet against the Evil Eye.

Among the Australian Aboriginals, all members of a tribe are said to be descendants of a particular kind of plant or animal, from which the creator goddesses or hero gods fashioned humanity, and which was recognised as their totem, or power symbol. Members of each totem group believed that spirits existed in specific territories in discarnate form until they entered a human body on conception. When a person died his or her spirit would return to the territory of origin no matter where the person was living at the time of death. When a woman who had married into a particular group became pregnant, the conception of her child was linked with a particular spirit from the local totemic place, which had entered her body. Totemic ceremonies were held at the time of the year when the totem species bore fruit or gave birth to its young at sacred sites where it was believed the ancestors resided. These secret rituals were believed to ensure the continuity of the totem species.

According to Native North American belief, all life is the manifestation of the Great Spirit, and as the most recent creation, humankind has much to learn from the older and wiser forms of life. The spirits of animals and birds (and even herbs) can act as guardians who endow those that they protect with their unique strengths and wisdom. Each person has his or her own totem animal or bird, after which they are named, for example Running Deer or White Elk Woman. These names might be taken from a creature who came near a person during an initiation ceremony in adolescence, or during a Vision Quest, a journey involving fasting and isolation to understand more about one's own spiritual nature. It is believed that the acquired wisdom of the creature is incorporated into the person, who might become more courageous, wiser or a healer.

Similar stories of the absorption of the qualities of a particular species also occur in Celtic mythology. A Hebridean tale recalls a fisherman of the McCodrum clan. He captured a selkie (a seal woman) by stealing her seal-

ABOVE: A 19th century painting of Mab, queen of the fairies.

LEFT: An ivory plaque found in the Assyrian palace at Nimrud representing Ishtar, goddess of war and sexual love.

A 15th century French illuminated manuscript depicting the Fairy Morgan showing King Arthur the infidelity of his wife Guinevere with Lancelot.

ABOVE: Ivory head of the goddess Hathor.

LEFT: A carved house post found in the village of Kitimaat on the north-west coast of north America. It describes the myth of the Bear-mother, a tale of the union of a young woman and a bear which resulted in the birth of two semi-human cubs. Their faces can be seen on the hands of this carving.

skin, and she lived with him in her mortal form. They had two children, but as the years went by she searched for her sealskin, for she knew that only by returning to the water could she survive. After finally finding it hidden in a cupboard, she wrapped herself in it and returned to the waves. It is said that the clan was thereafter called McCodrum of the Seals, and that its members were gifted with the sight of the fairy people and were as at home on the water as on land.

Power of the Totem

Perhaps as a sign of the continuing struggle that modern women have to integrate all the demands on their energies, a significant number that I have talked to on the subject have found working with a personal totem creature a valuable integrating focus for their lives. A particular species can represent not only the qualities that the woman most admires, but also strengths lying dormant within her that resonate with the chosen creature. On the other hand, as on a true Vision Quest, a creature may choose to adopt a woman, perhaps forming a psychic link on a day in the countryside, or during a visit to an animal sanctuary. Interestingly, a significant number of women in all age groups increasingly identify with the fiercer creatures, such as bears, lions, tigers, wolves or eagles, seeing them as having a protective as well as an empowering role in their lives. One nurse who regularly travels late at night in London says she surrounds herself by her protective pack of wolves and consequently seems less vulnerable to drunks and the unwanted attentions of human predators.

Women may also recall their first symbolic power animal, a teddy bear or fluffy toy rabbit from childhood, who drove away nightmares and usually remains among their most treasured possessions. Some also remember an invisible animal friend with which they played when they were four or five years old.

You may find that your power animal changes at significant times in your life, or that though other creatures move close, your special creature remains as your guardian throughout adulthood.

My own power animal last spring was a sleek male blackbird who would come and sit on the table outside my caravan while I worked. If I was indoors in the van and forgot to take a break, he would hop on to the steps outside the glass door and call until I went out. He was very assertive but uplifting, and many times his early morning song at the bedroom window

energised me and spurred me out of lethargy. I also made friends with the female bird, brown and more muted, who transmitted quite different energies. She would sit just behind my chair for hours but, unlike the male, would not take food from my hand. If I was indoors and anxious or stressed, she would be on the tree opposite and, when I looked up, I could feel sympathy flowing from her. However, if I was busy she would not appear.

Discovering your Power Animal

Your totem may be an animal or bird indigenous to your region, or one from another part of the world that attracts you. If you explore your ancestry, you can often trace the roots of your fascination. For example Ellie, a banker living in southern England, identified with a moose; her great-grandmother was Norwegian. Your creature may even be one that was indigenous to your home region hundreds of years ago.

Alternatively, your focus may be a mythical animal, such as a unicorn. I have listed in this chapter both magical creatures and animals and birds that are common to a number of cultures and have deep mythological significance.

You may see your power animal regularly in dreams; perhaps it has been present in them since childhood. Or there may be a particular creature with which you feel a resonance when you visit a particular animal park, which perhaps comes over to stand near you, quite unafraid.

§ If you are not aware of a specific animal that is close to you spiritually, you can allow an image to build up out of the light as you gaze into a candle flame.

§ Play music of the sea, the rainforest or bird song, whatever feels right. You may be surprised at the creature you 'see' with your inner eye or sense as you sit quietly, but do not try to rationalise. Your unconscious wisdom is a good guide to the strengths you need in your life at present. Reading the list in the next section may also trigger a connection.

- Alternatively, begin by studying indigenous wildlife either roaming free or in a bird and animal sanctuary. In my local sanctuary in the New Forest, I can observe otters and foxes in their natural habitat while I remain behind glass. Equally, they can observe me. Others, like the deer, roam free and will sometimes come close and offer their heads to be stroked. Go in the early morning or just before dusk, when the park is quiet and you will not be disturbed. Early and late in the season are good times too.

- If you do not achieve results with the above methods, go to a wildlife park with more exotic creatures, choosing a place dedicated to conservation, where the animals are free and happy; a caged creature will not be able to make a connection and neither will you. Find out as much as you can about your chosen creature by reading, watching videos, joining conservation groups and collecting pictures and artefacts that you can use as a focus when you need to summon the particular strength of the creature.

- Find a small statue or model of your power creature that you can hold or place close to your bed. You could select a small ceramic model or charm which can be placed in a tiny cloth bag to carry with you. Or you can craft your own animal from clay or wood. Shops selling ethnic goods, whose profits go to indigenous workers, tend to have artefacts that communicate the spirit of distant lands because they are filled with positive and not exploitative energies.

- Each morning and night as you lie in bed, allow your animal to come into your mind; in time it will appear spontaneously when you need its power. It is said that a new shaman must first find her or his helper spirit in the form of a creature to act as a guide to otherworldly journeys. Your own power creature may begin to work through your dreams, showing you exotic places or centuries, leading the way but remaining close and protective.

Mythological Power Animals and Birds

Bird of paradise: courage, splendour

Birds of paradise are now protected in New Guinea and on its neighbouring islands. The female birds are dull, but the males have brilliant plumage. It may have been these birds or a similarly rainbow-plumed creature that inspired stories of the legendary Bird of Paradise, who according to myth perched in the Tree of Life, especially in legends from the Far East. In Slavonic folklore, Mater Slava (Mother Glory) or Mater Sava (Mother Owl) was depicted as a brilliantly coloured bird with each of her feathers shining in a different hue; she would lead armies to victory or to glorious death.

Dragon: sovereignty, inspiration, guardianship

According to the early myths of lands from the Middle East to Central America, the original Dragon was a representation of the Earth Mother (see Gaia, page 14). Dragon-slaying myths have evolved to represent the struggle to defeat the Mother Goddess worship that continued long after the establishment of monotheistic patriarchal religions. Christianity has many examples of dragon-slaying saints – female as well as male (see Saints, page 250). In the Classical world, however, dragons were said to hold the secrets of the Earth and to guard rich treasure. To the Celts they were the emblem of kingship. In China, dragons heralded good fortune and brought rain in spring.

Phoenix: rebirth, perfection

The phoenix is of Arabian origin, but can be found in the tales of many lands. In Ancient Egypt it was the bird of the Sun God Ra and a sign of resurrection, as the sun was seen to be reborn with each new day. The phoenix burned itself on a funeral pyre every five hundred years and a young phoenix rose golden from the ashes.

To the Chinese, the phoenix is one of the sacred creatures, like the dragon, and in China and Japan its appearance was once said to foretell the coming of a great emperor or sage; images of the phoenix were carried to ensure long life and health. In the Western world, the phoenix concept was adopted by mediaeval alchemists, and the resurrected 'glorious phoenix' was the symbol of alchemy's ultimate aim of turning base metal into gold. The

bird is described as having brilliant gold, red and purple feathers, and as being of the size of a huge eagle.

Thunderbird: instinctual power, fertility

Thunderbirds, a magical form of the eagle, are most usually associated with Amerindian tradition. To many Native American nations, the thunderbird symbolises the power of nature; it is the bringer of rain, which pours from a lake on its back as it flies, while its flashing eyes create lightning and its vast, eagle-like wings bring about thunder. Japan also has a thunderbird that resembles a giant rook. It is a bird of the sun, creating thunder and lightning, and guarding the approaches to the heavens.

Unicorn: purity, healing

A pure white horse with a spiral horn in the centre of its forehead, the unicorn was first described in 398 BC by the Greek, Cresias. He travelled throughout Persia and the Far East and told of a creature he encountered that was remarkably similar to the fabled unicorn. Cresias said that the dust from its horn had healing properties, a power that was also mentioned in stories from many other lands. In China, the unicorn was thought to 'see' the evil in human hearts and to kill the wicked with a single thrust of its horn, hence its associations with holiness and purity. The unicorn of myth could run faster than light and walk across grass without disturbing it.

Power Animals and Birds from the Natural World

The creatures listed below all have powerful female associations, and are empowering for women particularly in the world of work. Each has traditional mythological qualities, but as you work with your chosen totem, you will discover unique strengths that mesh with your own evolving spirituality.

Bear: protection, connection with the wise ancestors

Bears were worshipped and sacrificed by early humans. Bear shrines and bear skulls and bones have been discovered buried with the remains of Neanderthal Man. Because bears hibernate in caves (which are regarded by

some cultures as the womb of the Goddess) and the female bear nurtures her young for many years, they are seen as possessing strong maternal qualities that are expressed as fierceness, especially in protecting the young. In Ancient Greece and Rome, bears were sacred to the moon goddesses Artemis and to Diana. In the cult of Artemis, maidens in yellow robes assumed the roles of bears at the annual festival of Brauronia. A number of far northern cultures, for example in Siberia, claim ancestry from bears. Indeed, many male and female shamans claim direct descent from a bear that has been killed at the time when the shaman or shamaness undergoes a ritual death and she or he is thus empowered with the spirit of the reborn bear.

Buffalo (bison): generosity of spirit, bringer of abundance

The buffalo may become the power animal of women who feel affinity with the Native North American world. To the nations of this world, the buffalo was the source of everything needed for survival: flesh for food, bones for cooking implements, weapons and tools, and skin for clothes and for covering tepees. Even the sinews of the buffalo were used for sewing. According to legend, White Buffalo Calf Woman (see The Medicine Women, page 243) not only brought knowledge of healing and agriculture to the Lakota nation, but also promised that she would return to lead the people into the revival of their spirituality after the sufferings that would come. Even though the buffalo herds were almost wiped out by the European settlers, a recently born white buffalo calf has become a symbol of hope for these Native Americans.

Bull: animus power, survival instincts

The bull is an icon that appears in early Neolithic art in images that depict the Earth Mother giving birth to a bull/Horned God figure as her son/consort. Bull dances and bull sacrifices, the origin of the bull fight, were performed in honour of the Mother Goddess in pre-Christian times in Mediterranean lands such as Spain; the vestiges of these ceremonies have survived as bull fighting. The bull is a lunar symbol and the Ancient Greeks called one aspect of Artemis, the Lunar Huntress Goddess, Tauropolos, which means slayer of bulls (see also Labyrinths for the Bull of Minos myth, page 279). The bull was also sacred to Freyja, the Viking Goddess of Love and Fertility.

Butterfly: transformation, renewal

The butterfly is often associated with the sixteenth-century mystic St Teresa of Avila, who likened the process of dying to a butterfly emerging from a chrysalis. Because of its transience, the butterfly is also a symbol of living in the present, a reminder to enjoy each day for what it is without always worrying about a past that cannot be changed or a future as yet unmade. According to early Greek myths, the butterfly is the mortal Psyche, whose name is Greek for soul. Psyche married Eros, the God of Love, but was only permitted to meet him in darkness; on her death, she was transformed into a butterfly, a common form for the human soul to take between incarnations.

Cat: sensuality, independence

Most of the lore is associated with black cats. Any unlucky connotations derive because two black cats pulled the chariot of the Viking Freyja. When Scandinavia was Christianised in the eleventh century, Freyja was downgraded to a witch and banished to the top of a mountain; as witches' familiars, black cats shared her fate. It is said, however, possibly because of Freyja's role as Goddess of Love, that a woman who keeps black cats will never lack for lovers. In contrast, Bastet, the Egyptian Cat Goddess, who accompanied the sun God Ra in his solar boat and protected him from the serpent Apep, gave the black cat more fortunate associations.

Crow: mature wisdom, magical powers

Crows were sacred to Athena, Greek Goddess of Wisdom, although she would not allow them to perch on the Acropolis in Athens since this was regarded as a bad omen. Generally, however, they are the sacred birds of the crone goddesses such as Cailleach Bhuer, or the Blue Hag, the Scottish Crone Goddess/fairy of winter who walks through the Highlands of Scotland in blue or white robes with her crow perched on her left shoulder. In Amerindian lore, the crow/raven is a teacher of magic.

Deer: sensitivity, swiftness of response

In the north of Scotland and the Scottish Isles especially, there is a long tradition of deer goddesses/fairies in the form of deer. These date back to the

hunter tribes, worshippers of the Mother Goddess as Mistress of the Herds, who released animals so that they might be hunted for food. This tradition continues to this day in northern Scandinavia, the Arctic Circle, North America and Siberia (see Shamanism, page 250). In European folklore, it was said that fairies would frequently assume the form of a deer to escape pursuit.

Dolphin: healing, spirituality

Many of the goddesses took this most intelligent of creatures for their icon; they include Aphrodite and Venus, the love goddesses; the sensual Ishtar of Babylonian mythology and Isis in Ancient Egypt. Women living in cities often first make contact with dolphins when they hear music into which the call of the dolphin has been interwoven. Dolphins are reputed to protect mothers and children and have proved powerful healers, especially of children and those suffering from deep emotional distress.

Dove: emissary of peace, love

A far more powerful totem than it superficially appears to be, the dove features in the Flood stories of the Chaldeans, Babylonians, Hebrews and Greeks as a symbol of peace and reconciliation. It is an emblem of Venus, representing faithful and committed love. The dove is also sacred to wise Athena, and is the symbol of Sophia, Goddess of Wisdom, linking her with the concept of the female Holy Spirit (see page 149). The cooing of sacred pigeons or doves in the oracular groves dedicated to Zeus at Dodona was used for prophecy by the priestesses.

Eagle: vision, limitless potential

In Amerindian lore, the feathers of the eagle carry the prayers of the people to the Father Sun. It was said that the eagle was the creature who could fly closest to the sun and not be burned. It could also (according to legend) look into the noonday sun and not be blinded. Because of this, and due to its association with Sky Fathers in many cultures, it is a totem that is adopted by women who have great ambitions or are very idealistic and work for the betterment of humankind. Eagle feathers are a symbol of healing wisdom.

Frog: empathy, fertility

The lifecycle of the frog is, like the butterfly's, one of transformation. In Amerinidan lore, the frog is the rain bringer. In Ancient Egypt, Heket, the frog-headed Goddess of Childbirth, gave life to the forms her husband created from clay. According to Romany legend, after the Crucifixion, Mary, Mother of Christ was comforted by a mother frog. Mary blessed it and said that thenceforth wherever a frog was found, the water would always be pure enough for humans.

Horse: stamina, a traveller

The horse, which was first domesticated in about 1750 BC, is a magical symbol of swiftness and power. Pegasus, the winged horse, was born from the neck of Medusa when she was slain by Perseus, and thus represents her transformed power. Epona was the Celtic Horse Goddess, frequently depicted riding a mare or represented as a mare with a foal; she was a powerful fertility goddess as well as a goddess of death and rebirth, and was adopted by the Romans.

Lioness: leadership, fierce nurturing power

Lion goddesses were important in Ancient Egypt and the Middle East. Ashtoreth, or Astarte, the Phoenician Moon Goddess and Goddess of War, is depicted with a lioness's head, as is the fierce leonine warrior Sun Goddess Sekhmet. In nature, the female lion is the killer of prey and cares for the entire pride of lions as well as her own young.

Owl: wisdom, the power of the night and the shadow self

The owl is called Night Eagle in Amerindian lore, being the bird who is Lady of the Night and Moon as the eagle is Lord of the Day and the Sun. In the Classical world, the owl was the special bird of the Greek Athena; in Roman times, it was the bird of Minerva, Goddess of Wisdom. The darker connotations of the owl originated in Rome, where the deaths of several Roman Emperors were foretold by an owl landing on the roofs of their palaces and hooting. The association with death also came from Celtic lore, in which the owl was regarded as the 'night hag', a form of the Cailleach, or Hag of Winter.

Pelican: devotion, worthwhile sacrifice

The pelican is famed for her maternal instinct. People once believed that when the mother pelican was reaching into her pouch she was ripping open her breast to feed her young on her own blood. Legends grew up according to which the pelican could revive infant birds who died by feeding them her life blood (it was said that she accidentally smothered some with her devotion). This image was adopted, after a vision by St Gertrude, as a representation of the sacrifice of Christ. The pelican with her brood also became a heraldic symbol of piety.

Stag: male principle, the hunter

The stag is the symbol of the Horned God, who was the son/consort of the Neolithic Earth Goddess. Cernunnos was a generic term, meaning Horned One, for the various horned gods of the Celtic tradition. He was Lord of Winter, the Hunt, animals, death, male fertility and the Underworld. Cernunnos's importance is in his continuing role as the male principle in witchcraft through the ages, in modern Wicca and in other neo-pagan faiths. The stag is a good power animal in the urban jungle.

Stork: life bringer, enduring love

Storks are said to carry unborn babies from the salt marshes where they grow to waiting parents. The strong association with birth came about because the stork represented woman as the bringer of life in the form of the Classical Mother Goddesses, Hera and Juno. Because the stork was also sacred to Venus, a nesting pair of storks on or near a home was considered to be a blessing from this goddess and a promise of enduring love. In many countries, the stork is encouraged to nest on house-tops. According to Scandinavian myth, the stork got its name at the Crucifixion. A stork was said to have flown around the cross, uttering cries of distress, 'styrka, styrka', which means strengthen.

Swan: renewal, artistic abilities

According to one Indian creation myth, the swan laid the golden cosmic egg from which Brahma, Hindu Creator of the Universe, emerged. A swan was said to carry Saraswati, Hindu Goddess of Wisdom and Music and the wife

of Brahma, whenever she travelled. The black swans of Australia are in some areas of that country considered the manifestation of the mother/sister female counterpart of Balame, the Aboriginal All-Father. In the Celtic tradition, swan goddesses/fairies were famed for their musical gifts and healing powers, and were identifiable by the gold and silver chains around their necks. In the Viking tradition, the Valkyries, beautiful maidens who served Odin, Father of the Gods, often assumed the forms of swans when they flew across battlefields in order to choose those who had died the most bravely to return with them to Valhalla.

Tigress: courage, longevity

Representing strongly animus power, the tiger is the totem of a number of younger women I have interviewed who function in highly competitive or chauvinistic workplaces or school rooms. The tiger is the King of Beasts in Eastern mythology. In China, the tiger is given the title of Lord of the Land Animals, and the souls of tigers are said to pass into amber after their deaths. In Japan, the tiger is believed to live for a thousand years. According to Malaysian legend, tigers contain the souls of sorcerers and therefore must not be referred to for fear of attracting bad magic.

Turtle: strong foundations, integration

In Amerindian lore, the turtle brought the Earth from the primordial waters. In Chinese myth, four turtles support the world on their backs. When they roll over to warm themselves in the sun, earthquakes or tidal waves occur. Because the turtle carries her home on her back and can live in water or on land, she is regarded as being complete in herself.

Wolf: altruism, defender of others

Legends abound of mother wolves suckling human children. Lupa was the Roman goddess she-wolf who suckled Romulus and Remus, the founders of Rome. The Victorian poet and author Rudyard Kipling recounts in the *Jungle Book* his tale of Mowgli, who was protected by a she-wolf. It is said that the female wolf is the fiercest of all creatures in defence of her young and her pack, from whom even a tiger will run away.

Vampirism and Women

VAMPIRISM, OR MORE specifically its mythology, contains powerful suppressed fears that touch the most primitive human emotions. Although vampire myths existed in countries as far apart as Australia, the frozen north, the Mediterranean, India, Japan and China, it was in eastern Europe that vampire lore was fuelled and entered the literature of Europe and America. All Turkish gypsies, for example, were believed to be vampires. This fallacy began when cases of vampire attacks began to filter into western Europe after Charles V1, Emperor of Austria, drove the Turkish armies out of eastern Europe in 1718.

Vampire myth in the eighteenth century and beyond not only touched deep, instinctive terrors of blood or being eaten or buried alive, but was also closely linked to unbridled sexuality (even in the twenty-first century, the love bite is still often considered as proof of a truly erotic relationship). For in the Gothic representation, and still to some extent in modern vampiric portrayals, women were helpless virginal victims, transformed against their wills by the all-powerful and usually male predatory vampires into sexually insatiable seductresses. This was not quite as liberating for the female of the eighteenth and nineteenth centuries as it sounds, for it could incite fantasies or even actual abuse by men who felt guilty about enjoying sex.

The current crazes for all things Gothic and vampire societies have ironically grown up at a time when it is known that blood spreads deadly diseases such as Aids. However, at its most spiritual level the modern vampire cult links with the energies of crone goddesses such as Hecate and the Hindu Kali. Even beyond cults, the vampire symbolism can, if consciously worked with in fantasy and dream, give expression to and empower the inner wild woman who is not ashamed or afraid of her own blood (especially menstrual blood) to take the initiative in sexuality. Because the vampire is by definition beyond conventional society, it can also help women to work through repressed anger and restrictive conventions.

Female Vampires

At the height of vampire fever, there were reports of actual as well as legendary female vampires, the most famous of whom was Elizabeth

Bathory. How many of her vile deeds are myth is uncertain, since the records of her trial were considered to be so horrendous that they were locked away and only partially survived. Moreover, most of the evidence at her trial came from the confessions of her alleged accomplices, who were tortured and executed. Most significantly, perhaps, Elizabeth Bathory was born in 1560 into a family of wealthy landowners in Transylvania, and married the older and equally rich Count Ferencz Nadasdy. When he died in 1604 and she moved back to her family lands near Vienna, Elizabeth became the target of envy of local male landowners who coveted her property and wealth. It is claimed that her vampiric career began when, because of her husband's frequent infidelities, she began to fear that she was losing her beauty. She discovered that when she hit a young servant girl across the face with scissors, the girl's blood made her own skin appear younger; thereafter, according to her accusers, she sought to obtain the blood of young girls to keep her youth. Her husband was apparently unaware of the source of her new radiance.

It is said that by 1610 Elizabeth Bathory had murdered 600 young women. Elizabeth apparently tortured her victims for months before they died, even sticking sharp spikes into them while they were in a cage on the ceiling so that she might bathe in their blood. The time between the first investigations of her crimes, her trial and the confiscation of her lands was a matter of months, and she was walled up for the rest of her life in an upper room of her own castle that had only air slits and a hatch for food.

Did Elizabeth Bathory's continuing beauty and perhaps a refusal to accept the sexual favours of local landowners attract spite from both them and their wives? Did they spread rumours that Elizabeth could only maintain her beauty by vampirism? Had her experiences with an unfaithful husband convinced her that it was better not to marry again, so that the only way to obtain her lands was by accusation that appealed to popular superstition?

Dracula Myth

Vlad the Impaler, the original male Dracula, was the inspiration for the first Dracula book in 1897 by Bram Stoker. The real Vlad allegedly lived in the fifteenth century in Transylvania and was called Vlad Dracul, or Vlad the Dragon, after the Order of the Dragon into which he was initiated before taking power (*dracul* could mean either 'dragon' or 'devil'). His viciousness

in impaling enemies – and indeed his own countrymen – on poles when he signed an allegiance with the Turks, the sexual tortures he inflicted on the women he branded as unchaste and his lust for eating live birds when he was imprisoned have created the powerful sexual and sadistic image of a male vampire. The novelist cleaned up the vile Vlad, portraying him as a Victorian Count in immaculate evening dress and white gloves – a rather more alluring figure than the prototype for innocent young ladies (and one bearing more resemblance to a predatory Victorian male).

In Bram Stoker's novel, the young solicitor Jonathan Harker awakens at Castle Dracula to find three young, beautiful vampire women around his bed; he is only saved from giving in to their sexual advances by their controller/husband Count Dracula, no less than the sanitised Vlad.

But nowhere is the transformation more stark than when, in the same novel, the virginal Lucy Weston is attracted to and bitten by Dracula. Lucy becomes a vampire herself after her death, and her transformation is described as 'purity turned to voluptuous wantonness'. Seductive women are still frequently called vamps.

Explaining Vampirism

A number of diseases not recognised until recent times may have suggested the presence of a vampire to superstitious people who were eager for a scape-goat for outbreaks of ill-luck, or for fatal epidemics in villages. The tradition of the sun being fatal to vampires, for example, may according to modern medical research have its roots in the rare genetic blood condition porphyria, which makes its victims extremely sensitive to light, causes pale skin and results in the incisor teeth looking bigger than normal. In the eighteenth and even the nineteenth centuries, vampirism was also a good excuse for putting away either in death or in a mental institution a faithless wife who suddenly displayed sexual desire or started an affair, particularly if the husband displayed signs of anaemia, as many people did at the time due to poor diet.

Modern Myths of Vampires

The contemporary American writer Anne Rice's vampire novels, especially *Interview with a Vampire*, which has been made into a film, explore the

theme of the outsider in society. *Interview with a Vampire* portrays the inno-cent female victim who is attempting to turn avenger, but who is crushed by the forces ranged against her that prevent her from expressing power and sexuality creativity.

The story, which begins in modern-day San Francisco, takes the form of an interview with Louis. Once an eighteenth-century Mississippi plantation owner, Louis was bitten by a vampire called Lestsat, who became his companion/foe over the ensuing centuries. The interview explores the agony of Louis' life as a vampire who retains human feelings. To me, however, the most fascinating character is Claudia, the daughter created through vampirism by Louis and Lestat. In the novel and film, Claudia is a slave girl whom Louis kills when he finds her weeping by her dead mother, who has died of the plague. Louis feels that it is better for her to be a vampire than to die, and Lestat binds her to them through his blood and that of Louis. Over the years, Claudia grows mentally and emotionally into a woman, but is trapped in the body of a five-year-old, although she acts cruelly, in accordance with her vampiric blood. Her growing struggle is for freedom to shed the daughter role (she plots the death of Lestat). She craves knowledge, enlightenment and physical maturity; her struggle ends when Lestat causes her destruction by sunlight.

One might say that Claudia represents powerless woman, forced to act vampirically to survive in an unequal world, and seeking authenticity for what she is; ultimately, she is destroyed by being denied true power and knowledge. This knowledge resides in the book in the male power icon Lestat.

Anne Rice has commented:

> '**W**riters write about what obsesses them. You draw those cards. I lost my mother when I was 14. My daughter died at the age of 6. I lost my faith as a Catholic. When I'm writing, the darkness is always there. I go where the pain is.'
>
> PEOPLE, 5 DECEMBER 1988

The pain of trying to hold on to the memory of her daughter, then letting go in Claudia's death, makes Anne Rice's Claudia an emotive character on many levels, especially for women struggling with identity issues.

Vampire Slayers, Mythology Reborn

Vampire slayers have appeared in myth from early times. According to Croatian folklore a potential slayer, or *kresnik*, would be indicated if a baby was born within a light-coloured caul, or membrane. A vampire slayer might begin to kill vampires from the age of about seven, with adolescence being the usual time for powers to awaken.

This dusty folk myth has been revived as a major teenage cult in the form of the incredibly popular US television series *Buffy the Vampire Slayer*, which has been spun-off into books, video games and all manner of role-playing exercises.

Buffy is not old or ugly, but blonde and definitely nubile, a rebel but every man's ideal daughter, apart from her violent, albeit justifiable forays, which wreak havoc with her High School career. Her Watcher, or protector, is the quiet and all-wise older man Rupert Giles, the librarian. Buffy is inevitably seduced by the handsome young vampire Angel, who is struggling to be a good guy according to whether the gypsy's curse on him that he can have a soul as long as he is unhappy is working. Buffy unfortunately reactivates the blood lust in Angel through a single, joyous night of passion, women's lust again getting everyone into trouble. Contrast the blonde slayer with the evil, dark Drusilla, with her hypnotic powers. It was said that Drusilla's family were killed by Angel more than a hundred years ago, and that he then turned her into a demoness. It was then that Drusilla began to terrorise people with her vampiric ways; indeed she was nearly killed by a crowd in Prague (more eastern European mystery). Another lady diverting her anger into thoroughly anti-social activities, or commercial interests cloaking the primitive myth in million-dollar clothing?

PART THREE

Women, Magic and Wisdom

❧

*Unfolding the mysteries
of female knowledge*

THIS SECTION LOOKS at myths about enchantresses and fairy women, as well as mortal women who have encountered other worldly beings.

When we were children we demonstrated clairvoyant powers more easily than we could fasten our shoelaces. As we jumped down steps and our rainbow spirit body danced in front of us, we could not understand why the adults were not laughing too. We could see essences in flowers and talk to fairy beings, and throw coins into wishing wells, knowing that even if no handsome prince materialised in the water over our shoulder, one day we would be happy and make all those dreams come true.

Reclaiming the Magic

Although our childhood may be gone, there are times when we know that the magical child is still within us and that when the tree spirits opened doors in the forest, we were not just fantasising, but glimpsing another dimension that coexists with our own. It is only as blinkered adults that we are arrogant enough to assume that we are the only or indeed the most evolved beings in the universe.

So this part of the book is in a sense a reconnection with those magical islands with mysterious enchantresses, with crystal castles beneath the lakes and fairy music heard through the mist. They exist in legend and are buried in our memories from childhood and in our genetic make-up, which may hold a blueprint of the folk memory of humankind.

Power Behind the Image

This part of the book is, however, more than a walk down the memory lane of past centuries, for the fey world also holds great potency behind its ethereal forms. The great goddesses of birth, death and transformation were, over the millennia, trivialised or demonised as wicked enchantresses like the Breton Vivien, Lady of the Lake, who bound

Merlin with his own magic, and the Greek Circe who turned sailors into pigs and whose island was filled with bones.

The powerful fate goddesses became in fairy tale benign godmothers whose sole function was to ensure that every embryonic princess found her prince after a turn or two around the wild wood convinced her that reality did not have much to offer. The Titan Goddess Themis, Ancient Greek Goddess of Justice and Order and the mother of the Fates and the Seasons, was scarcely recognisable by Elizabethan times in the petulant and petty-minded Titania, Queen of the Fairies, in Shakespeare's *Midsummer Night's Dream*. But the power is not gone, rather it remains to be explored as our deep memories are reactivated by the stories.

Dark Wood

Fairies and women are obviously linked in the patriarchal mind, for men regarded women as having supernatural powers, connected with their ability to give birth and their innate intuitive abilities. As women were accorded less respect in society, so this 'irrational' side became associated with evil, and female fairies were increasingly portrayed as evil temptresses of innocent men.

Moreover, in more superstitious times, some men cynically exploited fairy myths as an excuse to cast off their wives or even kill them. In Ireland as recently as 1895, Michael Cleary burned his feisty 'fairy wife' to death, claiming that his true wife had been stolen by fairies. Other brides allegedly abducted by fairies may have been sent to distant workhouses if their bridegrooms discovered that they were pregnant by another man. As late as Victorian times, servant girls and female farm workers were too often regarded as the property of their employers and were hastily married off to fellow workers with the Master's blessing as a way of offloading a pregnant and therefore useless worker.

In spite of this dark interpretation, the fey world is one of both enchantment and great potential for exploring our own otherworldly aspects – for we may be sisters of the fey women who resonate with the rainbow form we carry within.

WOMAN AS ENCHANTRESS

I N THIS SECTION, I have concentrated on three enchantresses: Circe, the most notorious witch of the Classical world, who turned men into tame beasts on her magical isle; Morgan le Fey, half-sister of King Arthur, who was regarded as the Sun King; and Vivien/Nimue, the Arthurian Lady of the Lake who bewitched the wizard Merlin.

All three enchantresses inhabited enchanted islands, marking their separation from the world. All three, according to the traditional (male) myth-weavers, used their magical powers for the purpose of gaining power over and destroying heroes/kings through seduction. Both the mediaeval chroniclers of Morgan le Fey and Vivien, and the Classical writers who described Circe, were unable to envisage how, except by witchcraft, female dominance over male power icons could have been possible. Nor could they imagine how such dangerous females could have any positive attributes. But search beyond the cultural bias and there emerge three powerful goddesses who acted as sacred guardians of fate and used their powers for transformation and restoration, a process that embraced destruction as well as creation.

Circe

Called in myth a sorceress, Circe was originally probably a sow goddess, a death and transformative aspect of the Great Mother. The fact that she turned the hero Odysseus's followers into swine would strengthen this mythological association. Her island Aeaea meant 'wailing', and her own name derives from the death falcon *kirkos*.

Circe was the daughter of the Greek Sun God Helios and the sea nymph Perse. According to the Roman writer Pliny, she commanded all the stars that controlled humankind's fate. Her island was a Bone or Death Goddess shrine not only to death itself but also to transformation, where the souls of men were symbolically transmigrated into her piglets. By this means, they might eventually be reborn in a more evolved human form, having learned acceptance and gentleness.

It is highly significant that the wild beasts on Circe's magical island, once sailors lured by her wonderful singing were, according to Homer, not at all ferocious but quite tame and 'knew what had befallen them'. Thus they

retained their consciousness or soul during their metempsychosis (transmigration of the soul). Circe shares many common qualities with the Sirens and Breton Morgana (see Women of the Sea, page 116).

According to Homer, Odysseus escaped the fate of his followers because he was given a sacred herb by the Messenger/Healer God Hermes. The herb can perhaps be regarded as a token of Odysseus's status as the chosen one to enter into sacred sexual union with Circe. Examples of a hero visiting the Lands of the Blest, or the Otherworld, meeting the Goddess and returning to the world are common in mythology. Moreover, Circe guided Odysseus in his descent to the Underworld to meet the Theban seer Tiresias, who was to give him the necessary knowledge to return home. Circe also gave Odysseus the animals that he needed to sacrifice to obtain safe passage on his Underworld journey (presumably, Odysseus did not mind that they were fellow sailors).

Robert Graves, a collector of myths whose most significant work was perhaps *The White Goddess*, says that Circe is a moon goddess because of her magical powers and her links with Hecate, the lunar Death Goddess, and he refers to Circe's spinning as a sign that she was a fate goddess. In other versions of the myth, Circe weaves human fate into the braids and tresses of her hair.

Of course, the Classical chroniclers stress that it was Odysseus (assisted by a *god*) who *compels* Circe to restore his companions to human form, and then the story becomes another example of the male outwitting the Mother Goddess representative, who naturally falls in love with him.

Circe was depicted in Classical myth as a jealous enchantress who was blamed for the demise of the lovely sea nymph Scylla, into whose bathing pool she put poison herbs. In other versions of the myth, Poseidon's wife was the one accused of turning Scylla into a hideous, avenging sea monster, the motive again being revenge for seducing 'her man' (see also page 35).

Morgan le Fey

Morgan le Fey is more usually chronicled as a malevolent fairy than as a goddess of fate in the myriad Arthurian legends that have spanned more than fifteen hundred years. 'Morgan the Fairy' has been described as the half-sister of King Arthur, or sometimes as his cousin. She is also identified as the mother of Mordred, who was conceived from her union with Arthur in the sacred marriage, the symbolic sacred sex rite of Sky Father with Earth

Mother (brother and sister consorts were common in pre-Judaic and Christian cultures). This union was a way of ensuring that the blood line was not diluted before the genetic consequences were appreciated. However, such a union did not translate well into mediaeval literature and served to demonise Morgan even further.

One of the best versions of Morgan's life is the late Marion Zimmer Bradley's well-researched novel *Mists of Avalon*. This recounts events from the feminist perspective through the eyes of Morgan le Fey. Ms Bradley makes Arthur and Morgan unaware of their relationship at the time of their sexual union, although the older Lady of the Lake, Vivien, plans the ritual mating for mystical as well as political purposes. According to the writings of Geoffrey of Monmouth, the twelfth-century bishop of St Asaph, Morgan was not Arthur's sister or his enemy, but his lover and chief of a sacred sisterhood of nine priestesses who ruled over Ynis Avallah, the Isle of Apples, synonymous with Avalon.

Some traditions see Morgan as a form of the Celtic Mother/Sovereign Goddess of the Land, to whom King Arthur is accountable. In this role she was called Matrona, and she was also Morgana, the Celtic Goddess of Winter and Death. From this latter title comes her association with the Breton Morgana, a vengeful creature of the sea and another victim of the process of demonising Druidesses (see Women of the Sea, page 116). The word fey, or fay, is linked with both fairy and fate, and Morgan has also been associated with the Irish triple-battle goddesses, the Morrighu, who traditionally protected hero kings. This is in fact Morgan's main function for much of her dealings with Arthur. As his half-sister, she nursed him as a child and she continued to watch over him from cradle to grave.

Certainly, Morgan was herself the priestess if not the Goddess of Sovereignty, bestowing through sacred sex the power and duty for Arthur to maintain the sanctity of the Earth (and therefore to uphold the Mother Goddess religion). Excalibur was given to Arthur by Morgan (or one of the other Ladies of the Lake who occupy the same role in different legends). Excalibur was one of the thirteen sacred Celtic treasures, the 'Sword of Nuada of the Silver Hand', whose sword hand had been cut off in battle. With a new hand fashioned of silver, he had gone on to lead his people to victory. The magical sword identified Arthur as hero king, a reincarnated solar deity, with his Round Table as a gigantic Sun Wheel. Morgan le Fey wove Arthur an enchanted scabbard that would protect him from serious wounding in battle as long as he possessed it. She later took back this gift in an action seen by her detractors, such as the fifteenth-century Malory who

wrote *Morte d'Arthur*, as spite or jealousy because Arthur loved Guinevere.

To Malory, Morgan was the bad witch in contrast to the 'good' Lady of the Lake, a splitting of roles. But in her role as touchstone of the sacred duty of kingship, Morgan felt that Arthur was dissipating the strength of the Sun Wheel by sending the knights who should have been protecting the land in an obsessive search for the Grail cup (see also Grail Women, page 62). This quest for the sacred chalice led many seekers to death or madness. Arthur also failed to uphold the Goddess religion. It was the scattering of the knights that allowed the treacherous Mordred to challenge the old King, who received a mortal wound without the protection of the scabbard and of Morgan, its weaver – although because of his own flaws Mordred also died in the combat.

As High Priestesss and Queen of Avalon, and in her more ancient role of the Goddess of Death and Rebirth, Morgan took the dying Arthur to Avalon for healing and restoration until he should be called again to become the sacred King. She was accompanied in the funeral barge by the other priestesses/goddesses of the sacred sisterhood.

Vivien

Vivien/Viviane, or Nimue, was the original Arthurian Lady of the Lake, the foster- mother of Lancelot and the alternative guardian of Excalibur. Vivien's lake is in the enchanted forest of Broceliande, near Rennes, Brittany, where the French Arthurian tales are set.

According to legend, Merlin several times left the court of King Arthur in the later years and went to Brittany/the Otherworld, where he fell in love with Vivien, who was one of the nine-fold sisterhood (see page 62). According to myth, Merlin taught her his magical arts to increase her occult powers. Her critics say she used feminine wiles to seduce him into revealing his secrets. She then used this sorcery to enclose Merlin in what has variously been said to be a tower, cave, tomb, enchanted wood, or nine magic rings, from which he cannot escape, so that he will never leave her. The tomb of Merlin can still be seen in the forest, and has become a modern-day shrine for petitions and offerings. It is a very spiritual place, suggesting not entrapment, but rather a shrine and sanctuary.

Why would Vivien so enchant Merlin? How could a master magician be bewitched? Was she really punishing Merlin by enclosing him in the tree because he wanted to leave her, as the myth-weavers suggest, or was she

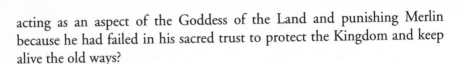

acting as an aspect of the Goddess of the Land and punishing Merlin because he had failed in his sacred trust to protect the Kingdom and keep alive the old ways?

In his *Idylls of the King*, the Victorian poet Tennyson described Vivien as an evil enchantress. However, Edward Arlington Robinson, a poet from Maine who wrote at the beginning of the twentieth century, believed that Merlin allowed Vivien to bind him. If Merlin allowed himself to be enchanted, it may be that he was giving himself into the hands of the Goddess of Death and Transformation in the person of Vivien. Thus he returned willingly to the earth and the Otherworld, which was not a prison but rather the womb of the Earth Mother in which he could await rebirth (see also Bone Goddesses, page 139).

Others argue that as a powerful Lake Lady, Vivien would have equalled Merlin in magical abilities, but that this would not have been acceptable to mediaeval or even later Victorian writers, such as Tennyson. We know from myth that Vivien was the daughter of King Dionas and reputedly the Goddess Diana's godchild, and that she was instructed in the mysteries of plants and stars and pledged as Lake guardian of the magical pool at Broceliande. She met Merlin when she was fifteen and he was very old, and he may have drawn on her youth and powerful psyche to strengthen his failing powers. Merlin may then have transferred his remaining magic to Vivien in readiness for his death.

The tower in which Merlin was enclosed has sometimes been described as made of glass, linking with the glass palace of Caer Wydyr in Annwyn, or the Otherworld, and the name for Glastonbury is Ynis Witrin, the Island of Glass. Merlin had also created a glass castle for Vivien, which was located near the present-day Chateau de Comper in the forest. It may be that the glass castles are linked symbolically and that the image of the glass tower is one that indicates a refuge from the world for Merlin rather than a prison. This remains the most mysterious of the enchantress myths, but one that speaks of spiritual transformation and rebirth and not just misplaced passion.

FAIRY WOMEN
The Goddess in the Fey Tradition

J UST AS CELTIC BARDS preserved the deities of the old religion as the heroes and heroines of their songs, legends and poetry, the Mother Goddess also survived in myth and secret worship as the Good Fairy, the Fairy Godmother or the Queen of the Fairies (see also Weavers of Fate, page 135 and Crone Goddesses, page 125). For example, in Slavonic folklore Rodenica, or Rozhenica, was originally the Lady and Creating Mother of the universe and her husband Rod was the Lord. In later myth, Rod was downsized to the status of household god/protector spirit and Rodenica became an ethereal white fairy who visited newborn children with her daughter to determine their future destinies.

Fairy Godmother

The Fate Goddesses, usually three sisters who are weavers or spinners of the Web of Destiny, appear in the fairy tales of many cultures, separated into the 'good' fairy godmother, protectress and granter of wishes, and the wicked fairy/witch. The bad fairy sometimes doubles as the evil stepmother who possesses magical powers, as in the tale of Snow White. Once the magical mirror proclaims the superior beauty/potential sexuality of the virginal Snow White, the Queen needs all the magical aids at her disposal if she is to remain the dominant female (the prize being, of course, the admiration of the dominant/wealthiest/most elevated man on the scene).

The aristocratic fairy was born in 1697 with the publication of the fairy tales of Charles Perrault in France. In Perrault's *Cinderella*, for example, the fairy godmother assumes the role of Cinderella's dead mother, using her magic to fulfil Cinderella's dream to go to the dance at the palace to win the heart of the prince. But Cinderella must be home by midnight or the magical props will disappear. Here, the fairy godmother doubles as guardian of virginity.

In these rather courtly stories, many of which were based on older, far more savage tales in which the heroine showed a great deal of initiative, the qualities of beauty, innocence and obedience were stressed. This meant that fairy power and protection were directed less into helping the heroine to

negotiate through the wild wood of life, and more into finding a prince who would supply the happy ending. The Disney versions of the popular fairy stories from the 1950s onwards, intended as much for adults as for children, reinforced the message that the right man was the road to bliss for modern women. This was not entirely in the cause of romance, but according to an official guideline. For in the post-war period women were being forced back into the home after their war service so that there would be enough jobs for the returning servicemen.

In the folklore of places where Celtic descendants are numerous, the Cailleach crone has survived in a fairy godmother role as the Bean Tighe. An Irish fairy housekeeper/grandmother who cares for mothers, children and pets, she will finish chores around the home while the family sleeps. Like her more terrifying sister, the banshee (see Bone Goddesses, page 142), she may be attached to a family for generations.

Powerful Fairy Women who were Formerly Goddesses

The Celtic Aine, fairy queen of Munster, continued even during the last century to be regarded as a powerful fertility icon, especially in the area surrounding the Hill of Aine. On St John's Eve (Midsummer), close to the Summer Solstice, local people climbed the hill as they had done for many centuries to pay tribute to the moon, for Aine was formerly a lunar as well as a solar deity. Then, carrying blazing torches of straw tied to poles, they walked in procession, led – it was said – by the fairy goddess herself, down the hillside and through the fields and cattle barns to bring fertility to the land, the animals and the people.

Fairy Queen Temptresses

As the goddesses were downgraded to fairies, some acquired the role of temptresses and abductors of innocent males (fairy kings were portrayed in the same way but more favourably).

In Scotland, myths tell of the *Bean chaol a chot uaine's na gruaige buidhe*, 'the slender woman with green kirtle and yellow hair', a fairy queen who had the abilities to turn water into red wine and to spin the threads of spiders into tartan. By playing her magical reed pipe, she would lure young

men into her fairy hill. Unless they left a piece of iron over the lintel of the entrance, they would be forced to dance and serve the pleasure of the fairy queen until she tired of them and sent them home. But they would find that although it only seemed as though one night had passed in fairyland, decades had gone by in the mortal world, and the fresh-faced milkmaid sweethearts to whom they had sworn eternal fidelity were now ageing great-grandmothers.

The most famous young male abductee, who seems to have actually gained from his visit to fairyland, was Thomas the Rhymer, whose ballad is still performed in folk clubs. The real or 'true Thomas', as he is sometimes called, was Thomas of Earlston (Erceldoune), a thirteenth-century poet who allegedly met the Queen of Elfland under a magical elder tree. In return for a kiss he was forced to go to fairyland with her, although other versions of the story suggest that Thomas was more than willing to be seduced. In a few accounts, the fairy queen became an ugly hag and the ritual mating of youth with the ancient Crone Goddess occurred to maintain the cycle of the seasons and ensure the fertility of the land. Thomas remained in fairyland for seven years, although only three days passed in fairy time. He was rewarded with the gifts of poetry and prophecy, and with a magical harp. It has been argued in recent years that Thomas was in fact initiated into a local witch cult, and that his visions of fairyland were shamanic.

Downsizing in Literature

With the coming of Christianity, the Celtic Goddess Maeve, Queen of Connaught and Warrior Queen, became Mab, Queen of the Fairies. Mab is a corruption of the Gaelic form of her name, *Medb*, which means 'she who intoxicates'. In her former role as a goddess of war, the sight of her would blind enemies, and she could be seen fighting in the centre of any battle on the side of her favoured clan and was able to outrun the fastest horse or the swiftest arrow. Compare her with the sanitised Mab in Shakespeare's *Romeo and Juliet*, of whom Mercutio, Romeo's friend, says:

> '*O then, I see, queen Mab hath been with you,*
> *She is the fairy's midwife, and she comes*
> *In shape no bigger than an agate-stone*
> *On the fore-finger of an alderman.*'

Mab did retain a little of her power in that she brought nightmares to humans when she visited. But she is pictured as 'driving her hazelnut-shell wagon across sleeping faces' (the hazel is the magical tree of wisdom and divination).

Mab is also sometimes associated with Titania, most famously in literature as the mortal-sized wife of Oberon, King of the Fairies, in Shakespeare's *A Midsummer Night's Dream*. In this play she is depicted as petulant, willing to let the seasons go to rack and ruin while she pursues her vendetta against Oberon.

> '*The green corn*
> *Hath rotted 'ere his youth attained a beard;*
> *The fold stands empty in the drowned field*
> *The Spring, Summer, the chiding Autumn, angry Winter,*
> *Change their wonted liveries and the' mazed world*
> *By their increase, know not which is which.*'

However, in the play Titania's power over nature is still acknowledged. For originally she was Themis, the Ancient Greek Titan Goddess of Justice and Order, and the mother of the Fates and the Seasons. She was also the daughter of Gaia, the Earth Goddess, and is linked with Diana.

Being Your Own Fairy Godmother – Making Wishes Come True

I believe we all have a spiritual guardian, whether we visualise him or her as an angel, a fairy godmother or a spirit helper. In carrying out wish rituals, we can tap into this source of power and encouragement. Most important, however, is the inner fairy godmother, the power of those personal strengths you will name here, which can make almost anything possible with belief and sheer determination. Therefore take the first steps in the real world, however small, and let the magic follow.

§ Surround a crystal or glass bowl of water with silver candles, and for your wish-pebbles use small crystals or glass nuggets, green for love, orange for clear identity, yellow for logic and matters of the mind, blue for success and wisdom, purple for psychic development and spirituality, brown for the home, family and security, grey for secrets, pink for babies, children and reconciliation, white for energy and new beginnings, red for change and passion, and black for acceptance and nurturing.

§ Light each of the candles in turn, naming a power or quality you already possess that will help you to fulfil your dream. If you allow the words to come without conscious effort, you may be surprised at the emergence of hidden talents you had never considered developing.

§ Next – in true fairy godmother style – you require a wand. You may already have a long, pointed clear quartz crystal, or another favourite sparkling crystal. Alternatively, you can make a true magic wand with a long, straight twig from a hazel, an ash or a willow tree, which you should rub smooth. Some people split the twig and secure a tiny crystal in the top, but this is not essential.

§ Place a crystal for each of the wishes you are going to make (as many as you like) in a smaller glass bowl.

§ Draw in the air nine ever-increasing, clockwise circles with your wand over the dish of crystals; at the same time, say each of your wishes out loud, beginning with the most important one.

§ Alternatively, you can recite the age-old magical chant, while visualising a brilliant star moving closer and closer as you speak:
'Starlight, star bright, first star I see tonight, I wish I may, I wish I
might, wish the wish I wish tonight.'

§ Cast your first wish crystal into the bowl of water, this time making
the wish silently, and continue until you have dropped all the crystals into the 'magic pool'.

§ Leave the candles to burn through and if the stars are bright, go
outside and repeat the star chant, choosing your special star and
reciting your wishes once more.

WOMEN AND FAIRIES

In Life and Literature

Seeing Fairies

OVER THE CENTURIES there have been thousands of fairy sightings.
Women and girls have reported by far the majority of the cases that I
have collected during my own research, which began twelve years ago with
an investigation into children's psychic experiences. This may be because
women have traditionally been more open to psychic phenomena, and also
because they are more willing than men to talk about their experiences. For
example, Lilian, who is now a healer and clairvoyant in her sixties, related to
me how as a child:

'I used to see fairies in our garden in Cheshire, but especially in the
woods. They were semi-transparent and tiny with wings. I found
myself looking at the little people in shadowy forms. They all looked
different according to whether they belonged to a tree, a flower or a
bush. Each species was the same colour and even the same texture and
would merge into the tree or flower.'

Lilian still sees nature essences in the lovely gardens she creates, as does Julie, a medium who described to me a particular place in Devon where, as an adult, she shared her fairy visions with her own children:

'They [fairies] are very fleeting, like butterflies, but not as small, about the size of squirrels.'

Moreover, fairies have come into the cities. Layla, who is in her early twenties and as a child lived in a council house in a northern industrial town, explained what she saw in her back garden:

'Faces and forms would appear at the sides of my vision. They would appear only for a fraction of a second, and when I looked again they wouldn't be there. . . .The Tree Men . . . were very strange indeed. For a second it would look as if somebody was entering or leaving through an invisible door on a tree trunk. The somebody would be very indistinct and transparent but definitely there. On one occasion a head poked out of a tree, saw me and promptly disappeared back inside.'

Fairies in Folklore

As well as sightings such as those described above, accounts of interactions with fairies (some of them very frightening) are found in folklore spanning hundreds of years from the Celtic world to Scandinavia and Eastern Europe. Many are remarkably consistent in content. Some recent alien abduction accounts by women bear strong similarities to these earlier tales of fey kidnappings. This section focuses on the folk tales that relate to fairies.

Women Who Act as Midwives to Fairies

Midwives were once surrounded by magical and mystical associations. In Greek and Roman times, they were regarded as seers. Although from the fifteenth century onwards they were frequently accused of witchcraft, in remote places, especially those where Celtic peoples predominated, some

did continue practising in secret, which may account for them being fetched in the dead of night (see Witchcraft, page 215).

In folklore, midwives were said to attend fairy births, which they were requested to attend, rather than being taken against their will. It is possible that these folk tales may have their roots in old stories that actually referred to the descendants of tiny, dark Neolithic people who lived in remote forest, marshland or mountain communities. According to Gillian Tyndall, author of *A Handbook of Witches*, a number of such communities might have existed in the Britain until the end of the Middle Ages, when the forests were cut down and the marshlands drained. Others tales undoubtedly referred to communities of outlaws or dispossessed peasants living in the forests. There are still vast tracts of Northern Scandinavia and the Slavonic lands that are deeply forested or mountainous and largely unexplored, and here the legends persist. If there was a difficult birth in one of these communities, one of the settlers might come into a town or large village to seek the help of a midwife, who would be taken in the dead of night, perhaps blindfolded, to a secret destination. Secrecy is a major feature of the legends.

There are also salutary tales of women who agreed to assist in fairy deliveries and who became curious about the fairy folk; a midwife might rub one of her own eyes accidentally or deliberately with the oil with which the fairy baby was washed. Afterwards, she could see fairy people in the everyday world, a gift that normally resulted in the brutal putting out of the offending eye when she acknowledged the fairy mother or relatives at a market days or weeks later. This again may be a folk memory of women who revealed the locations of outlaw communities to which they had ministered. Of course, these stories may be true.

Fairy Abduction of Young Mothers

Nursing mothers were, according to folklore, in great demand to suckle fairy babies both because their milk was said to be richer than that of the fairy mothers, and because it was hoped that it would transmit to the fairy baby the soul that it lacked. They were also said to suckle mortal babies that were abducted to fairyland. Similar experiences are recounted in modern alien abduction accounts.

The time of giving birth was traditionally regarded as very magical and dangerous not only for both mother and child, but also to all who came into contact with the woman, a peril that was supposed to persist from childbirth until the churching or purification ceremony of women in church

forty days after the birth. In Europe until the nineteenth century, nails were hammered into a mother's bed and a child's cradle to deter fairies, which were supposed to fear iron. A fire would be kept burning at all times, and milk from a cow fed with straw from the childbed (which also increased the fertility of the cow) would be given to the mother and child. No new mother would leave home after dark before the christening for fear of being spirited away by the fairies.

According to a variant of the changeling myth, fairies might substitute a mother with a block of wood disguised by glamour, or illusion, to resemble her human form but which would be constantly crying and moaning. Many a woman suffering from post-natal depression may have been treated harshly by superstitious relatives who believed that she had been enchanted by the fairies. Beating was one recommended method of revealing the changeling form in wives as well as in children.

In some stories, a baby was sometimes left behind when the true mother was kidnapped; if it failed to thrive, the father might blame this on the changeling wife who was not taking care of it, rather than on natural causes. Infant mortality remained high until after World War I, and infanticide, cruelty to wives (and to a lesser extent undetected wife murder) were common until Victorian times. A wife who consistently produced sickly boys who did not survive, or girl children for a man who desperately needed a male heir, might suddenly disappear: 'spirited away forever by the fairies' was the official and often unquestioned explanation for her disappearance. In our own age, there have been horrific cases of bride burnings by husbands and relatives among the Asian community, and of young women killed during exorcisms of evil spirits. There are still parts of the world where the value of a woman, except as a bearer of sons, is low and this is a reminder that it has not that long been otherwise in Western society.

Brigit Cleary

Fairy abduction as an excuse for wife murder or beating may sound like pure speculation, but we do know that in Tipperary, Ireland as recently as 1895, Bridget Cleary was tortured and burned to death by her husband Michael. He claimed that his wife had been stolen by the fairies, and that she had been substituted by a changeling. He insisted that after he destroyed the enchanted block of wood (Bridget) his wife would return on a white horse at midnight. Seven of Bridget's neighbours and relatives, including her father and aunt, were also involved and later convicted of her death. A

hundred years later, Angela Bourke, a professor at University College, Dublin and author of *The Burning of Bridget Cleary*, stated that the case demonstrated the clash 'between two different world views, two ways of dealing with troublesome people, two ways of accounting for the irrational, at a time of profound social, economic, and cultural change'.

Bridget Cleary's crime was that she was economically and socially independent by her own efforts, rather than by birth, and was therefore offensive to a traditional community. Presumably, however, had the case gone unpunished, her death would have been very profitable for her husband and family, who would have inherited her money.

Brides in Fairyland

A woman on her wedding day or night was said to be considered a great prize by the fairies, as she was still a virgin but at peak fertility. Until mediaeval times, a woman would be accompanied to the church by identically dressed bridesmaids, so that any watching fairies could not identify the true bride.

Abductions of women probably did take place, but the culprits were probably more worldly. In parts of mediaeval Europe, the local Lord was allowed the use of his serfs' brides on their wedding nights. Rape by wealthy landowners and their sons was a real threat for country women – especially servants in big houses – even in Victorian times. It could be that the traditional return of the abducted bride from the fairies after a year and a day, bearing a babe several months old, was an acceptable way for a husband not to appear cuckolded. She might have been placed in a distant workhouse for the duration of the pregnancy with the collusion of the husband (or father in the case of an unmarried girl). Unlikely? In the UK during the earlier decades of the twentieth century, unmarried mothers as well as those suffering from post-natal depression were routinely assigned to mental hospitals and in some cases disappeared for the rest of their lives.

A typical bride abduction story, which was made into a ballad, was that of the Scottish Colin, whose wife was taken by the fairies, but who was said to return invisibly each day to milk the cows and do the chores. Only her singing could be heard. In other versions of the story she returned after a year and a day with a baby. Was Colin keeping his bride locked away because he had discovered on their wedding night that she was pregnant by someone else, albeit by rape? Did he let her out to do the housework, but allowed no one to see her, only to hear her voice? Or was she truly a bride of the fairies?

PART FOUR

EXPLORING
THE
GODDESS
WITHIN

❧

*Encountering the inner
divinity*

ONCE WE HAVE identified the archetypal goddess forms and tried on the different masks, some of which may feel strange at first, others like coming home, it is time to assimilate their powers into our lives, rather than treating them merely as visitors, albeit welcome ones. This part of the book therefore offers the goddesses house room, so that their energies are available to strengthen, support and enfold us as we work, play, make love, laugh, cry, quarrel and dream.

Welcoming the Goddesses

Your new lodgers will not be possessing spirits or control freaks, even if they will wake you much earlier than normal with plans and challenges and mountains to be climbed before breakfast. Every one of these goddesses or powerful women is your sister, friend, mother or great aunt psychically twice removed. You will be welcoming home part of yourself, and initially it may be a crowded, bumpy ride to enlightenment as you try to merge all the different energies and make sure that everyone is fed and comfortable. Take your time, and as you work through the exercises in this chapter let your emerging powers find expression in physical activities as well as spiritual ones. Walk, swim, cycle, and explore new places and new projects that you may previously have avoided.

We are taught in Western society to split off light from darkness, age from youth, life from death. The Crone is ignored, offered Prozac or given a facelift. The Bone Goddess, her older sister, waits at the grave to take us from the arms of the Crone. She is the gentle grandmother who eases our passing, yet modern society only lets her out at Halloween, once the sacred Celtic Festival of the Dead, when we can laugh at plastic skeletons and light our pumpkin heads to banish the darkness. But in pre-Christian times the Crone and bone goddesses were revered, as they still are in some indigenous societies, as healers of pain and sorrow. Given courage and help from our goddesses, we can connect with that deep female wisdom which assures us that death is just one stage on the

Wheel of Life. If we can welcome the Crone into our lives whatever our age, she will bring kindness and protection and take away all fear.

There is a saying in the *I Ching*: 'Be not sad. Be as the Sun at midday.' By embracing the joy of every moment and accepting the ageing process in ourselves and our relations, we will see the sun and bone mothers go hand in hand, promising that we will never lose our way.

Exploiting the Wisdom Within You

You may find goddesses in other sections of the book that inspire or strengthen you at times when the world seems particularly dark or frightening, when you need energy for a specific project or opportunity, or wake up and know you must be outdoors in the wind and sunshine even for a short time to connect with the wildness within you.

You may also find it helpful to create goddess cards; there are commercial sets, but it is good to make your own. You can stick on to one side of plain white cards images of goddesses downloaded from the Internet or bought as postcards. When you feel uncertain about something, place the cards face down and select one that feels right. You may be sure that the goddess who comes to you will inspire and guide you through the day. You can work with ten, twenty, or a hundred cards. However many or few you use, your intuitive wisdom will ensure that you choose the relevant goddess energy for your specific need.

As well as doing the exercises suggested in this section, you can collect power symbols such as shells, crystals, and statues of the goddesses and totem animals that symbolise their powers. Keep them in your special place as a focus for meditation or quiet contemplation.

WOMEN OF THE SEA
Power and Unpredictability

SEA WOMEN, like the tides they ruled, were reputed to hold the power of life and death over those who sailed across the oceans or fished in them. Rich shoals brought prosperity, while the sudden ferocity of the waves meant the loss of lives and craft. Although the mighty, trident-bearing Poseidon, or Neptune, is the stereotypical image of a sea god, the sea is the womb from which all life came and thus many ocean deities were sea mothers.

Throughout the ages, offerings have been made to sea goddesses to ask for the return of sailors and fisherfolk safely to shore. The wives of sailors would collect sea water in a flask or bottle when their husbands set sail. At the time when the boat was expected to begin the homeward voyage, they would pour the water back into the sea, saying: 'I return what is yours, return mine to me.' In some parts of the world, the first of a catch is still thrown back as an offering to the Sea Mother.

Sea Mothers

Sea mothers have survived in a number of cultures for which fishing is the main source of income, and some date back thousands of years. In Peru, Mama Cocha, or Mother Sea, the Whale Goddess, was originally worshipped by the Incas and has been revered through the ages by the people living along the South American Pacific Coast. Yemaya-Olokun of the Yoruba peoples in West Africa is similarly loved as a sea goddess, as well as feared, for she is also primary deity of Santeria, the form of voodoo practised in Cuba and Brazil (see Women and Voodoo, page 263).

The Brazilian Yemaya, or Iemanjá, is called the Womb of Creation and is the bringer of dreams and prosperity. Altars are created on Brazilian shores on New Year's Eve, and offerings of candles and food are laid on them. These are accepted by Yemaya on the morning tide, for she is an elemental force who not only lives in but is the sea.

In Western magical tradition, fires are created below the high-water mark; these are then surrounded by and eventually consumed by the sea. In

this way, the four ancient elements of water, air, earth and fire are combined, although the superiority of the primal waters is recognised.

Sedna

Because of the importance of the sea as the main source of food, the most powerful spirit in Inuit cosmology was a very ancient fertility mother, the Old Woman who lived under the Sea. She is given different names throughout the Arctic: Nerivik in Alaska and Arnarquagssag in Greenland, but her most common designation is Sedna the Sea Mother, divinity of the ocean and all sea animals.

There are different versions of Sedna's origin, but in all of them she is regarded as the source of the creation of marine life. In the most common myth, Sedna was a beautiful Inuit girl who refused all suitors until she fell in love with a handsome hunter, who let his kayak sway on the waves while he sang to her in her hut. He offered her necklaces of ivory and a tent covered with the finest furs if she would go and live with him in the land of birds. He lured her into his canoe and abducted her, revealing his true form as Kokksaut, the bird phantom. Her father Angusta, who was searching the oceans for his lost daughter, found her weeping alone on an ice-flow. He took her in his canoe, but Kokksaut pursued them. When Angusta refused to hand back his daughter, Kokksaut changed into his evil bird form and created a terrible storm. The waves demanded the sacrifice of Sedna. Angusta became afraid that he had so offended the sea and spirits of the air that he would be killed, and cast Sedna into the waves. When Sedna tried to cling to the boat, her father seized an ivory axe and cut off her fingers. The girl sank into the water. Three times she tried to reach the kayak, but her father hacked at her wounded hands until she was lost beneath the waters. Her fingers became seals, and her knuckles walruses and whales.

The Inuit believe that Sedna controls storms at sea and can either provide or withhold sea creatures for the hunt. When the people do not catch seals or other sea creatures, a shaman dives in astral or soul form to the bottom of the sea to entreat Sedna to set the sea animals loose. He passes first through the kingdom of the dead, then through an abyss with a wheel of ice and a boiling cauldron of seals.

The shaman finally enters a tent under the sea, which is furnished with the skins of the finest sea animals. There, the dark, gigantic Sedna – for she is no longer the beautiful maiden but the Sea Mother/Crone – listens to the magical chants of the shaman and tells him either that the tribe must move

to another place to seek the sea creatures, or that she will send shoals to the current hunting grounds. The shaman combs the tangled hair of the Sea Mother, since she cannot do this herself with her damaged hands. Out of her suffering and the betrayal by her lover and her weak father, Sedna emerges as a fertile Sea Mother who has transformed her pain and suffering into food for the people, though she exacts high standards of them and their shamans.

Stella Maris

Because of the ages-long importance of the stars in navigation, there have been a number of goddesses who bear the title of Stella Maris, or Star of the Sea. With the coming of Christianity, the title was given to the Virgin Mary and she has retained her patronage of sailors and fisherfolk. The name Mari has been used for sea goddesses in different lands, all of whom are described in a similar way, as wearing a blue robe and a pearl necklace, and being fringed with pearly foam. One of the most famous images of Stella Maris is on a Spanish prayer card, which depicts her as a voluptuous goddess wearing a crown and a robe of stars. She is called La Diosa del Mar, Goddess of the Sea, although she is a representation of the Virgin Mary. Similar images of the Virgin crowned with stars are found in many Mediterranean coastal towns and villages and as far west as the Atlantic coast of Brittany.

In an annual ceremony in Venice on Ascension Day, the Doge of Venice ritually casts a golden wedding ring into the waters. This ceremony is a relic of the Sacred Marriage, which in seafaring communities often takes place between the sea and the people.

The Ancient Egyptian Mother Goddess Isis was known as Stella Maris when her worship spread to Rome, and for many centuries she and the Virgin Mary were interchangeable in seafaring communities, especially where representations of her were dark-skinned (see The Black Madonna, page 224). Isis was probably first called Stella Maris when the Greek Alexander the Great conquered Ancient Egypt. Even before this, she had been associated with Sirius the Dog Star, whose rising in mid-July heralded the flooding of the Nile and the return of fertility to the land. In Western ceremonial magic, Isis is worshipped as a deity of the sea and is invoked by priestesses; she is said to rise over the waves in her veiled or hidden aspect (see also Isis, page 176).

Goddesses Who Became Vengeful Temptresses

In earlier times, a goddess of the sea would be worshipped in all her aspects and moods: as giver and taker of life, alternately benign and vengeful, as pure maiden, and as sultry siren and brooding hag. But with the rise of the Sea Fathers of the Classical world and with Christianisation, her role became split between innocent fairy mermaids/Mary of the Sea and the temptresses/pagan goddesses who dragged sailors beneath the waves and seduced the unwary (or the more than willing, as the case might be).

Cliodna

Clionda of the Golden Hair was the daughter of Manannan, Celtic Sea God and Lord of the Isle of Man. Like her father, she once ruled over the sea. She was also Queen of the Land of Promise, a realm of the Celtic Otherworld in which there was perpetual peace and harmony. When she was downsized to a fairy queen, she took mortal lovers to fairyland, never to return. However, she fell in love with the young mortal Ciabhan so deeply that she left the Otherworld to live with him. One day while he was out hunting, her father sent a fairy minstrel to enchant her and carried her back in a magical sleep. She is reputed to be seen on seashores either as a huge wave or as a seabird seeking her lost love. As Sea Queen, Clionda still rules over every ninth wave, and she is said to heal the sick with her magical birds.

Sirens

> '*There is no home-coming for the man who draws near them unawares, for with their high clear song the Sirens bewitch him, as they sit there in a meadow piled high with the mouldering skeletons of men, whose withered skin still hangs upon their bones.*'
>
> HOMER, *ODYSSEY* 12. LL. 39

The Sirens are very ancient goddesses; it was said that they sang while Anake, Goddess of Unalterable Necessity, wove the web of the universe (see Weavers of Fate, page 135). They were great seers and also, like Circe, Death

and Transformation Goddesses; on their island there were heaps of white bones (see also Bone Goddesses, page 139), which were re-formed into more perfect form by their magical singing.

The Sirens were beautiful half-women, half-birds; they had taken wings in order to help Demeter search for her daughter Persephone, who had been abducted by the Underworld God Hades. Their beautiful singing was originally said to induce a state of forgetfulness of the everyday world in sailors who heard them and then remained on their wonderful island. But that was not good for the social order of the ideal Greek male, who was constantly reminded that a woman's fidelity was important for him. So the Sirens became evil temptresses, blamed not only for seducing sailors against their will, but also for the wrecking of ships that steered on to rocks not through human error or bad weather, but because their sailors were lulled by the Sirens' enchantment.

Morgans or Morgana

In Brittany too, there is a whole tradition of powerful sea fairy goddesses who cause storms and drag sailors to their deaths beneath the waves in unsuccessful attempts to satisfy their own passions.

The Morgana legends first appeared at the time when Brittany was Christanised in the fifth century and certain powerful Druidesses and noble-women would not submit to the patriarchal power of the Church. The first Morgan was Dahut, daughter of Gradlon, the King of Cornouaille in Brittany, who created Ys, a beautiful city built below sea level with walls to keep back the water. A dyke was opened to allow fishing boats to leave and enter.

Dahut was probably a Druidess who still worshipped the old gods and so was in constant conflict with Corentin, the bishop of Quimper. She was accused of bringing disrepute to the city with her unbridled passions and, it is claimed, caused the destruction of the city by handing the keys to the dyke, which she had stolen from her father, to her lover the Devil. Satan flooded the town and the waves drowned all the citizens except Gradlon and Corentin, the noble bishop, and Dahut, who clung to the back of her father's horse. But the bishop told Gradlon to cast Dahut into the sea or he too would be drowned. Gradlon, who was weak (like Sedna's father), pushed his daughter into the sea, leaving her to perish. Dahut did not die but was transformed into the vengeful Marie Morgana. Other versions of the tale assign the role of the condemning cleric to St Guenole, who was the first missionary.

Cliodna Sea Ritual for Power

Sea rituals can be practised by using tidal rivers. If you live a long way from the ocean, you can make sea water using sea salt. But at a day on the shore, either alone or with someone with whom you are in tune, you can establish a potent connection with this primal power.

- Working on the ebb tide takes away sorrow, pain or guilt. On the incoming tide you can attract love, happiness, health or prosperity. The point of tide turn is the most powerful of all.

- When you ask for power from the sea, make an offering of something that will not pollute her, such as flowers, fruits, crystals or coins. You can obtain pure silver coins from a museum shop, or use a small gold or silver earring or charm.

- Decide which power you need the most – for example courage, perseverance, ingenuity, righteous anger. The power may be bound up with a particular cause, such as righting an injustice in your life or gaining promotion.

- Name your desire, following the rhythm of the sea, so that you make your wish/empowerment as each wave crashes on to the shore. Finish on the ninth wave.

- Find a double shell on the shore (or buy one) and in it place your offering.

- Bind the shells together nine times with seaweed or with natural twine, repeating your empowerment, which can either be quite specific, such as 'Let me pass my exam,' or more general, like 'Fill my life with light.'

- Then cast the shell on to the ninth wave, if possible at tide turn, saying: 'Lady of the ocean, Goddess of the Sea, I return what is yours send power to me.'

- Look where the wave hits the shore and you may find a special stone, a gift from the Sea Goddess that you can use as a charm.

> ⚡ If you have made your own sea water, cast *your* stone (a shell, or a white stone if you do not have one) and a few drops of salt water into any flowing stream or water course while making a wish.

Virgin Goddesses
The Power of Separate Identity

THE VIRGIN, or Maiden, was originally an aspect of the Great Goddess associated with the waxing moon, representing the Springtime, and the Goddess in her pre-childbearing role (see Seasonal Goddesses, page 20 and Moon Magic, page 186).

Virgin goddesses were, unlike mother goddesses, whose principal role was regarded as nurturing others, separate and complete within themselves. Although they might have lovers and even bear or rear a child, they did not pour their energies into others or give themselves exclusively to any man, child or deity. Even their sexual drives were channelled mainly into personal psychic and spiritual energy. The virgin state in this sense thus represents not celibacy, as it came to in later Classical philosophy and Christianity, but a reservoir of undiluted power, an identity not eroded by emotional ties and attachments. In human women the virgin state was traditionally manifested in heightened prophetic and magical powers. Temporary abstinence from sex is still a recognised preparation for both men and women before ceremonial magical work.

Gradually, as the Sky Gods became supreme and the Mother Goddess role was reduced to that of wife and consort, the virgin goddesses were no longer recognised as maidens by choice, and they needed permission of the Father God to eschew matrimony. In return for freedom from male domination, virgins both divine and human no longer enjoyed the freedom to decide whether and when to have sex, or practised sacred or ritual sexuality as priestesses.

By Roman times, this downgrading of women, which had begun at the time of Plato and Pythagoras in the later Greek era, resulted in an increasing call for male sexual restraint. This caused a backlash against women, who

came to be regarded as temptresses of virtuous males unless they were either married or practised total celibacy. The virgin goddesses too, became untouchable, and earlier tales of their lovers or even love children were now attributed to priestesses of the Goddess. For example, according to early myths Artemis, who was also called the Great She Bear, bore a son called Arcas, or Little Bear, but his mother was later said to be one of Artemis's maidens, Callisto, who was supposedly seduced by Zeus. Arcas, however, became the constellation close to Ursa Major, the Great Bear, which was the constellation of his true mother.

Some of the priestesses of goddesses associated with love and fertility who had previously practised sacred sex in the temples were downgraded to temple whores; examples were the maidens of Aphrodite, the virgin Love Goddess. At the other extreme, the Vestal Virgins, the priestesses of Vesta, Goddess of the Sacred Fire, became unsullied maidens, although the first Vestal Virgins did practise sacred sex and even had children.

Sacred prostitution originally signified the union of a man with the Goddess, and his dedication to her and a commitment to protect the land through ritual sex with her priestesses. The Sumerian Inanna, who later became the Babylonian Ishtar, the Morning Star, was Goddess of Love, Fertility and Rebirth; she had temple prostitutes who were highly respected as manifestations of the goddess on earth, and they were virgins in the sense that they chose to make love as a holy gift. Prostitution originally meant to stand in the place of.

With Christianisation, virgin and whore completely splintered into the Virgin Mary and Mary Magdalene stereotypes – even though there is no firm evidence to link Mary Magdalene with the sinning woman mentioned in the Gospel of St Luke. But the idea that Mary Magdalene was not only the first to see Jesus after the Resurrection, but also may have had a sexual relationship with him, even as his wife, condemned her in the eyes of the later patriarchal Church Fathers. For Jesus himself had to be celibate as St Paul himself was – if he had indeed married Mary or taken her as a lover, she must have been the seducer.

The Vestal Virgins too, in spite of their purity, were cruelly treated when Rome was Christianised, and some date the fall of Rome from the destruction of the six-hundred-year-old sacred fire and the dismissal of the virgin priestesses in AD 394.

Power of Virginity

The fourth-century Christian chronicler St Jerome (AD 340–420) described how the Roman Sibyls, or prophetesses of Erythrae and Cumae, drew power from their virginity. In Ancient Greek myths, the prophetess Cassandra was one of the daughters of Hecabe, the Trojan Queen associated with Hecate, the Crone Moon Goddess. Hecabe's virgin daughters were famous as diviners and spell casters. Cassandra, who was later captured by the Greek King Agamemnon and foretold his downfall, paid a high price for her virginity. She was promised the gift of divine prophecy by Apollo if she had sex with him, but she refused. Apollo spat in her mouth and said that although she would prophesy the truth, no one would believe her.

Virgin Goddesses of Ancient Greece

The three Virgin Goddesses of Ancient Greece and Rome had their origins in an ancient tradition of Triple and Earth Goddesses that existed before the creation of the Classical pantheons. In the Greek world, Artemis was Mistress of Wild Things, while Athena was Goddess of Wisdom and Justice and Hestia the deity of Sacred Fire (both ritual fire, and fire as the centre of the domestic world). In the Roman world, they were called Diana, Minerva and Vesta, but their roles were similar, though with the passage of time increasingly sanitised.

Artemis, Mistress of the Wild

Artemis dates from Neolithic times and is a form of the ancient Mother of the Herds, who released animals for the hunt, and protected pregnant creatures and their young, including human mothers in childbirth.

The early goddess connection is revealed in the myth of Actaeon, who was, according to later Greek myth, turned into a stag and torn apart by Artemis's female hounds, symbolising the ritual sacrifice of males by the priestesses at her temples, and specifically the annual death of the Horned God. According to later legend, Artemis was born from the union of Zeus and Leto and was the twin sister of Apollo, whom she helped to deliver, thus linking her with the ancient midwife goddess role, a function shared by Hecate. When Artemis was three years old, she asked Zeus to allow her to always remain a virgin and he granted her wish. Artemis was also a death

goddess in the sense that she released women from suffering and pain with her silver arrows. She was very much a woman's goddess, and men were not allowed to attend her rituals.

As the Great She Bear, Artemis was worshipped by her virgin priestesses at the time of the new moon as well as at her festivals. Bear worship is said to be the most ancient of all known forms of religion (see also Totem Animals, page 79). Orion, Master of the Hunt, the one man Artemis was said to have loved, was ritually slain by Artemis and has his place in the sky close to Ursa Major; the issue of this sacred coupling may have been Arcas. Perhaps Artemis slew Orion because she loved him so much that she realised she was in danger of losing the detachment and virginity she valued above all else. The worship of Artemis as Diana continued especially at Ephesus on the west coast of what is now Turkey, and no man could even enter her temples. At Ephesus, her worship merged with that of the Virgin Mary, whose tomb was said to be located there with the establishment of the church of Our Lady of Ephesus in AD 431.

Diana is also known as Queen of the Witches, and is still evoked in Wiccan rituals and in the Italian-inspired American Dianic craft, which has a powerfully feminist basis.

Athena, the Wise One

In many ways Athena, or Athene as she is often called in Greece, is the goddess who underwent the greatest transformation under the Sky Gods. It has been speculated by some researchers that she was originally the Serpent Goddess of the Minoans in the second millenium BC. She is associated with Ariadne, the Serpent Goddess Weaver of Fate, and also with Medusa, whose image she bore on her shield after the serpent-headed monster was killed by Perseus, apparently at her behest. Medusa was once part of the Libyan Triple Goddesses Ath-enna, who was associated with the Egyptian Neith, the primal goddess whose name meant 'I am sprung from myself'. It has been suggested that Medusa, the veiled Goddess of Wisdom, was Athena's mother or the destroyer/crone aspect of Athena herself (see Serpent Goddesses, page 35). Medusa was also identified with Metis, the goddess Zeus swallowed so that he could give birth to their daughter Athena through his head (a male virgin birth had to involve a certain amount of ingenuity). Athena was born fully grown and armed for war. She became the ideal Greek goddess: impartial patroness of art, science, literature and learning, and of the city of Athens, and symbol of wisdom, justice and intel-

ligence, a creature without emotion or weaknesses. She was a powerful seer and was allowed, like Zeus and her Roman equivalent Minerva, to wield thunderbolts. In her warlike aspects, she demonstrated her fierce roots, although her efforts were directed towards negotiated glory, and the olive, symbol of peace, was sacred to her.

Over time Athena became increasingly purified in myth, while her supposed and somewhat earthy lovers Pan and Hephaestus, God of the Forge and Fire, retreated into the background. It was said that she retained power by the grace of Zeus because she did not dissipate it through the despised role of temptress. She became the unattainable ideal for human women who, unless they became priestesses, were inevitably sold into marriage by their fathers.

Minerva, Roman Goddess of Wisdom and Learning, had the same virtues as Athena, and shared with her the same totem, the owl, symbol of wisdom, prophecy and also warnings.

Hestia, Mistress of Fire

In many ways, Hestia is the truest natural virgin. She is a very ancient goddess, who was the eldest daughter of Cronos, or Saturn, God of Time and Fate, and Rhea, the Earth Mother. Swallowed like her brothers and sisters (except for Zeus, whom Rhea hid) by Cronos, she was regurgitated by her father and therefore was, like Athena in Greek legend, reborn of the father and thus under his protection.

Hestia was revered as a domestic goddess at the heart of the home. *Focus* was Latin for the hearth, and the hearth formed the spiritual as well as the physical centre of both Greek and Roman homes. Pythagoras likewise located the fire of Hestia at the centre of the Earth. She became the Spirit of Greece and later, in the guise of Vesta, the guardian of Rome. For hundreds of years in both civilisations, her sacred fire was carried across oceans with colonists and soldiers and always kept tended. She was beyond any man or god and was married to her duty. In Rome, Vesta's priestesses were likewise expected to dedicate their childbearing years to her service.

Vestal Virgins

The eternal fire of Rome was kept burning in the round temple at the foot of the Palatine Hill tended by specially dedicated Virgins. If this ritual fire

went out at any time apart from the occasion of the annual rekindling at the New Year, this was regarded as an indication that the maiden who tended it was impure (since chastity was demanded of the priestesses). The priestess would then be executed by being ceremonially buried alive. This may have been a way of avoiding the scandal of a birth if one of the priestesses had become pregnant.

Six virgins, chosen from maidens between the ages of six and ten coming from important Roman families, took vows of chastity and promised to serve as Vestal Virgins for thirty years, after which time they were allowed to marry (though few of them actually did). It has been suggested that at one time they may have practised sacred sex with the High Priest of Rome, the Pontifex Magister, who oversaw their welfare as well as the major ritual calendar in the city. The annual festival at the temple, the Vestalia, was observed on 9 June, when women brought offerings to the temple.

The rewards for obedient, worthy Vestal Virgins were great, as they were guardians of the good fortune of Rome and so were honoured by all; in return for their chastity, they were allowed to administer their own financial affairs. On 15 May, the Vestal Virgins cast straw effigies into the Tiber as symbols of the spirits of the Corn, thus ensuring the continuing fertility of the land.

The last known Vestal Virgin High Priestess was Coelia Concordia, from AD 380. Because of the emphasis on the purity of the Vestal Virgins, they are believed to have inspired Christian convents, in spite of their cruel treatment at the time of the destruction of the shrine.

An increasing number of modern women are choosing celibacy (at least for some periods of their lives) as a way of channelling their power into a career or spiritual life, and even those who make a permanent commitment to a partner may keep a separate home as a way of defining their own boundaries.

A Special Place

For many women, the process of maintaining a separate identity while juggling a career with emotional and home commitments can be difficult. Creating a personal space, whether it is an area in the garden marked out by a circle of stones and shielded by trees, a room, or a curtained off corner of a bedroom, is a simple but potent way of marking a boundary between yourself and others, and between your everyday and spiritual life.

֍ On a table or plinth you can create a personal altar to your own spiritual powers and personal identity.

֍ On the table you can display treasures such as crystals, beeswax candles, incense, flowers, oils, stones and shells from the sea, or feathers from beautiful birds.

֍ You might choose to add a statue that suggests a women who is loving but complete within herself, perhaps a Madonna, a Hindu, Ancient Egyptian or Classical figure, a beautiful shell as a symbol of the Goddess, or a totem animal that conveys to you either power or stillness. Your private area can reflect the passing seasons with fruits, flowers, berries or leaves, or you can create artefacts specifically for a sea or fire goddess, or a mistress of wild things.

֍ You could add symbols of one of the virgin goddesses: for Hestia, for example, you might keep a small oil lamp or dish with a small, flat beeswax candle, and burn this while you meditate or sit quietly in your space.

֍ When you have even a few minutes, light beeswax candles, lavender or rose oil, sandalwood or jasmine incense, all of which are especially evocative of female goddess energies.

֍ Between your fingers hold a favourite crystal, such as amber, which is believed to contain the power of many suns and the souls of tigers, or a stone found by the sea (see Crystal Divination and Magic for suggestions, pages 166–170).

֍ Allow images to form in your mind's vision, sounds to pass through

your inner ear and sensations to permeate through your fingertips. You will find that solutions to questions, though unvoiced, come spontaneously at these quiet times, when you are filled with harmony and energy.

§ Whenever you feel overwhelmed by responsibilities or the demands of others retreat to your sanctuary; all the positive energies that you have built up over weeks of quiet contemplation will strengthen and empower you.

§ If you are feeling especially vulnerable or drained of enthusiasm, light a shallow bowl of dried sage, sweetgrass, thyme or cedar on the altar and cup the smoke gently over your face to cleanse your aura (psychic energy field). This exercise will fill you with optimism and renewed vigour. (Avoid if pregnant.)

§ When you extinguish the candles, remember to send the light from the bee goddesses and the fire of Hestia into your innermost being.

§ If you are facing a challenge of some kind, you can pass a tiny, clear quartz crystal through the oil and candle flame and carry this as a talisman.

CRONE GODDESSES

Teachers of Wisdom and Understanding of Life's Mysteries

Who is the Crone?

IN MYTHOLOGY, the lifecycle of women is frequently likened to the lunar cycle of waxing, full and waning moon, a cycle that ends with two and a half days of darkness until the crescent is visible in the sky once more. The Triple, or three-aspected, Goddess that appears in many cultures as the Maiden, Mother and Crone, or Wise Woman, is a personification of these stages of the lunar cycle. As the Bone Goddess, she enters the Underworld in the days of the dark of the moon, and is reborn as the Maiden on the crescent.

The Crone signifies wisdom and experience. As the Dark Goddess, she holds the keys to the mysteries of life, death and rebirth, and will accompany us through dark times and fears and even hold our hands when we meet her even darker and yet more wonderful sister, the Bone Woman. Some spiritualities combine Bone Goddess and Crone, and there is considerable overlap between them. Both of them may be found in the Underworld, or inner psyche, but the Crone's role is primarily that of wise guide for women once their childbearing years are over and into the wisdom of old age. However, the Crone does not only represent the lives and concerns of older women; she is identified with all inner journeys of personal exploration by women at any stage of life.

The Crone is also mistress of magic and divination. It was traditionally the Wise Woman of any community who held the repository of herbal and healing knowledge and passed it on to her daughters when they reached maturity. Among the Native North American Plains Indians, a woman cannot become a Medicine Woman until she is past middle age, and she keeps her role until she dies. In Amerindian myth, it was Grandmother Spider Woman who wove and maintained the interconnecting web of all creation, and who made Dreamcatchers to hang over the cradles of babies to filter out negative night energies and fears. In traditional societies such as some of those of the Far East, older women are still greatly honoured and suffer fewer menopausal symptoms than women in the Western world, although as older Asian women are drawn into Westernised society and stresses, this is changing. For in the Western world youth, sexual desirability and beauty are prized above wisdom, experience and serenity. To counter this, Croning ceremonies are becoming increasingly popular, especially in the US, and are very empowering.

The association of the Crone with ageing and eventually dying made her in earlier times a powerful and loved figure, who was said to care for people as they passed into death and guide them. In my own research on ghosts, I have found that the vast majority of family apparitions are well-loved grandmothers who act as guardian angels to favourite grandchildren and appear as death-bed visions in the last moments of their lives.

Grace, who is in her thirties, told me that when her father was dying, he had been very frightened. He and Grace's mother Matty were atheists, and had laughed at Grace when she had visited a Spiritualist church. One evening as the sun was setting, Grace was sitting by her

father's bedside; he was restless since his pain relief was wearing off. Suddenly he sat up and looked into the corner of the room. 'Hello Gran', he said, and all the pain and ravages of the long illness seemed to leave him. 'Yes, I've got my muffler, It's cold out there. OK, I'll come then shall I? We mustn't be late if Granddad's cooking kippers.' He closed his eyes and minutes later he was dead. Matty refused to accept this as anything more than the ramblings of a dying mind, stirring up memories of childhood. But Grace saw a golden glow in the corner, and witnessed a transformation in her father. I have come across many similar accounts that describe the Crone, in some familiar grandmotherly or grandfatherly guise, easing someone's passing.

The Underworld, typified by the Celtic Otherworld, was the place in which some awaited rebirth. Others chose to remain in this world in which the old gods still ruled and where heroes and heroines could become deities, doing so with the help of wise teachers, of whom the Crone was pre-eminent. It was said that some of these teachers had never lived as mortals, nor ever would. This other world was reputed to be a place of spirit, which heroes might visit during their lifetimes to gain wisdom, and to which King Arthur went to be healed: a place of feasting, music, laughter and restored youth and energy.

In later Classical myth, the other world was divided into the dark, sorrowful Underworld for mortals, and the joyous Elysian fields for heroes, and by Roman times the Crone had become associated with all that was to be feared and avoided.

The most dramatic example of the demonisation of the Crone and the emphasis on the pains of the Underworld is provided by the story of the Viking goddess Hel, Queen of the Dead. When the monks recorded the Viking legends (and Christianised them) from the eleventh century onwards, Hel was cast as mistress of what was very definitely a Christian Hell, with an emphasis on ice and on dreadful tortures for wrongdoers. In this Hell, Hel plotted the downfall of the gods. Yet earlier legends tell how she received and restored all deities and humans, except those slain in battle, who in the Viking world were accorded special status. She even gave shelter to the slain Solar God Balder, so that he could be healed and reborn as the new Sun God.

Hel may have been an ancient form of the Mother Goddess, for she was worshipped and loved by ordinary people, even after the coming of the

missionaries, in deep caves symbolising the womb of the Earth. Older people and the bereaved, especially those who had lost children, asked her for help. Her shrines were places of prophecy, like the oracle at Delphi, and were often sited in areas of subterranean volcanic activity.

In other lands too, the Christian Church, with its fiery pits of hell beneath the ground, identified the Crone Goddess with a hideous old witch who practised black magic at the dead of night and demanded blood sacrifices. Because a wise, powerful woman was a threat to patriarchal society, by the Middle Ages many wise women/midwives and old women living alone in villages were burned or hanged. Their healing wisdom was replaced by the rising male medical profession which knew little about hygiene and cared even less about painless childbirth. The ancient Graeco-Roman Crone Goddess Hecate, once deity of birth and regeneration and patroness of midwives, as well as Queen of the Witches, was blamed for fuelling the evil practices of mediaeval midwives and nurses, who were accused of worshipping her and killing babies at her behest.

Hecate

When we talk of Crone goddesses we think mainly of Hecate, Goddess of the Crossroads where three paths – past, present and future – meet, a remnant of her significance as a Triple Goddess. Offerings were left to her at crossroads to ask her for blessings and to bring good fortune. She was protective especially of sailors, and in her ancient role as animal mother also of hunters, as well as those falsely accused of wrongdoing.

Hecate was one of the elder gods, a Titan; she was the daughter of Tartarus, the original Underworld, and Nyx, or Night, daughter of Chaos. Originally, she had the power over the Heavens, the Earth and the Underworld, linking them in her person of Hecate Triformis. She was also Triple Goddess of the Moon, and carried a torch through the skies, as she did in her role of Underworld guardian and guide.

After the War of the Titans against Zeus, Hecate was the only Titan deity to retain her authority; gradually, this was eroded, as the worship of Apollo the Sun God and Zeus took precedence over the goddesses. She became associated more and more with the sad, dark abode of lost souls and wandering ghosts guarded by her hell hound, the three-headed Cerberus, who stood at the gates of Hades. As she was absorbed into the myths of Rome, she was portrayed as uglier and more aged. Crossroads, once sources of prophetic power, became increasingly frightening, evil places where

suicides and witches were buried. Hecate became identified with cemeteries and mills, the latter a relic of her former life-giving and regenerative role.

Hecate as the wise guide and initiator of women's mysteries may be found in the myths that describe her as Persephone's companion in the Underworld. She did not rescue this maiden goddess and some may ask why, if she really was so kindly. But if we view the fall of Persephone into the Underworld as an initiation from innocence and unawareness into experience through suffering, then it is understandable why Hecate could only comfort her while she learned the lessons that were necessary for her rebirth. One of Hecate's most important roles in women's lives is not to make false promises, but to help us through the different stages of our lives. If we can learn from wise Hecate and stand back while our loved ones make their own mistakes, being there to comfort and advise them if asked, then we and our families and friends have learned wisdom indeed.

It is said that Hecate will act as adviser and mediator in any woman's journey into her own psyche, in which she confronts her fears and emerges stronger. Hecate may also be invoked in rituals to banish sorrow, fear or self-destruction, especially during the waning moon.

Cailleach

The Cailleach, or Veiled One, is the name given to the Celtic Goddess in her winter or Crone aspect. In Scotland, Ireland, Wales, England and France, it is likely that the cult of the Cailleach is many thousands of years old, and that it far predates the Celts. Like the Native American Grandmother spirits, Cailleach created the landscape, casting stones from her basket as she flew through the sky and thereby forming mountain ranges. She was the original Old Woman who was tossed up in the basket in the children's nursery rhyme. Associated with cairns and standing stones, which some believe were created as part of her early worship, the Cailleach was reborn each Halloween, the beginning of the Celtic winter and New Year, and travelled through the land, striking the earth with her staff on which a crow perched. She called down the snow, so that the soil might rest and grow strong again. On May Eve, the beginning of the Celtic summer, she threw her staff under a holly tree or a gorse bush (both were her sacred plants) and turned herself into a stone once more.

One of the Cailleach's most intriguing aspects is that of the Crone form of the Irish Triple Goddess Garbh Ogh, a giantess who lived for many centuries, and who was said to hunt the mountain deer with a pack of

seventy dogs, all of whom had the names of different birds. When she chose to die she piled stones around herself in a single cairn and, according to a Celtic poem, 'set her chair in the womb of the hills at the season of the heather-bloom and breathed no more'.

GODDESSES OF THE SUN

Greeting to you, Sun of the Seasons
As you travel the skies so high,
With your strong step on the wing of the heights,
You are the happy mother of the star.
FROM THE SUN WOMAN OF IRELAND, A TRADITIONAL GAELIC PRAYER.

THIS CHAPTER IS about the sun goddesses who dance and laugh and tell us that we should enjoy every moment of joy, and spiritual and emotional – as well as actual – sunshine that comes our way.

Although traditionally the moon has been regarded as female and associated with motherhood and fertility, there were also many sun mothers, a number of whom have survived in indigenous cultures that have followed the same way of life for thousands of years. Walo, an Australian Aboriginal Sun Goddess, lived with her daughter Bara and her sister-in-law, the world mother Madalait. Although her daughter originally travelled with her on her daily journey from the east, their combined power caused the Earth to become a desert and so her daughter waits at home until she will become the new goddess. Another Aboriginal legend, from the Wotjobaluk tribe of Victoria, Australia, tells how the Sun Mother carries a bark torch through the skies and returns to the west each evening to feed her waiting infant. In other cultures too, the Sun Mother has a Sun Daughter. The Celts believed that when the end of the world came, the Sun Mother would give birth to a daughter who would herald a new order.

Sometimes the Sun Goddess was pictured as a maiden. Among the Inuits, the Sun and Moon were sister and brother, Seqinek and Aningan, or Akycha and Igaluk. Their path around the heavens was a perpetual race in which the Moon, at first close to his sister the Sun, lost ground until she

finally overtook him at the end of his cycle; this is said to explain why the moon can sometimes be seen during the day. In Hungarian folk myth, Xatel-Ekwa, the Hungarian Solar Goddess, was so passionate that she baked her suitors with her ardour.

The stumbling block to accepting female sun gods is thousands of years of prejudice. The sun gives us warmth and light and encourages the crops to grow; it is nurturing, creative. Sun goddesses were said to regularly visit fields and hilltops as lovely, golden-haired women to oversee the progress of people, animals and the land. The life-giving female functions of the sun are, however, overshadowed by the Classical patriarchal view of the sun as a symbol of dominance and power; of Apollo in his chariot, always above humankind unless he is stopping to seduce a nymph or to usurp the power of the Earth Mother at the oracle at Delphi.

The conquering Sun God was adopted – along with many other female-unfriendly symbols – by collectors of myths from the eighteenth century onwards. The moon image became a weak reflection of male solar energy – and was thus always female – in spite of the existence of male lunar gods such as the Slavonic Triple Moon God Myesyats, who represented the three stages of the lifecycle. Meanwhile, the sun goddesses were done away with because they did not fit into the patriarchal view of the world.

Some goddesses were both solar and lunar deities, for example Isis, the Egyptian Goddess, and the Celtic Aine (see Isis, page 179 and Fairy Women, page 100). Aine's sister Grainne was a Celtic Solar Crone Goddess who was said to wake the fertility of the Earth every Spring. The top of her sacred hill at Leinster, like that of the hill of Aine, was the venue for torchlit processions and bonfires at the Summer Solstice and at the first grain harvest at the beginning of August, ceremonies that persisted into the twentieth century.

Sun Mothers in the Northern Tradition

Because light and warmth are especially vital in the northern lands, the concept of a loving sun mother is perhaps natural for people who live in these parts. Desert places, for example those of the Bedouins of Afghanistan, often have an evil-tempered, withered sun goddess who wreaks destruction unless she is restrained by her husband.

In Lapland, where the solar goddess tradition has continued, the Sun Mother Baiwe, or Beiwe, blesses the land with vegetation and brings fertility

to the reindeer as well as to human mothers. Baiwe is depicted not in human form, but as a geometric design that may, for example, be shown in the centre of a shaman's drum as a lozenge with rays emanating in all directions. Her special festival is the Summer Solstice, when sun-rings or grass garlands are woven, butter is rubbed into doorposts and a special sun porridge, rich in dairy foods, is the centre of a family feast (fats are especially important in this cold region). At the meal, the father of the family prays for bright sunshine over the birch forests, and that the reindeer will give milk. A Lapp hunter who is lost will erect a sun ring on a pole to contain the sun, so that she will not set before he has found his way home.

Saule, the Baltic Sun Goddess

Parts of the Baltic were not Christianised until the early fifteenth century and Lithuania, Estonia and Latvia have retained a rich folk history and customs. In these lands, the pagan Solar Goddess Saule, Queen of the Heavens and Earth, who was said to be dressed in and crowned with gold and to drive her chariot across the skies, is still remembered in folk rituals at the Spring and Autumn Equinoxes, and at the Summer Solstice, which is known as Rasa, or Kupolines. Traditionally, throughout the autumn and darkening days, ceremonies were performed and offerings made so that Saule would not be defeated by the powers of darkness. The Christian Advent at the beginning of December now marks the traditional time when Saule began her long journey of return; on the feast of St Lucia, the Northern Goddess of Light Saule once danced with her daughters, the planets. Can you imagine Apollo having such fun? She returned in triumph on Kaledos, the Mid-winter Solstice, and her celebrations continued until 6 January, the Christian Epiphany. Saule had a strong maternal role, caring personally for lands, herds and people – unlike her inconstant husband Menulis, the Moon, who would disappear for three days each month. In Christian terms, Saule has merged with Mother Mary in her personal care for her people, but in folk tradition she is still invoked in her own right as guardian of shepherds, the harvest, women's work, fertility, healing and single mothers.

Japanese Sun Goddess

Perhaps the most powerful sun goddess of all was the Japanese Amaterasu Omigami. The chief deity, or kami (essence of divinity), she was one of the

children of Izanagi and Izanami, the kami who created Japan as the most beautiful place on Earth and sent their offspring to be the spirits of nature and the elements – the wind, mountains, waterfalls, the ocean, animals, birds and trees. Her name means Great August Spirit Shining in Heaven, but she is also called Shinmet, or Divine Radiance, and O-hiru-me-no-muchi, Great Female Possessor of Noon. She reflects great compassion and vulnerability, as well as power. According to legend, her brother Susanoh, or Susanowo, God of Storms and Earthquakes, was so jealous of her that he destroyed her fields and her golden palace and its wondrous gardens. She understood his bitterness and did not strike back. But when he raped her sacred virgins and defiled her temple, she shut herself in a cave and the world became dark, thus demonstrating that she was the source of life. The other gods were afraid and tricked her into opening the cave, so that light was restored to the world. Amaterasu is said to be all-seeing; it is said that the affairs of humanity sometimes make her temporarily despair and return to her cave, causing an eclipse.

Exercise to Draw Down the Sun Goddess

In witchcraft there is a popular ceremony known as Drawing Down the Moon, in which a priestess takes into herself the power and wisdom of the Moon Goddess. However, you can also utilise the creative, courageous power of the golden sun goddesses, especially if you know that you have a challenge or obstacle to overcome in your life.

§ Visualise your Sun Goddess in any way you find helpful: she can, for instance, be a powerful maiden outrunning her brother – this image can help if you are facing a lot of prejudice at work from chauvinistic colleagues. You might see the Sun Mother caring for the land and her children, which can energise you if you have to be particularly creative or suddenly need to give extra input to a family member if he or she is temporarily vunerable.

§ On a sunny day work out of doors, using bowls of water and crystals to reflect the sunlight. If it is a darker day, improvise with Perspex rainbows on glass, golden candles, mirrors and fibre-optic lamps, so that you create a pool of 'sunlight' in which to sit.

♦ Breathe in the golden light through your nose slowly and gently, exhaling darkness through your mouth.

♦ As you continue breathing, visualise the light spreading to every part of your body, from your toes right to the tips of your fingers and the crown of your head.

♦ Now allow the light to extend beyond your body, forming a shield of golden rays all around and above you, so that you are enclosed in a shimmering sun sphere.

♦ Cease to breathe in the golden light when you feel that you are completely filled with the radiance, and allow the energies to flow between your body, the pool of light and the golden sphere.

♦ If you face opposition or spite, shake your fingers and see golden sparks emanate from your fingertips like miniature sun rays. Extend your arms in a circle over your head so that you create a psychic protective force field of sparks all around you that will gently repel any malice.

♦ Make a sign, perhaps touching the place between your eyes and just above them, which is regarded as the third psychic eye, the Brow chakra, a spiritual energy point. Or you may prefer to touch your heart or make a circle in the palm of your hand.

♦ As you do this, say: 'When I touch my brow/heart, I will invoke the power of the Sun Goddess.'

♦ Visualise her once more before you, then gradually allow the radiance and the Goddess to fade, knowing that you can recall her at any time when you are in need, just by making your psychic sign.

♦ If ever you feel afraid, stand in front of a mirror, framed in sunlight or golden candles, and your goddess will appear behind you in your mind's vision. Your aura, the energy field most visible around your head, will shine even more brilliantly, and you will know that you are protected and filled with confidence.

SPINNERS AND WEAVERS OF FATE

I N MANY CULTURES, the goddesses of fate were spinners and weavers of the destiny of humankind and of the other deities. Above and beyond the power of even the mighty Sky Fathers, the Fates pose unanswerable questions about whether we follow preordained paths or are free to create our own fortunes.

In Native North American wisdom, Grandmother Spider Woman spins the interconnections between all life in her cosmic web. A remarkably similar image is described by the Greek philosopher Plato: he relates how Ananke, Goddess of Unalterable Necessity, spun the universe and wove the web of fate and time with shimmering threads while the Sirens sang. The sun, moon and planets formed the whorls on her spindle, and people moved up and down the threads between life, death and rebirth as she created. In Hindu myth, Maya, the maiden form of the Triple Goddess and mother of the Buddha, was symbolised as a spider in the centre of the Web of Fate, the worn threads of which she constantly formed and replaced.

Spinning and weaving were essential arts before the Industrial Revolution, and were practised in every home by peasant and noble woman alike. The craft became entwined with the mystique that accumulated around female creativity, which was passed on from mother to daughter in an unaltered and unbroken tradition. As women worked in groups both within the family and in cottage industries, they talked together and shared secrets and dreams; their emotions were woven into the fabric, which empowered or protected the wearer. Even today, mothers, sisters, aunts and grandmothers may make a first shawl, a christening robe or a wedding dress for a family member, endowing it with love and hopes. As a consequence of such practices, it was envisaged by early myth-makers that the mother goddesses must also be spinners and weavers who fashioned human destiny in the same way. Because these goddesses of fate pre-existed the various pantheons of deities, they were not subject to their changes, rises and falls in fortune.

The Ancient Egyptians claimed that Isis, the Mother Goddess, taught humankind the art of spinning, and she too has links with Fate and Fortune. In the British Museum, London, there is a bronze figure of Isis-Tyche, which was created in the second century BC in Cyprus. Tyche was a goddess of luck and chance. The cornucopia, the horn of plenty which she

is holding, stands for the riches that she can give mankind if she chooses to. Frigga, the Viking Mother Goddess who had knowledge of the fate of all but would not reveal the deeper secrets even when asked to do so by her husband Odin, gave flax to the people and taught them how to spin. Her jewelled distaff may be seen in the stars in what we now call Orion's Belt.

Sisters of Fate

The Fates, the original fairy godmothers, were three sisters or Maiden, Mother and Crone in a number of cultures; they are a form of the Triple Goddess. The Greek Fates, the Moerae, were daughters of Ananke, and like her were said to have existed before Time. The first sister, Clotho, assumed the role of Creator and spun the golden thread of life and placed it upon the loom, representing an individual's birth. Lachesis the Measurer set the parameters of each destiny and assigned good and evil characteristics to it. Atropos the Destroyer cut the thread with her shears when she ordained that the time of death had come. Like their mother, the Moerae sang with the Sirens as they worked, Lachesis of the past, Clotho of the present and Atropos of events and deeds still to unfold. In times of danger, rituals and charms were used by individuals, especially soldiers in battle, to entreat Atropos not to cut the thread of life so soon. The Roman Fates were the Parcae: Nona spun the thread of life, Decuma gave it to the chosen person and Morta cut it.

In the Baltic world there are seven goddesses who create destiny, a process that begins when the High God gives a distaff to the first goddess. Each goddess works at spinning or weaving in sequence, from teasing out the first threads of new life until the completion of the winding or shroud sheet. The fourth goddess tells stories to distract the other weavers, while the fifth encourages the goddesses to work harder and end the life earlier.

Such accounts of the fate goddesses seem quite definitely to place the power of destiny in their hands. They suggest that we can do little but wait for the pattern to unfold until the final knot is cut. But this is to misunderstand these shadowy goddesses. No one would deny that some people begin with great opportunity and others with overwhelming obstacles; that a promising avenue or relationship can be shattered by an unexpected loss or illness; that the offer of a lifetime or a lottery win, or blinding love or an unpremeditated response to the urgent needs of another can change the whole picture overnight. However, it is the human life moving through the

loom that causes the pattern to form in a unique way, as our threads combine or tangle during interactions with the related strands of others' destinies.

Fate the Challenger

Nowhere is the importance of human free will clearer than in the role of the Viking fate sisters, the Norns. According to the Vikings, fate is not preordained but is determined by a number of factors: our own actions past and present and those of our forebears, who have made us what we are both genetically and in terms of inherited memory patterns, which are increasingly seen as one and the same as the intricacy and comprehensiveness of DNA strands becomes better understood. Each conscious decision or action or unconscious prompting alters the pattern of the web of our personal fate as it is being woven.

The first Norn is called Urdhr, and she has knowledge of the past, which influences not only our own present and future but also that of those involved with us and ultimately our descendants. The second Norn, Verdhandi, reveals present deeds and influences. These are also strongly implicated in our future direction and decisions. Skuld, the third Norn, holds the secrets of what will come to pass given the intricate web of past and present interaction. She is constantly tearing and re-forming the old patterns as words are spoken or repressed, opportunities taken up or missed and obstacles overcome. Our personal fate, or *orlag*, is constantly being changed as each new day adds to the web of interaction, and tomorrow's future becomes the present and ultimately the past. In the Norse tradition, the role of the Norns is beyond even their own conscious control, and they act as challenges, not judges or restrainers of free will. They wove, according to *orlag*, the collective eternal law of the universe. In Shakespeare's *Macbeth*, in the guise of the 'Weird' or 'Wyrd' sisters, they point out to the hero Macbeth the possibility of attaining his heart's desire through his own wicked deeds and the option of blaming it all on fate, in this case the witches:

> First Witch: *All hail, Macbeth! hail to thee, thane of Glamis!*
> Second Witch: *All hail, Macbeth! hail to thee, thane of Cawdor!*
> Third Witch: *All hail, Macbeth, that shalt be king hereafter!*

The witches/Norns are not foretelling a fixed future, but one that depends on the deliberate decisions made by Macbeth and the Thane of Cawdor. Macbeth was already Thane of Glamis. His elevation to Thane of Cawdor came about because the Thane committed an act of treachery, thereby forfeiting his life and title. As a favourite of King Duncan, Macbeth was a likely candidate for elevation. As for becoming King, the seeds of ambition were already within Macbeth, as was the ability to kill Duncan. The hags were merely revealing one potential path, which Macbeth could have rejected. He could alternatively have decided to wait and, given the bloody times and his own strong constitution, the succession may in any case have come to him by default a few years hence. Or he could have made a good career as the favourite of the King, in the course of which he would probably have picked up other honours and riches.

Most acts of 'blind fate' do not depend on external forces, but are the direct or indirect results of acts and omissions by ourselves or others. Moreover, our reactions to fate are crucial in deciding the future path that we take – in many situations, we can choose from several options, which will in turn affect future opportunities or obstacles in different ways, changing the pattern on the loom.

Knot Ritual for Empowerment: the Seven-knotted Hair

After first coming across knotted hairs at Merlin's tomb in the Forest of Broceliande, I discovered a whole folk history of knot empowerments in Breton legend. Although at Merlin's tomb the knotted hairs were affixed to the trees on the tomb, I found that releasing knotted hairs from a high place or into rushing water could bring a swifter release of the energies needed to bring an urgent need or wish from the thought plane to actuality.

Using human hair makes the ritual personalised, although I do not think that you should use the hair of others without permission: even with the best intent, this is an infringement on free will.

Traditionally, seven knots were tied either in a single strand, or seven hairs were bound together with seven knots. The latter is easier than using individual hairs unless you are very nimble-fingered. Tying

the hair is a means of focusing and concentrating energy into a tight ball. Although the hair can, in the authentic manner, be plucked from the head, you may prefer to cut it or even cheat and use dead hairs from your hairbrush – these will soon be filled again with vitality by your chant.

- The wish or empowerment, for example 'Give me courage', or 'Bring me success', is spoken once for the first knot, twice for the second, three times for the third, and so on until the seven knots have been made.

- The knotted hair is then released from the top of a windy hill with a final cry of the words of power, or cast on to an ebb tide or into a fast-flowing stream (a waterfall is best of all).

- If the empowerment relates to freedom or an abandonment of redundant anger or guilt, then you can throw the hair into a fire or burn it in a candle flame.

- If the need is less urgent, tie the knotted hair to a tree or bush and let the wind tease the knots into untying in their own time.

- In love empowerments you can bind together your own hair and that of a lover with seven knots, or plait the fourteen hairs in a circle.

- The hair of a pet can be used for a protective or healing purpose.

BONE GODDESSES

Rebirth and Renewal

THE BONE GODDESS is perhaps one of the oldest and most elusive goddess forms, which has survived in shamanic practices in Siberia and also in folk myths, especially in Eastern Europe and Scandinavia. She is akin to such figures as the male Grim Reaper, but she is a much more positive figure because she not only calls people to death, but also restores them to life in a new and more perfect form. She is an image that can be helpful to

any woman who is undergoing major changes, whether physical, emotional or spiritual, when a path or stage in her life has become redundant or destructive.

The dark time of the moon – which lasts from the time of the new moon until the crescent in the sky can be seen – is the time associated with the Bone Goddess, the older sister or mother of the Crone. As mentioned in an earlier chapter (see page 126), the two characters are sometimes combined in myth.

Origins of the Bone Goddess

In the remains of Neolithic villages in south-eastern Europe, archaeologists have discovered small, featureless, doll-like figures made of white bone or stone in which a regular pattern of holes was carved out. Some anthropologists believe that these may represent the White Lady of Death and Rebirth. Many more such figures may have been made of bleached wood, which would not have survived the millennia.

Another ancient form of the Bone Goddess is the Bird Goddess, who is sometimes called the Bird of Prey Goddess; it was believed that she hatched the cosmic egg and that she pecked away, vulture-like, the flesh of humans whose lives were done so that their spirits might be freed and reborn. Stone Age goddess figurines dating from about 3000 BC, which have the claws and faces of birds and the antennae and circular eyes of bees, have been excavated from megalithic tombs in Europe. Chambers in barrows, or burial mounds, dating from the third millennium BC onwards contain human bones that face west, which is believed to be the direction of death and rebirth. Two of the most famous of these burial mounds are the West Kennet Long Barrow, near Avebury Rings, and the artificially created Mother Goddess hill at Silbury, Wiltshire, which was built in around 3600 BC.

Hunters in the frozen north still return the bones of seals and other animals to the places where they were killed so that the Mother of the Herds can restore them to life.

Bone Goddess in the Classical World

The role of the Bone Goddess survived in the myths of many lands, especially in the tradition of Cauldron Goddesses (see page 237). Rhea, the

Titan Earth Goddess and wife of Cronos, God of Time, performed this role as a kind of elder stateswomen to the younger Olympian gods. She restored the life of her infant grandson Dionysus in a perfected form after he was ripped to pieces and his remains were boiled by the other Titans. This savagery was supposedly carried out at the behest of Hera because Dionysus was the result of Zeus's infidelity with a nymph called Semele. Rhea reassembled his bones and sang magical chants over them to restore him to life.

This tearing apart and reconstruction was in fact a ritual death and restoration – in many cultures, this is a symbol of the transformation of an individual through suffering and death into a new life, as is the case in shamanism, where the experience may be acted out in a trance by initiate shamans (see page 250). The adult Dionysus died as God of the Vine and Grain each winter as a sacrifice, and was reborn in the spring to restore fertility to the land (see also the Celtic Lughnassadh corn sacrifice, page 23). In the Ancient mystery cults that celebrated the annual death and rebirth of the grain in cultures including Greece and Egypt, a sacrificial victim was torn apart by the priestesses either symbolically or actually and brought back to life as the new spirit of the grain. Initiates into these mystery cults underwent a personal transformation. The Roman writer Apuleius described his own initiation into the cult of Isis:

'I approached the very gates of death and set my foot upon Proserpine's threshold yet was permitted to return. At midnight I saw the sun shine as if it were noon. I entered the presence of the great gods and worshipped near them.'

Celtic Bone Goddesses

One of the most dramatic forms of the Bone Goddess in Celtic myth is that of the Morrigu, the Goddesses of War, who swooped over battlefields as crows or ravens to gather the slain. Badb the Crone was known as the Crow or Vulture Goddess; she also assumed the form of a wolf, a bear or a huge woman with her foot placed on either side of a wide, fast-flowing river, indicating that either side could win a battle according to her choice. The

other Morrigu were Nemhain, whose name meant frenzy and Macha, the Raven Goddess (see also Celtic Spirituality, page 57).

Banshees

The figure of the banshee is a direct descendant of the Bone Goddess, and her appearance is reported even in the modern world, not only in Celtic lands but also in America, Canada, Australia, New Zealand and South Africa, where Celtic people have settled. The name banshee means 'woman of the fairy', a literal translation of *bean sidhe*.

Also called the White Lady of Sorrows, the banshee is depicted wearing a grey, hooded cloak or a ragged veil; her eyes are red from weeping. From Scotland, and from West Virginia, where there are many families of Scottish descent whose banshee has travelled with them from their native shores, come accounts of sightings of the banshee mounted on a white horse, especially near rivers. She is also seen in Brittany, Ireland and Scotland as the phantom washer-woman who is constantly cleaning blood from shrouds. Her special wail heralding a death, called a 'keening', has been described as quite musical and immensely comforting, especially if a person has been ill and in pain or is very old and is fading away. It is claimed that some beautiful Irish funereal music is based on the songs of the banshee.

Like other hag and bone goddesses, the banshee can appear as a hooded crow, a stoat, a hare or a weasel, all creatures that are considered unlucky near a sick room. In Cornwall a banshee is said to be seen flapping her cloak outside the window of a dying person, and for this reason is sometimes mistaken for a crow or owl.

Slavonic Tradition of the Bone Goddess: Baba Yaga

Baba Yaga is probably the purest form of the Bone Goddess (see also Kali, page 71). In the fairy tales of Eastern Europe and Scandinavia, the old hag is not actually the wicked witch, but retains the transformative powers of the hag goddesses as a dispenser of justice. Baba Yaga is one of the most famous fairy hags from the Russian tradition, a witch with iron teeth who lived in a hut that danced on giant chicken legs and was surrounded by a fence made of human bones with skulls on top. She rode through the skies

in a mortar and pestle and was benevolent – although still terrifying – towards the deserving but harsh to those who had done evil or who were selfish. She would help those who were resourceful and pure of heart and devour the wicked.

In one Russian myth, a young girl, Vasalisa, who was protected by the talismanic magical doll her mother had given her before her death, was sent to Baba Yaga for a coal to restore the fire and was rewarded for her efforts with a blazing skull to rekindle the fire. However, the fire also burned her wicked stepmother and sister.

German myth tells of Mother Holle, a Crone form of the Mother Goddess Frige (Hulda, or Holda, and Frigga in the Viking sagas). Like Baba Yaga, she had huge teeth and a terrifying appearance. She controlled the weather and in her form of Bertha, the shining one, cared for the souls of dead children and guided them to rebirth.

Bone Goddess and Shamanism

In shamanism, the Bone Goddess restores the symbolically dismembered initiate to a new life as a shaman or shamaness by singing magical chants, spells and incantations over his or her bones.

One of the most vivid examples of this tradition comes from Yakut shamanism in Siberia. Here, the Bird of Prey Mother nests in the branches of the World Tree. She has iron feathers, an iron beak, hooked claws and the head of an eagle. On the branches of the World Tree she hangs the soul of the newly formed shaman (who is in a deep trance) out to dry; when the soul is ripe she tears off the flesh and feeds it to waiting demons. She then reassembles the bones and sings life into them (see also the chapter on Isis, who re-formed the bones of her consort Osiris, page 178). In other shamanic traditions of the far north of Asia, the shaman's bones are symbolically boiled in a cauldron before the flesh is restored.

Burying the Bone: Transforming Negative Experience

In earlier times a bone marked with a symbol of a seemingly irresolvable quarrel or bitterness was buried in soil to allow the matter to come to an end and be transformed by Mother Earth. This is a gentle but potent method of marking an end, whether to sorrow or anger, or to the garbage of self-destruction running constantly in our heads.

§ You can use an animal bone or a bird or fish skeleton, which can often be found on beaches at low tide. If you prefer not to use bone, find a white stone or bleached twig in the shape of a bone.

§ Scratch on to the bone either a word or a symbol representing the obstacle that stands in the way of your happiness, success or healing. As you work, allow the redundant emotions to pour into the bone.

§ When it is dark, find a place in your garden, or in a window-box if you live in an apartment, and bury the bone as deep as possible, saying: 'It is gone, it is done, peace come.'

§ Plant a fast-growing herb or flower, such as lavender or rosemary, on top of the bone to represent the energies that are now released for positive growth.

§ The next morning, initiate a new project or make the changes you have planned but feared.

§ If the old sorrows creep back, repeat the ritual, using a smaller bone or stone each time, and planting even more herbs until a luxuriant growth is achieved.

SOPHIA
Goddess of Wisdom and Female Soul of God

'*Sophia is the great lost Goddess who has remained intransigently within orthodox spiritualities. She is veiled – denigrated and ignored – or else exalted – and pedestalled as an allegorical abstraction of female divinity.*'

CAITLIN MATTHEWS, *SOPHIA: GODDESS OF WISDOM*, 1991, AQUARIAN BOOKS.

Who is Sophia?

Sophia is the Greek word for wisdom. Sophia's name is used for the Divine Feminine God's female soul. She has been described in many different ways through the ages: as the Virgin Mother of God who existed before Creation; as Hathor, the Ancient Egyptian Goddess of Wisdom; as Grandmother Spider Woman in the Native North American tradition; as the Holy Spirit who, as Mother, formed the Holy Family with God the Father and God the Son; and as the Platonic abstract World Soul whose microcosm was the human soul. Her symbols are the Grail cup, source of spiritual nourishment, and the dove, which was also the icon of both Aphrodite, Goddess of Love, and the Holy Spirit. To mediaeval scholars, Sophia was Lady Sapientia, whose seven virgin daughters represented the seven Liberal Arts, including mathematics, astronomy and rhetoric, which formed the core of men's academic education until the sixteenth century. Finally, she was Christianised as St Sophia, or the Holy Sophia of Mother Russia, who is much loved in the Orthodox churches of Eastern Europe.

Sophia and the Patriarchal Religions

Whatever the religion or philosophy in which Sophia was named or described, she was the essential Great Goddess. In Greek philosophy, Judaism and Christianity, however, she was compartmentalised and either idealised as divine inspiration, or denigrated as the cause of the bringing of

145

sin to the world. In Kabbalistic wisdom, she was known as Shekinah, and was the separated and alienated female aspect of God, trapped in matter in the lowest sphere on the Tree of Life, Malkuth, because she would not leave her people alone in exile.

The Great Goddess embraced within herself darkness and light, good and evil, and birth, death and rebirth; she was both transcendent, existing before and independently of creation, and immanent, manifested in and as her creation. Her place as a subordinate in a monotheistic patriarchal religion was therefore totally untenable. For her existence raised the central question that if God was a man and a Monad (complete in himself) where had he come from, in relation to the tradition from earliest times of a Mother Goddess giving birth to her son/consort? If, also, God was wholly good, where did evil spring from?

The supreme male god birthing process is far from natural: in the Genesis creation myth, the male God produced creation seemingly by remote control; there was no fashioning of people out of clay and cradling them, and no planting of herbs and making sure that everyone had water and food. But Sophia was the blood and the flesh, as well as a divine creating force, although you have to piece together what is a gigantic jigsaw representation of her that got strewn all over the world, and re-form some of the pieces that were trodden out of shape, to see her movement through the major religions of the West.

The East was more comfortable with the concept of goddesses. For although Sophia is mainly portrayed in patriarchal religions in her heavenly aspects, sullied only by her contact with matter, she was also the powerful Dark Mother as manifested in the Black Madonna, the Hindu Kali and the earth goddesses who brought forth life with their menstrual blood. To her, the despised filth and sediment, or dust and earth that brought forth the first humans, were beautiful materials, made of living matter and thus sacred.

The idea of Sophia as a fierce goddess was very different from the image of the supreme Creator God who made the world in six days and then stepped back from his creation. Unlike Sophia, who embraced dark and light, good and evil, birth and death, the One God consigned all darker aspects of humanity and divinity to the realms of Hell and sent women to church to be purified after childbirth (see also Eve, page 274). Sophia therefore had to be either angel or demoness, not both. This meant in effect that Sophia in religion could be acknowledged only as Sophia the good, and this resulted in her disempowerment.

The purification of Sophia into a sanitised muse is illustrated in the *The White Goddess* by the twentieth-century writer Robert Graves. This is actually a book that is worth reading for the scholarship and inspirational insights it gives especially on Celtic goddesses and on the Tree Alphabet of the Druids. Moreover, Graves brings back the Goddess into consciousness after centuries of marginalisation. He was certainly inspired by Sophia, but to him and to others in his circle, the White Goddess Sophia's divine wisdom was the inspiration of male poets, writers and artists. She was in Graves's view represented on Earth by an idealised woman, usually the mistress or object of adoration of the writer or poet (wives were rarely spiritually uplifting). But the inspiring woman herself is not viewed as innately creative, reflecting the loss of the acknowledgement of Sophia's active energies.

Thus the different theories created by male theologians and philosophers in order to slot the all-encompassing Sophia into a male-orientated universe have caused a huge web of complex and frequently contradictory images. Rather than trying to untangle the philosophies obscuring Sophia, I have focused on several significant strands that illustrate how various religions and philosophies, as well as individuals, have attempted to integrate the Divine Feminine into their own world views.

Biblical Sophia

Sophia, the Greek translation of the Hebrew Hochmah, is the feminine personification of wisdom in the Old Testament. However, the real biblical Sophia was obscured, perhaps deliberately, in English and other translations of the original texts throughout the world, which substitute the abstract term Wisdom for the name of Sophia. In the Hebrew tradition, Sophia was considered to have been with God from the beginning of Creation. In Proverbs 8: verse 27 onwards Sophia (or Wisdom, as she is called), says:

> '8:27 *When God prepared the heavens, I was there: when he set a compass upon the face of the depth:*
> *8:28 When he established the clouds above: when he strengthened the fountains of the deep:*
> *8:29 When he gave to the sea his decree, that the waters should not pass his commandment: when he appointed the foundations of the earth:*

8:30 Then I was by him, as one brought up with him: and I was daily his delight, rejoicing always before him.'

FROM THE ST JAMES'S BIBLE.

Sophia in the Classical World

Sophia is often closely identified with Athena, about whom I wrote in Virgin Goddesses (see page 121). As I said there, it has been suggested that Athena was originally the serpent goddess of the Minoans in the second millenium BC, daughter of Metis/Medusa, the veiled Goddess of Wisdom and thereby herself a form of the veiled or heavenly Sophia. Athena married Hephaestus, who was himself the virgin-born God of Fire. But when Hephaestus would have impregnated her, Athena the eternal Virgin disappeared and his seed fell to the ground. The Earth Mother Gaia nurtured it and from it Erchtonios was born; this god sometimes took the form of a serpent. He was cared for as a son by Athena, a myth that directly influenced the Gnostic account of Sophia's daughter or Sophia giving birth without impregnation to Ialdaboath/the Demiurge, who had the head of a lion and the body of a serpent.

It is in Gnosticsm, in one of the many versions of the story, that this virgin-born son creates the imperfect world. This made it evil Sophia's and not God's fault because she insisted, it is claimed, on trying to usurp or emulate God's creative functions. But just as Metis was the real creator of Athena, so Sophia secretly planted in the Demiurge the embryo that would be attached to the soul and body of every human, who could thereby be saved through gnosis, or knowledge, at least according to Gnostic doctrine.

Sophia as the World Soul

To the Greek philosopher Plato (428–347 BC), Sophia was the World Soul, the spirit of the Planet that brought beauty and harmony to the universe and pervaded all creation. But the fact the she was created by the Monad (the male principle) and subject to his limitations was a distinct down-grading of the all-encompassing creative energies of the Mother Goddess. Moreover, her continuing role is also more passive: she feels the pain of the universe and all humanity and mediates between the Creator and the created.

In his unfinished work *Timaeus*, Plato describes the creation of the world by the Demiurge (who, unlike the Gnostic Demiurge, is not flawed) from the four elements earth, air, fire and water; in the centre of the world he placed the World Soul, so that it extended and formed the edges. The Greek historian Plutarch (AD 46–120) identified the World Soul with the Egyptian Mother Goddess Isis, and associated it with Nature and thus the source of evil, which was inherent in Nature but not in the (male) Creator God.

Sophia and the Holy Spirit

St Sophia, the official Christian adaptation of the Gnostic Great Mother Sophia, is symbolised by the dove of Aphrodite, which became the sign of the Holy Spirit. From early Christian times in parts of Eastern Europe, and in a more recent, generalised revival of this belief, Sophia has been associated with the Holy Spirit, thus creating a true Holy Family. The concept of a Holy Spirit descending in tongues of fire or as a dove was hard for ordinary people to relate to after worshipping the families of pagan gods such as Mother Isis, Father Osiris and son Horus, who were very popular in Rome at the time when Christianity became the official religion in the early fourth century.

Both the Old and the New Testaments contain references to the female Spirit of Wisdom, who gives birth and nurtures her spiritual children, and this designation has been applied to Sophia by some theologians. This is an ideal slot for the Goddess, and certainly as Holy Spirit she is empowered and has a central place in religious life. But the Virgin Mary, another form of Sophia, also offers (especially to women) a flesh and blood person who, by ascending into Heaven in her bodily form, became divine and mediates with God and Christ on behalf of humanity. She too has been seen as part of the heavenly Holy Family, with the Holy Spirit as the power that overshadowed her at the conception.

Sophia and the Gnostics

Gnosticism is the umbrella term for a number of Christian mystery religions that flourished in the Mediterranean region in around the second century AD, and in spite of persecution survived in various forms and places until the Middle Ages.

Gnosticsm was concerned primarily with the question of the nature of

evil and suffering, and some sects aimed for mystical union with Sige, or Silence, the primordial Goddess who was said to exist at the beginning of all things. Sige had contained within herself the Creator Logos, the Word, who in Genesis initiated the creation of the world. The union with Sige would, it was believed, reveal the secrets of God and raise the divine spirit within the individual human from the evil matter of the body in which it was trapped, and place it in its rightful place in the heavens. Sige gave birth to Sophia, the Great Mother, mother and wife of God. Sophia in turn produced a male spirit, Christ, and a female spirit, Achamoth, Goddess of Wisdom, and it was said that the World Soul came as light from the smile of Sophia. The idea of the Mother Creator persisted even into the mediaeval European world with the heretical but popular icon of La Vierge Ouvrante, statues of Mary that opened to reveal the Holy Trinity within her body.

The positive result of Gnostic beliefs was that women were ordained as priests and bishops and allowed to carry out baptisms. The negative side was that the persecution of the Gnostics set back the cause of women in the Church as well as acknowledgment of the power of Sophia. She was subsequently eradicated from conventional New Testament writings because the Gnostics had espoused her so fervently. Gnosticism was not finally wiped out until the thirteenth century with the persecution of the Cathars in Italy and southern France, whose kings claimed sovereignty through Christ's son by Mary Magdalene. However, Sophia was not completely obliterated because Mary Magdalene was linked with the Black Madonnas, another form of Sophia.

Other Gnostics identified Christ with Sophia herself, the female Logos, whose spirit or essence entered the man Jesus and left him at the Crucifixion, having redeemed the Fall she unwittingly initiated by her creation of the Demiurge. Her sorrow at her creation caused her to retreat to the higher heavens. Sophia sent Christ to Earth in the form of her dove to enter Jesus at baptism, through the feminine element of water.

Sophia was, however, also sometimes viewed as the mother of Jesus, a return to the ancient mother/son/consort motif. She may also have been Jesus's metis (wisdom) that was absorbed by him. As mentioned previously, the theologians had problems finding a large enough slot for the Great Mother that would not challenge the supremacy of the male God.

How could this belief system work? The Demiurge, ldabaoth or Jehovah, as he was also called, son of Achamoth, or Sophia, was a jealous god who either made the imperfect world, a theory that has been mentioned earlier, or energised the imperfect creation of Achamoth. Yahweh here was not the

overall supreme God of the Old Testament. Nonetheless, like the Yahweh of Genesis, he would not allow humans to eat the fruit of the Tree of Knowledge because he wanted them to be kept in ignorance. Achamoth therefore sent her own spirit to Earth in the form of Sophia (in the mother/daughter alternation that appears throughout feminine mythology) to teach people to disobey the jealous god through the person of Eve, the lower or human manifestation of Sophia. Eve gave the forbidden fruit to Adam because this was necessary, since it enabled people to gain knowledge of good and evil so that they could understand their own natures and choose goodness and exercise free will rather than remaining puppets. To reconcile the evil side of Yahweh with the biblical Supreme God of Goodness, Gnostics formulated the existence of a higher, perfect Father, who was unknowable. By this circuitous route, they explained evil and the need to suffer to gain experience.

St Sophia

In Catholicism, Sophia, or Sofia, has become identified with Mary or the Mother Church. Indeed, Mary was given many of the attributes of Sophia and a number of churches dedicated to Mary were on sites once sacred to the Goddess Athena.

In Eastern Europe and Russia, Hagia Sophia, or Sanctus Sophia, meant Holy Female Wisdom rather than St Sophia. The Russian Sanctus Sophia churches at Kiev and Novgorod linked Mary and Sophia not only in the forms of worship, but also in the icons in the churches. The Russian Orthodox Church instituted a special mass for Saint Sophia, or Holy Wisdom, on 15 August, the day the Virgin Mary (or Sophia) was taken back into Heaven. Sophia is especially revered in Eastern Europe, where she is associated with Mother Earth.

In the sixth century, a magnificent shrine dedicated to the Holy Wisdom Sophia, considered to be one of the wonders of the world, was built in Constantinople (now Istanbul) in Turkey. It proved very embarrassing to later Church authorities because of its splendour, which was more befitting, it was said, to a pagan goddess.

The official story of St Sophia is unconvincing and vague on dates. It tells of her three young daughters Faith, Hope and Charity, who were martyred, with their deaths being followed by that of their grieving mother. Her feast day is on 1 August.

SACRED FIRE OF RITUAL AND HEARTH

Goddesses of Protection and Inspiration

∽

Sacred Fire

E VIDENCE OF HEARTHS dating to as far back as 400,000 BC has been found in Ancient China, and we can only guess at the origins of the sacred fire ceremonies that have been a feature of almost every culture. Women have traditionally been the guardians of fires of the home, and as priestesses have tended the eternally burning flames of states, cities or countries, as in the case of the Vestal Virgins of Rome (see page 122). The family hearth was the centre of the home not only for living family members but also for their wise ancestors. In Ancient Greece, a bride would take fire from her mother's hearth for lighting her new hearth in order to keep the Goddess Hestia's flame alight and transfer protection and good fortune to her new home. At the beginning and end of every feast, offerings would be made to Hestia and cast on to the flames. Gabija, the Lithuanian Goddess of the hearth fire, was similarly honoured when salt was thrown on the fire each evening after the main meal, and some older Eastern European people continue this tradition.

Ritual fires also marked the passage of the year and gave symbolic power to the sun and to the solar deities. For example, at the Mid-winter Solstice, the shortest day of the year on around 21 December, great bonfires would be lit by early tribespeople to give power to the sun and persuade it not to die. This ritual is the origin of the yule log and the present-day Christmas celebrations. In Druidic times, ritual fires were kindled from nine different kinds of wood, willow, hazel, alder, birch, ash, yew, elm, rowan and oak; an oak spindle was used to generate the flame.

Fire Goddesses

Fire goddesses were fierce deities, guarding their fire against those who would steal it, although significantly in one Maori myth, Mahuika, the fire guardian, was willing to share her knowledge with humankind. She only became angry when she was tricked by the young, arrogant hero who wanted to possess all the fire, her total power, rather than accepting only

what he really needed. In this myth, Maui-Tinihanga, or Maui of the Many Devices, a demi-god hero, went to Mahuika, the ogress clan mother, who kept fire in her fingernails. Each time he asked for fire she gave him one of her fingernails of fire. Maui deliberately extinguished the flames and it was not until he demanded the last nail that she created a huge conflagration.

In Papua New Guinea, a similar tale is told of the ancient goddess Goga, who carried fire within her body. A boy stole the fire, hurting her as he tore it from her breast. As she chased him, he dropped the burning torch on to a tree, which blazed upwards. Within the tree slept a snake, which was also set alight. Although Goga brought down torrents of rain, the tail of the snake continued to burn and so the first human fires were lit.

Pele, Goddess of Volcanoes, Fire and Magic, is still revered in Hawaii by those who claim descent from her and who still set up altars near lava streams. She is often described as a hag sitting by the fires in her volcanic cavern, which is lit only by a single blue flame.

These fire goddesses lacked the calculated cruelty of Zeus. When in Greek myth Prometheus, a Titan, stole the fire from Hephaestus because Zeus had denied mortals its use, Zeus punished Prometheus by chaining him to Mount Caucasus, where an eagle ate his liver by day. The liver was renewed each night so that his torment could begin anew on the next day.

Brighid, Goddess and Saint of Fire

Nowhere is there a more dramatic example of the merging of Christian and pagan practices than in the character of Brighid, the Triple Goddess of the Celts and patroness of healers, poets and smiths, who became St Bridget, or Brighid of Kildare (see also Saints, page 246). In spite of the fact that she was born in the fifth century, St Bridget was known as the midwife of Christ and was said to have walked before the Virgin Mary bearing a candle into the Temple at her Purification and the presentation of Christ (see also page 278). This was the actual Purification that took place after Jesus's birth, and in spite of all the evidence to the contrary, the tale persists – a sign of St Bridget's importance in Christianity.

1 February, the Festival of Lights that in Christianity is called Candlemas, coincides with the Celtic fire and light festival formerly dedicated to the pagan maiden goddess Brighid and is also St Bridget's special day.

Brighid was once a sun goddess, born according to legend at sunrise. As she entered the world, a shaft of fire blazed from her head and linked Earth

with Heaven. The holy fire at the 'saint' shrine in Kildare, dedicated originally to the Goddess and later to the Saint, is believed to have burned
unquenched for more than a thousand years. It was tended first by nineteen
virgin priestesses called the Daughters of the Sacred Flame, and later by the
nuns of the Abbey at Kildare. The Goddess and later the Saint were said to
care for the fire on the twentieth day of the cycle. Unusually for an early
monastery/convent, which generally contained both monks and nuns, the
women remained entirely apart from the men and even their food and
provisions had to be brought to them by village women. In AD 1220, the
local Bishop insisted that the nuns must be under the rule of a priest and
that the fire could no longer be kept alight.

Fire Divination

Dion Fortune, the twentieth-century occultist and founder of the
esoteric Society of the Inner Light, described how it was possible
to create a divinatory fire known as the Fire of Asrael, the Dark Angel.
The fire was made of cedar, sandalwood and juniper wood. This fire,
said Ms Fortune, gave visions of past worlds. You can, however, make
a fire of any of the nine sacred woods, although ash, hazel, rowan and
oak are particularly associated with divination.

You may see past lives and visions relating to the present or future.
You need not fear Dark Angels, for the process taps into inner
resources and most definitely does not conjure anything other than
good ideas and insights. In the embers, you may see images that
suggest solutions to aspects of your life that are not clear-cut, or about
which you have received conflicting opinions that have clouded the
issue.

Fire divination was used by Druidesses and also has a long tradition in Tibet.

⚬ Ask a question or concentrate on an aspect of your life and through
half-closed eyes look at the embers and flames.

⚬ Allow images to form. The key to successful scrying, whatever
medium you are using, is to reprogramme the mind so that it can
return to the pictorial way of expressing the ideas of childhood,

rather than trying to verbalise and analyse what you see. With fire divination, you tend to perceive a whole picture rather than separate images.

❧ Sketch the images or write down a very brief description of them, however unlikely the concepts. This information is coming from the collective pool of wisdom that we can access when our subconscious minds take charge.

❧ If you are working with a friend, partner or family member, you can alternate reading images and build up a whole series of pictures that, if formed into a story in the order in which they appeared, will offer direction as to future joint ventures or present concerns. You can poke the fire between readings to create a new formation.

❧ You may see visions of past worlds, usually aspects that shed illumination on your current stage of life. They may be actual past worlds or symbols of current concerns. Whatever their origins, they are usually helpful and may continue in your dreams.

❧ You can also burn a stick endowed or etched with symbols and make a wish. Look at the direction the smoke takes and the nature of any flames.

❧ In the Western tradition of fire divination, the future of the venture under question was considered promising if a fire or your wish-stick burned vigorously and the fuel was quickly consumed.

❧ It was also considered to be a good omen if a fire was clear, if the flames were transparent rather than dark red or yellow, and if they crackled.

❧ A fire (or wish-stick) that burned silently, was difficult to light, or smoke blown about by the wind indicated that the coming days and events might need caution and perseverance to be successful.

PART FIVE

WOMEN
AND THE
ESOTERIC
ARTS

～

*Goddess wisdom and
spiritual evolution*

T HE DIVINATORY FORMS described in this section are a fast track to the knowledge and experience of women in other times and places who looked at the same moon, turned over the jewel-like images of the Tarot, held a crystal between their hands, or meditated on the hieroglyphs in Mother Isis's travel bag. For it is the case that every young woman who looks into the mirror and asks, 'When and how will love come?', and every betrayed wife who mists the crystal with her tears, connects with an ocean of other smiles and sorrows. As you work with the disciplines in this section, therefore, you will not only obtain answers to questions, but also establish connection with and gain comfort from the compassion and unshakeable optimism of other women through the ages.

Reactivating the Inner Self

While you work with some of the more formal divinatory arts, your inner imagery system, which you last used as a child, will be reactivated. You will once more see images in the clouds and rippling on sunlit water, or pictures in the marks left by the tide in sand or in the mist around a candle flame. The images that will flow into your mind will offer you insights in symbolic form into your future as well as into your present world.

Once you have taken the time to explore the divinatory forms in this section, you may find that what you thought was your set course for the next thirty years is only a mirage; the true way may be far more circuitous and difficult, but it can promise enlightenment, fulfilment and an awakening. Some sources that will enable you to develop these magical arts further are given in Further Reading (see page 285).

The more we explore magic, the more powerful and inspired we become in every situation, and the more our innate goddess energies permeate every aspect of our being. Some women have developed their natural inspirational abilities through mysticism or alchemy, so that their paths to spiritual awakening follow definite, preordained steps. Women are particularly gifted in these arts, for it is said that while a male mystic

will see a vision, women will live it with all their senses. Moreover, these arts can be practised by anyone – past female mystics, for example, were not always remote women: the fourteenth-century wife and mother Margery Kempe was said to talk 'as easily to God as to the neighbours'.

Being Strong

The pursuit of spiritual awakening has not been without cost. Witchcraft is the story of the oppression of women who wanted something more from their lives than the mundane world offered. Herbalists, wise women and midwives have been singled out for persecution, particularly (but not only) between the fifteenth and late seventeenth centuries, as have other explorers into spirituality. We are their inheritors, and we will not allow ourselves to be tortured or imprisoned for looking into our crystals or for dancing in the moonlight and drawing its power into us.

We should not be too complacent. There are still many places in the world where woman are not free. Even in relatively liberal lands such as Australia, America and England, if you are poor and inarticulate and are perhaps bringing up children alone, you may get a visit from social services if your child talks about your magic cards at school, or tells of the old man or woman who stands in the corner of the bedroom (few university courses in social science teach about ghosts).

For the vast majority of us, the magical world will bring joy, wisdom and healing both to ourselves and to others with whom we come into contact. For as society is increasingly able to encourage the spread of responsible and accurate information about the paranormal, so sensationalism, secrecy and prejudice should melt away. With them will go the protection present taboos offer to those who hide perversion behind the name of magic and witchcraft.

ALCHEMY
Transmuting the Spirit into Gold

'*Alchemy is a universal art of vital chemistry which by fermenting the human spirit purifies and finally dissolves it. Alchemy is philosophy; it is the philosophy, the finding of the Sophia in the mind.*'

MARY ANNE ATTWOOD, THE NINETEENTH-CENTURY ALCHEMIST.

THE WORD ALCHEMY comes from *chyma*, Greek for the casting or fusing of metals. It was also known as *theurgy*, the Divine or Great Work. Although alchemy has an image of being a male preserve, women have always played a significant role in this discipline. One of the founders of the Western alchemical tradition was Maria Prophetissa, also known as Mary the Jewess, who claimed kinship with Miriam, the prophetic sister of Moses. She lived more than a century before the birth of Christ.

The fundamental aim of alchemy in the Western world was to create the 'Philosopher's Stone', a substance that would transform base metal into gold. It was believed that this discovery would bring the key to knowledge, enlightenment and healing. The aim of Eastern alchemy was to make a perfect elixir of gold that would give immortality as well as the ability to use celestial knowledge for human benefit to those who drank it.

Western and perhaps also Eastern alchemy was influenced by the Ancient Egyptians, who were skilled metalworkers and invented alloys and metal tinting. There were many prominent women alchemists in Ancient Egypt, and they in turn derived much of their knowledge from an earlier Mesopotamian tradition. An alternative theory places the origins of alchemical knowledge at around AD 200, in the Gnostic community in Alexandria, which was known for its alchemical expertise. Women were allowed to study in this community because of its devotion to Sophia as Goddess of Wisdom (see Sophia, page 145).

Although alchemical wisdom flourished in the Greek and Arabic worlds, it did not reach Western Europe until the late tenth century; the flow of knowledge increased throughout the early Middle Ages, being transmitted to Europe by the Crusaders as a result of their travels to the East. Alchemists

of this period were skilled in chemistry, biology, herbalism, medicine, philosophy, astrology, magic and Kabbalistic (Jewish esoteric) wisdom.

At this time, women in religious orders were able to study science, especially in Germany; the most notable of these women was the twelfth-century mystic Hildegard von Bingen. With the increasing domination of the male clergy, by the early fifteenth century this avenue had been closed to women, and with the rise of the Protestant religion, many of the orders of nuns were destroyed and their books burned.

Women alchemists in Western Europe were often the self-taught daughters of liberally minded male alchemists. One of the problems for women who were able to practise alchemy during the Renaissance in the fifteenth and sixteenth centuries was that they were in danger of being accused of witchcraft by taking an interest in esoteric or scientific matters. For this reason, women who wrote alchemical tracts did so as men under one of the exalted Classical names, which suggested that their work could claim authority from antiquity. Even male alchemists, unless protected by powerful churchmen or nobles, had to work secretly because of fears of the Inquisition (although more than eighty per cent of those accused of witchcraft were female). In 1575, Julian, Duke of Brunswick burned to death an unnamed female alchemist because she refused to give him the secret of creating gold, and in 1641 Martine de Bertereau du Chatlet, a prominent French mineralogist, was executed for witchcraft; there were countless other such cases.

The Feminine Principle in Alchemical Philosophy and Practice

Central to alchemy was the union of the male and female principles (represented by sulphur and mercury) to produce the Divine Hermaphrodite. In this sacred marriage, Venus joined with Mercury, or King Sol with Queen Luna, and they are pictured stepping naked together into an alchemical bath of the kind invented by Maria Prophetissa and still called *la bain de Marie* in France today. It was thought that by nurturing the Hermaphrodite by various processes and refinements the Philosopher's Stone might be obtained. A predominant image connected with alchemy was the figure of the Virgin Mary/Aphrodite/Sophia, Goddess of Wisdom, mingling her blood with the maternal milk that poured from her breasts to nourish the Hermaphrodite. This links with the alchemical symbol of the pelican – the

archetypal perfect mother – feeding her young with blood from her own breast.

There was also a wild female form in alchemy that both fascinated and repelled male alchemists as society increasingly valued compliant women. Melusina was a terrifying creature, part-animal and part-woman, a figure of the earth that both devoured the dead and gave life to the newly born in the continuing destructive/creative cycle that lay at the heart of alchemy. She was the fierce All Mother, womb and tomb, the Hag, the Bone Goddess who tears apart and reforms the initiate alchemist and who must be faced and incorporated into the journey of the soul towards perfection. In some alchemical illustrations, her vulva is portrayed not as a cavern of delight but as a terrifying place of destruction.

By the eighteenth century in Europe, the gentler concept of the Soror Mystica, the mystical sister, had evolved. She was a feminine companion of the experimenter with whom it was forbidden to have sexual relations. Magically, the Soror Mystica could be seen as his Queen Luna, and psychologically she was his anima, or feminine side. Of course it was incredibly ego boosting for a male alchemist to have a legitimised emotional liaison with a willing female who shared his spiritual interests and who was not distracted by having to cook his dinner, tend his children or worry about paying the bills. Thus he enjoyed deeply meaningful encounters with what was the equivalent of Robert Graves's White Lady, who in her human form acted as a foil for male poets (see page 147).

With the rise of formal scientific practice at the beginning of the nineteenth century, chemical alchemy begin to decline. Philosophical alchemy became the antidote to the depersonalisation of the material sciences and now formed a separate discipline. A key figure in the new movement was Mary Anne Atwood, who in 1850 published *A Suggestive Enquiry Into The Hermetic Mystery*. She merged the new spiritual arts of spiritualism and hypnotism with ancient alchemical teachings. However, after only a hundred copies of her work had been sold, Mrs Atwood attempted to buy back and destroy the rest, fearing that she had revealed too much secret knowledge. Since the aim of individual alchemists both ancient and modern was the perfection of the soul, she felt that it was important for them to follow the intricate path of discovery themselves, rather than being exposed to knowledge without the necessary practical experience. From then on, she kept silent about her studies until she died in 1910 at the age of ninety-seven. However, copies of the book still exist, and a reprint was published in 1960 by the Julian Press. In some ways, her work fore-

shadowed that of the psychologist Carl Gustav Jung, who believed that alchemical literature could be of great value in understanding the human psyche.

CRYSTAL DIVINATION AND MAGIC

OVER THE CENTURIES, women have incorporated crystals into their folk magic. In Scandinavia, Denmark and lands in which the Anglo-Saxon influence was strong, including Germany and the UK, clear quartz crystal spindle-whorls were used in spinning; when turned, the spindle would catch the light and suffuse the thread with rainbows. Spinning and weaving magic by chanting spells and incantations as garments were sewn was said to infuse them with protective or empowering charms, and this practice remained popular until mediaeval times. Frigga, the Viking Mother Goddess (Frige in the Anglo-Saxon tradition), was patroness of spinning and could read the magical Web of Fate. Her jewelled distaff may be seen in the stars close to Orion's Belt (see also page 136).

This spinning magic was thought to have been amplified by the specific powers of the kinds of crystal from which the spindles were fashioned. Clear crystal quartz channelled the power of sunlight and moonlight (for important ventures, thread would be spun first in bright sunlight and then at the time of the full moon); it was also a source of the life force, bringing health, energy and clarity of purpose. Spindle-whorls were also made of amber and jet. Amber was called the tears of Freyja, the Viking Goddess of Love, Beauty and Fertility, and was reputed to endow the wearer of the magical garment with courage, confidence, radiance and sexual magnetism. Jet was used for adornments and amulets since the Bronze Age, and was thought to be fiercely protective, especially for sailors and those who crossed the seas for the purposes of trade or conquest.

Crystals and Divination

In the sacred groves of Ancient Greece, oracular priestesses interpreted the sound of the water running over stones. Talking stones or crystals have also been used in many traditions to seek answers, whether through interpreta-

tion by a clairvoyant or – as with the method suggested in this section – by drawing on personal intuitive wisdom from the seeker.

A stone or crystal, part of a set collected from sacred places where Earth energies were powerful, would be selected from a bag of divinatory stones apparently at random. Because crystals contain demonstrably living energies, they can when held transmit impressions received through the fingertips from the cosmic well of wisdom in the psychic art of psychometry, an extension of the physical sense of touch. These impressions can stimulate visual images and words clairvoyantly and clairaudiently.

Women who are in close touch with their intuitive processes and will trust wisdom coming from non-logical sources seem – as I have seen during the course of my work with women's divination over eleven years – to be able to use this method almost instantly. In contrast, many men want to know what a crystal is supposed to mean and so block their own powerful intuitive responses.

Our ancestors did not work with polished stones, but were gifted at interpreting from the glints of crystals or gems in seemingly ordinary pieces of rock the kind of information we now seek in highly polished and refined crystals. In time, you may find that a bag of stones from a shore where earth, sky and water meet, gathered on a sunny day to add the power of fire, can be just as powerful as polished stones in triggering your intuitions.

Choosing the Right Crystal

We can select the appropriate crystals for a given situation without using our visual sense at all. In fact, we are probably tapping into another psychic ability, psychokinesis, or telekinesis, whereby our unconscious mind influences which crystals we choose that will suggest an answer to a current situation.

Divinatory Crystals

I have listed ten basic crystals for discussion here, but you can add many more crystals of different shades and kinds. I have over one hundred and fifty crystals in my own divinatory bag; it does not matter what mix of colours and types you have – the right crystal (or crystals) to answer your question will invariably be the one you select.

In my experience in hundreds of readings, the colour of a crystal is an important pointer to the best strategy to adopt in resolving an issue. But the unique message comes from the impressions received by holding the crystal and allowing it to speak through your psyche, which draws through the unconscious mind on the wisdom of your ancestors.

If possible, buy the crystals you will use in divination at times when you are happy or harmonious, perhaps on a holiday or a day away from your normal routine. In the section on crystal healing I have suggested ways of cleansing and empowering crystals.

Crystal Divination

• Whether you are using ten crystals or more, place them all in a bag made of a natural fabric. Ask a question or focus on an issue and allow your hand to take from the bag the crystal that feels right.

• Before you consider the crystal's colour, hold it between your hands with your eyes closed and allow sensations to flood your mind, maybe feelings of heat and cold, sunlight or rain.

• Let images form in your mind's vision and accept them, however unlikely. You are using the latent visual image system that makes children such superb clairvoyants and its insights may be totally unexpected, but are always accurate.

• You may also hear snatches of songs or poetry, phrases or just a single word in your mind's ear through clairaudience, for the psychic senses are closely related.

• Open your eyes and hold the crystal to the light. Even an opaque stone or crystal will reflect patterns on its surface and if you allow your unconscious wisdom to take over, then you may gain further insights. The images that appear in a crystal, whatever its shape and size, are transmitted by a process called eidetic imagery, whereby the mind can externalise an inner image.

• To these impressions, add the colour meaning. I have suggested under Further Reading (see page 285) several crystal and crystal divination books that you can refer to if you wish to study the art further; my own book, *Crystals talk to the Woman Within*, is written specifically from a female perspective.

• If the issue you are trying to resolve is complex, you can take a second crystal, or three or four more if you have a larger collection. Work with each crystal in turn, creating impressions by combining the imagery, perhaps as a story.

Listed below are crystals, arranged according to colour, that I find particularly effective for divination, along with the possible meanings that may be gleaned from them. There are many more crystals, and if you go to a shop selling minerals and handle different stones, even ones of the same colour and type may convey subtly different energies.

White

Clear crystal quartz
Fluorite
Snow or milky quartz
Zircon

These are the crystals of individuality and pure potential. Now is the time for new beginnings, for innovation and originality. You will be filled with pure energy and creative power, the animus or yang that women need to succeed in important aspects of their life. Anything is possible right now if you believe in yourself and your abilities, if you throw your heart and soul into any venture, whether it be related to love, career or simply connecting with life. On a spiritual level, you may be particularly connected to your higher consciousness, and may spontaneously channel wisdom from angels, spirit helpers or devic nature spirits, who will guide you as you move from the mundane to mystical experience. Opposition and self-doubt will disappear, and although others may not share your vision, if you remain true to it and yourself then you cannot fail.

Black

Jet
Jasper
Obsidian
Smoky quartz

It is a time for waiting and listening rather than for speaking your mind, for accepting life as it is and people as they are rather than trying to change the status quo. This pure yin or anima energy is not weakness, but a counter to white energy, encouraging inner stillness. Absorb rather than react to impressions and experiences, and in time the way ahead will be clear and many problems will be naturally resolved. Do not resist the natural endings of phases or experiences in your life; by closing a particular door, energy that is perhaps being wasted on a person or cause that will not bear fruit, you will open the way to new beginnings. Get plenty of rest to avoid becoming exhausted.

Red

Blood agate
Carnelian
Garnet
Jasper

This is a time when you will be up on your horse, maybe in battle dress. You may need to confront the status quo (perhaps a chauvinist or three who is blocking your path?). It is definitely a time for positive change and progress, for being courageous and strong whatever the challenge, and for concentrating on important issues and determining your own agenda and priorities. You should not be intimidated by any of those grown-up playground bullies. Assert what it is you want and need and insist on recognition of your worth. Refuse to accept second best, and express anger creatively rather than allowing it to bubble inside or be repressed as a migraine.

Orange

Agate
Amber
Beryl
Carnelian

This is a crystal of the warm sun, and it is the stone of fertility and abundance in any and every area of your life. It confirms your unique identity and worth and says that you should be confident in your own ability and value yourself for what you are now and what you have achieved. So it is

important not to allow anyone – with subtle carping or criticism 'for your own good' – to undermine you or to deter you from living life in your own way, according to your values. The orange crystal bears some similarities to the white crystal, and they may appear together at a time when your identity is perhaps being eroded. Orange crystals are, however, much gentler than white ones, and are to do with harmony and integrating the different aspects of your life in a creative way. You may find expression in actual creative ventures, such as writing, painting, drama or healing.

Yellow

Citrine
Jasper
Rutilated quartz
Topaz

You should listen to your head rather than to your heart and be very logical, using the clear light of dawn to clear away indecision, inertia and illusion, and especially the ego trips of others that keep you from doing the work and allow them to get the credit. It is a time for career or personal goals, and maybe for learning new skills or updating your technological ones. Clear and focused communication is vital, especially if others are muddying the waters. Your own doubts may be clouding your intuitive decision-making processes, so check the facts and find answers through deduction and a rapid assimilation of the actual evidence, rather than listening to what others, even experts, tell you; others may on this occasion be less than open. Negotiate your way through any difficulties.

Green

Aventurine
Bloodstone
Jade
Malachite

Trust your emotions and listen to your heart, for in this case they are the best guide to the intentions of others and to your own needs, which may have been temporarily sidelined. A green and yellow crystal together suggest that you need to balance both approaches. You may be concerned with family or love matters, and these are areas of your life that will become especially rewarding. Money-making schemes and any projects that will bear fruit over a longer period are also well augured, and may thus be begun now. The same applies to any environmental work that may improve your area or help with conservation of a particular species over the next few years, as well as in the short term. Follow your heart, which is very different from being swayed by sentiment or the emotional pressures of others. Make connections with the natural world. Even a day in the countryside or the garden will be restorative; follow the flow of life as new opportunities unfold.

Blue

Azurite
Blue lace agate
Laboradite
Turquoise

You are to the fore of leadership matters and this is a time when your own horizons will naturally expand. For now, a conventional approach will be most successful, especially in matters of promotion or where you are negotiating with authority. Goals can be achieved through the existing power structure, and it is a time when you will receive perhaps long overdue official recognition of your achievements. Making it on other people's terms is not always right, but on this occasion you have succeeded perhaps in spite of entrenched prejudice. Now you can make new, fairer rules for future interactions. Fight injustice through official and legal channels. Do not doubt the wisdom of your actions or your ideals even if they are not popular.

Purple (Violet/Indigo)

Amethyst
Fluorite
Lapis lazuli or lazurite
Sodalite

These are the crystals of the inner world, where dreams and contemplation are the truest guides to action. Any psychic or spiritual work will be rewarding, and you may find that the psychic abilities which you had previously

doubted are naturally unfolding. Natural healing abilities may also be increasing, and if this crystal appears regularly in your readings, you might consider developing your healing or clairvoyant abilities with a course of study (see Useful Addresses, page 289). Rise above any pettiness that may surround you at home or at work, and enclose yourself in a circle of purple protective light by breathing in the colour of this crystal. Make extra time for meditation, sitting by the light of a purple candle and letting insights come.

Pink

Coral
Rose quartz
Rhodochrosite
Sugilite

You may find yourself acting as peacemaker at work or at home and should let go of any resentments, guilt or regrets of your own. Forgive yourself as well as others if your (or their) conduct has recently fallen a little short of the angels. You may find that happiness lies in friendship and in spending time with people who make you feel good about yourself, so that your own natural reservoir of harmony and gentleness does not become depleted. Quiet pleasures, the company of children or animals, seashores and woodlands, as well as time spent in holding your crystals and letting them speak to you, will bring you inner harmony, which is important because you give so much to others. Ask for and accept help and support for yourself as well as giving it, especially from friends or family.

Brown

Desert rose
Fossilised wood
Leopardskin jasper
Tiger's eye

Brown stones are not at all dull, but hold rich stores of wisdom that are linked especially with Earth energies. This stone indicates that you are very grounded and that you can succeed in any venture because you can translate it into what is possible, beginning where you are with the resources you have. You may want or need to spend time at home, working on the home

ABOVE: Indian miniature of Vishnu and Lakshmi surrounded by female servants.

LEFT: 15th century book illumination of two witches riding on broomsticks, from *Le Champion des Dames* by Martin le Franc.

LEFT: Alberich curses Wotan and Loge, a scene from *The Reingold* by Wagner. Above the three Weavers of Fate are shown.

BELOW: A 16th century painting showing a fortune-teller at work by Lucas van Leyden.

RIGHT: 'Venus of Willendorf', a female idol made from chalky sandstone painted with red chalk, c. 2000 BC.

BELOW: Terracotta figurine of a Mayan woman weaving.

or in securing or improving your finances. Vulnerable family members and friends may need practical help, and giving it will be rewarding for you. New ventures involving a step-by-step approach, or learning or improving a creative art or practical skill, such as pottery, sculpture, or textile work, or design, cookery, wood carving, or carpentry or a whole host of other DIY activities, may be therapeutic as well as leading to future money-making or money-saving opportunities. Make small changes or improvements initially. Act with caution rather than with flair.

HATHOR AND MIRROR MAGIC

HATHOR WAS THE Ancient Egyptian Sky Goddess of joy, love, music and dance, and she was also protector of women. In the ancient world she promised good husbands and wives to all who asked her. She appears in statues and on tombs wearing a sun disk held between the horns of a cow as a crown. Her sister and alter ego is the fierce solar Lion Goddess Sekhmet.

According to later myths, in which the Sun God Ra had been elevated to supreme creator (although in earlier myths he was the son of Nut, the Sky Goddess), Hathor was allowed to see through the sacred eye of her father/consort Ra. In this way she had knowledge of everything on the Earth, in the sea and in the heavens, including the thoughts and the deeds of humankind. These powers were, however, probably inherent in Hathor.

As a sky and solar goddess, Hathor also carried a shield that could reflect back all things in their true light. From this shield she fashioned the first magic mirror. One side was endowed with the power of Ra's eye/Hathor's own all-encompassing vision to see everything, no matter how distant it was in miles or how far into the future. The other side showed the gazer in his or her true light, and only a brave or pure person could look into it without flinching.

Mirror Divination

Hathor can be invoked in mirror divination, one of the oldest forms of scrying, which means seeking eidetic or psychic images within a reflective

surface. When interpreted, the pictures seen in the mirror will provide answers to questions that have been formulated either consciously or, usually more significantly, unconsciously and that become apparent during the divination.

Mirror divination is an especially potent way to discover the identity of a future partner, for questions about love, fidelity, marriage and permanent love relationships, fertility, and family concerns, and for discovering the location of an item or animal that is lost or the truth about a matter that is hidden from you. Although men can scry in mirrors, Hathor as protectress of women makes this a particularly female-friendly art.

Modern women do not generally call the Goddess to enter the mirror to reveal her hidden wisdom, as their ancestors did right through to Victorian times. Rather they invoke the clairvoyant powers of Hathor to amplify and channel innate intuitive powers.

Beginning Mirror Divination

- An oval mirror on a stand is ideal because you can angle the mirror to reflect candle light, which forms the best lighting for scrying work.

- The hour before sunset is the traditional time for scrying because the dying sunlight is mingled with the candle light.

- In ancient times, mirrors were made from polished metal, or agate, and a large, unadorned polished silver, bronze or pewter tray can make a very effective alternative to glass for scrying. However, while you are practising, plain glass probably provides the clearest focus.

- Silver-coloured frames are customary for scrying mirrors.

- You may wish to keep your Hathor mirror exclusively for scrying, covered with a soft cloth when not in use.

- To distance yourself from the everyday world, have a bath before you begin scrying in water containing rose petals, rose essential oil or rose bath essence. Roses are sacred to Hathor.

- After you have dressed, you can circle turquoise eye-shadow around your eyes: in Ancient Egypt, this was believed to increase the power of the inner clairvoyant eye and to ward off all harm.

- Place the mirror on a table of medium height and surround it with tiny turquoise crystals, Hathor's own stone of power, and with jewellery made of gold, the sacred metal of Hathor. Gold is both empowering and protective and represents Hathor's solar aspects. For this reason, some practitioners prefer to use a gold-framed mirror.

- On one side of the mirror, light a pink candle and on the other an orange one, so that the light is reflected in the mirror in the twilight.

- Position the mirror so that it faces a plain wall, if possible with a west-facing window to the side so that the rays of the setting sun mingle with the candle light on the surface of the glass (Hathor was Queen of the West).

- Light rose incense on either side of the mirror and sit slightly to one side, so that you do not see your own face reflected unless you are seeking to discover yourself in your true light (most women are pleasantly surprised when they do, as we tend to sell ourselves short image-wise).

- Ask a question of Hathor and wait for the images to form either within the mirror or in your mind's eye. Both types of image are equally valid, and with practice you can cast the images from your psyche into the mirror, using the eidetic powers we all possess. In this way, you can see the images more clearly, uncluttered by the background distractions of the mind. To do this, visualise the image in a tunnel of light passing from the centre of your brow, the location of the psychic Third Eye.

- Alternatively, begin by visualising the image on the surface of your magic mirror, then gradually see it receding deeper within the mirror and becoming three-dimensional.

- Either way, you may see single images or whole scenes.

- If this method does not work, close your eyes, open them, blink and look at the mirror, naming whatever image you perceive in your

mind. Once you see an image either look away or close your eyes again, open and blink. Continue until you have evoked five or six consecutive images.

ᔥ When you feel that you are tiring or losing concentration and can get nothing more, blow out the candles, polish and cover your mirror, and in a notebook or on a sheet of paper draw the pictures you saw or write down words to describe the images in the order they occurred.

Interpreting Images

ᔥ If the pictures do not make sense, join them with a spiral line and as you do so begin to weave a story with them, or write down words to express the emotions they evoked in you. Do not force logical connections but just let the words flow.

ᔥ Alternatively, using plain paper and felt-tip pens, draw the pictures into a backdrop like a collage or frieze.

ᔥ There are traditional meanings concerning the positions of images in a mirror. I tend not to use them myself, but the rules established over centuries can offer guidelines while the technique is unfamiliar.

○ An image moving towards the scryer suggests that the event will occur or person appear very soon.

○ An image that is moving away implies that an event or person is either moving away from the scryer's world, or that a past issue or relationship may still be exerting undue influence on the scryer.

○ Images appearing on the left of the mirror suggest actual physical occurrences that have already influenced the everyday world or may influence it in the near future.

○ Images appearing in the centre or to the right tend to be symbolic.

- Pictures near the top are important and need prompt attention.

- Images in the corners or at the bottom are less prominent or urgent.

- The relative size of the images can indicate their importance.

What do the Images Mean?

The images will shed light on the question you asked, or perhaps reveal an issue that you thought had long been buried or was irrelevant, but which may actually hold the key to moving forwards. We all have personal image systems, built up from childhood and modified over the years. An image system is never fixed but most people's do have common factors, based on meanings that are passed down in the knowledge. This knowledge may be contained in our genetic make-up.

Workplace Protection with a Hathor Mirror

Hathor has become the natural protectress of business women and indeed all working women in the modern world, specifically through the symbol of her mirror. A tiny Hathor mirror can act as an amulet against physical threat as well as malice. To repel hostility, you can use a highly polished gold medallion on a chain, or a make-up mirror that you have placed facing outwards on your desk. I use a scarf that has tiny mirrors sewn on to it.

⚶ On the back of the mirror, scratch or stick a drawing of the symbol of the protective eye of Horus, the Sky God, sometimes called the Eye of Ra.

⚶ Empower your protective mirror with the power of Hathor by passing it through an orange candle flame and through the smoke of rose incense. Then sprinkle it with water to which a few grains of salt and a single drop of olive oil have been added.

🙵 As you do this, say: 'May he/she who seeks to harm me see reflected back their own weakness and malice. Look on thy true self and depart in peace.'

🙵 If you are unavoidably in a dark, dangerous place or are under threat from spite, gossip or envy, hold your mirror so that the eye is facing you and the shiny surface faces outwards, then repeat the mantra silently until the subject of the threat moves away.

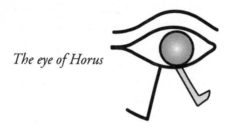

The eye of Horus

ISIS, MISTRESS OF ENCHANTMENT
Goddess with Ten Thousand Names

OF ALL THE GODDESSES of the ancient world, the Egyptian Isis has been the one whose worship as the Great Mother rivalled that of the Virgin Mary, and at one time seemed likely to replace Christianity in the Roman Empire. Isis has been honoured in many forms, as Goddess of the Moon, Stella Maris, Goddess of the Sea, Holy Virgin, Sacred Bride, Mother of Nature and, perhaps most importantly in the Westernised ceremonial magical system, as Mistress of Enchantment.

Isis was immortalised as Lady of Magic in the novels of the twentieth-century occultist Dion Fortune. In the modern world too, Isis is a central figure in goddess-focused organisations such as the Fellowship of Isis, which has members worldwide (see Useful Addresses, page 289). However, her widespread appeal over the millennia perhaps resides in the fact that she was a wife and mother as well as a great goddess. Like her consort Osiris, she was regarded as being mortal as well as a deity, dwelling on Earth as well as being

Queen of Heaven; she also (as Osiris did) promised ordinary people, not just great Pharaohs and kings, hope of immortality.

Although Isis was one of the great goddesses of Egypt, her worship became equally popular in the Greek and Roman worlds, particularly among women, and spread throughout Europe as far north as England. Paris was her special city.

Egypt became part of the Greek Empire when it was conquered by Alexander the Great in the third century BC. His successors, the Ptolemite kings, were anxious to incorporate Egyptian religion into their own so that they could win the support of ordinary Egyptians who had become disillusioned with the might of the Pharaohs. In this new dynasty, Isis was worshipped as wife of the god of the Ptolemites, Serapia. The cult of Serapia and Isis spread to Greece with Egyptian traders who had settled in the fourth century BC at Piraeus, the harbour town of Athens. However, whatever her forms or locations, she was still Mother Isis.

Mother of All

Isis was known to the Egyptians as Au Set, Lady of the Moon and Mother of the Crops. She was regarded as the throne of the Pharaohs in a literal as well as a symbolic sense, cradling the Pharaoh as she did her infant Horus, who was believed to be manifested as each Pharaoh. Isis was therefore the Queen Mother to mortal rulers for four thousand years, enfolding them in her protective wings as she did the mummified body of Osiris. The solar disc between two bovine horns on her headdress indicated her status as Moon Mother, who provided maternal milk to all and combined sun and moon, power and protection, within her.

By the time of Ancient Greece, Isis had been elevated to 'Oldest of the Old, from whom all things arose'. The Greek Sky Gods had usurped the earlier matriarchal focus and there was a need for a personalised Gaia to whom women especially could relate, and Isis fulfilled this function. Her elevated status also strengthened her unifying role among disparate peoples who needed to be welded together under a single political system.

Inevitably, there were attempts even in Egypt to limit Isis's all-encompassing power, especially in the later years of the Egyptian dynasties. During this time, it was said that she derived her innate supreme magical powers, which enabled her to restore her dead husband to life, partly from Ra by tricking him into revealing his power name.

The worship of Isis was also temporarily suppressed after the conquest of Egypt in 31 BC by the Roman emperor Octavius (Augustus); when her suppression proved impossible to enforce, her worship was restored (again for political reasons). As supreme goddess, Isis incorporated into her self the identities of other powerful goddesses, such as the Graeco-Roman Athena, Goddess of Wisdom, and Tyche, Goddess of Good Fortune.

Some Roman statues show Isis as remarkably homely rather than awesomely beautiful, and this characteristic was as much a source of her power as her more ethereal portrayals. Roman tombstones at Athens and elsewhere portray women members of her cult wearing the special fringed shawl knotted between the breasts and holding the *sistrum* (rattle) used in religious ceremonies.

The policy of grafting Christian festivals on to pagan ones to make the new religion more acceptable to the vast majority of people meant that the Purification of the Blessed Virgin Mary on 2 February, part of the Christianised Candlemas, was close in form as well as date to the festival of the pre-Christian Isis as Queen of Lights. Likewise, the Assumption of the Virgin Mary in August, when she ascended and was crowned as Queen of Heaven, mirrors the rites of Isis held in Ancient Egypt to celebrate the rise of the Dog Star Sirius that heralded the flooding of the Nile. The annual flood was caused, it was believed, by the tears that Isis shed for her dead husband Osiris, who was killed by his brother Set.

Isis the Empowerer

As the devoted wife, Isis searched through the land and reassembled the dismembered body of her husband Osiris, except for his phallus, which she magically recreated using chants and amulets. Then she breathed life into Osiris, so conceiving her son Horus; this was in a sense a virgin conception and birth since she was the initiator and the life force.

As the perfect mother, Isis suckled her infant in the papyrus swamps, hiding him from his evil uncle like the Old Testament prophetess Miriam, who stood watch over her mother and baby brother Moses, and like the Virgin Mary who fled with Jesus to Egypt to protect him from Herod. Early Christians identified the Virgin Mary with Isis, and she is undoubtedly the source of the numerous Black Madonna statues of mother and child found throughout Europe and the Mediterranean regions (see The Black Madonna, page 224).

In all these roles Isis is the initiating force, and the power of the woman

as mother, wife and weaver of magic survived the downgrading of the female and has links with the empowering Shakti energy of the Hindu goddesses.

Isis the Enchantress

The second-century writer Apuleius, who was born in the Roman colony of Madura in Morocco and was initiated into the mysteries of Isis, described Isis as an ethereal goddess of magic in his semi-autobiographical work *The Golden Ass*, which was translated by Robert Graves from Latin. Apuleius wrote:

> '. . . the apparition of a woman began to rise from the middle of the sea, with so lovely a face the gods themselves would have fallen down in adoration. Her long thick hair was crowned with an intricate chaplet in which was woven every kind of flower. Just above her brow shone a round disc like a mirror or like the bright face of the moon, which told me who she was. Her mantle was embroidered with glittering stars on the hem and everywhere else and in the middle beamed a full and fiery moon.'

This image of Isis is one that has formed the basis for recent art and literature, and for her role as Lady of the Magical Arts in the late-nineteenth and twentieth-century Western magical tradition, notably the Golden Dawn occult society. In her novel *The Sea Priestess*, Dion Fortune distinguishes – in accordance with the Western magical tradition – between Isis veiled, the heavenly Isis, Lady of the Moon, and Isis Unveiled, the Goddess of Nature, Mother of the Sun. William, the hero of the book, has been initiated by Morgan le Fey, a sea priestess of Isis who has been reincarnated in the twentieth century. He watches as Morgan draws down the power of the full moon into herself and becomes transformed into Isis:

> '. . . and as I looked I saw her change from silver to gold and a glowing aura of all the colours of the rainbow sprang out free around her . . . she glowed with life like a glorious Dawn . . . I knew this was Isis unveiled and dynamic'.

Afterwards, Morgan disappears, it is suggested back into the sea. Isis is here associated with Binah, the Mother or the Great Seas, the third sphere on the Kabbalistic Tree of Life.

ORACLE OF ISIS AND THE EGYPTIAN GODDESSES

HIEROGLYPHS, pictorial representations of words and phrases of power, contain magical and spiritual meaning. In Ancient Egypt, it was believed that the energies contained within these representations were released when they were written down or spoken aloud (runic symbols have the same power, see page 199).

I have used hieroglyphs as a form of divination for about eight years, but as my interest in and knowledge of Isis and the Egyptian goddesses have increased, I have realised that the basic system which I have been using is far more effective when it is interpreted through the imagery of Isis and the goddesses associated with her, especially for female divination.

Bloodstones and turquoise are Isis's special crystals and you can paint the twelve hieroglyphs central to this method on to small, oval crystals. Alternatively, you can etch them on to wood: sycamore is the tree of Isis, but you can use any wood to create discs about the size of a large coin. Your divinatory hieroglyphs will act as amulets, and you can carry with you the one that you select in your reading; at night, you can place it under your pillow to protect and also empower you while you sleep. Another option is to draw or paint the symbols on to stones. As Isis is Goddess of the Sea, you should collect these from a seashore, if possible on the day or evening of the full moon. Round shells of equal size are also potent.

Silver is the colour and metal of Isis, so if you are working in the early morning or evening, light silver candles. The water lily is Isis's flower and you can float the candles on a crystal bowl filled with water and lilies; this will enable you to gain extra insight from the light images cast on the water.

Using the Oracle of Isis

To obtain an answer to a question, first place the marked crystals in a silver bag and then select one. If you choose to select a hieroglyph each day, you may find that the same one appears regularly if a particular issue is dominant, or if specific opportunities are coming into your life. Through psychokinesis (mind power), your unconscious wisdom will ensure that you receive the message you need, which may or may not be the one you want or expect.

In Ancient Egypt, each of the symbols described below was worn as an amulet for protection or power, set in different precious jewels or metals. As well as offering strength and growth to the living, the hieroglyphics on tomb walls or on amulets placed in a coffin promised resurrection to those who had died.

Ankh, the key, is the symbol of eternal life. This is the special amulet of Isis, representing her union with Osiris and thus the uniting of birth and death (it was her magical incantations that restored him back to life and potency).

For modern women, the ankh signifies regeneration through personal creativity. It may be a good time to persevere with an avenue that seems unpromising, or to breathe new enthusiasm into a stagnant relationship, rather than abandoning it. The ankh advises taking a long-term view of any relationship or venture, and choosing what is of worth rather than the most exciting option or the one offering instant returns.

Perseverance is the key.

Wedja means fire, and because fire was used by the Ancient Egyptians to forge metal and smelt gold, it represents prosperity. The hieroglyph was based on a bow-drill that was turned in a shaped piece of wood (the lower part of the hieroglyph) to produce fire by friction, thereby generating vitality from itself rather than from an external source of fuel. Sekhmet is the lioness-headed Goddess of Fire; she is courageous and determined and answerable to no one, not even to her consort Ra.

To women, the wedja says that they can succeed through their own efforts and initiative, especially if others are being unhelpful or even obstructive. It is particularly relevant to financial and career matters, and it

augurs well for self-employment, for seeking more independence within an existing work structure, or for taking a course to improve qualifications or knowledge in a field of interest that might prove profitable. Make sure that others do not take credit for your ideas and effort.

Independence is the key.

Seneb as a symbol was the first letter in the word *seneb*, meaning health, although the hieroglyph shows a bolt of cloth, linking it with the Weavers of Fate (see page 135). Tait was the name given to Isis in her role as a weaver and binder of the threads of fate. Both healing and destiny are therefore contained in the meaning.

This hieroglyph symbolises the power of a woman to heal emotionally as well as spiritually, and it may appear at a time when you need to bring healing to whatever situation or place is under stress in your life. Right now, you are the weaver whose actions will affect those connected with you, and it is possible for you to reconcile even disparate elements or warring factions into harmony. This may also be a changing point in your life, and because you are central to the design, you will bring necessary change to the lives of those around you. Although this is something that they may fear, it will be beneficial to a family or group as a whole. Take time to plan, do not be rushed into any decisions until you are ready, and use divination regularly to see how the web is forming. You may also find your innate healing and divinatory abilities emerging.

Integration is the key.

The Boat Because the Nile was central to the life of the Ancient Egyptians, 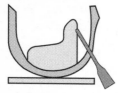 the boat was the main means of transport – and not just for mortals. The sun god Ra crossed the sky each day in his solar boat. Ma'at, the Goddess of Truth and Natural Law, rode in the sun boat and even Ra was subject to her law and to her allotting of the day and night, time and seasons.

For women today, this hieroglyph advises resourcefulness and adaptability in the achievement of a goal. Whether in career matters or in the social environment, it may involve temporarily sharing the boat with someone who acts in a superior manner, or continuing to be cooperative in spite of prejudice. Remember that it is Ma'at who is the force behind the Egyptian cosmos (although Ra assumes sole credit for creating the universe). You are more powerful than you reveal or realise, and the time

will come when you can steer the sun boat in your own way and eclipse your personal Ra.

Cooperation is the key.

The Scarab To the Ancient Egyptians, the scarab was a profound symbol of 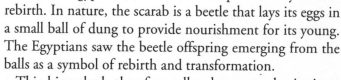 rebirth. In nature, the scarab is a beetle that lays its eggs in a small ball of dung to provide nourishment for its young. The Egyptians saw the beetle offspring emerging from the balls as a symbol of rebirth and transformation.

This hieroglyph therefore talks about new beginnings, perhaps after a setback or loss of confidence, drawing on all your existing talents and resources, which are not lost, but can be applied in a new, more fruitful way. Begin from where you are now with whatever material you have to hand, and do not fret for the past or for burdens shed.

Transformation is the key.

Nefer symbolises happiness, good fortune and beauty, and is based on a musical instrument that resembled a primitive guitar. In Ancient Egypt, the perfect form and harmony of the instrument represented fulfilment and pleasure. Hathor, to whom Isis is closely connected, was a goddess of music and dance, of joy and creativity.

This hieroglyph symbolises personal joy and fulfilment that may not accord with the views or harmony of others. Follow your dreams and remember to enjoy the present as well as planning for the future. The good fortune promised will be gained through the fulfilment of your personal destiny. Creativity and what is of beauty and of spiritual worth should be a guiding principle, for in this way you will experience harmony.

Happiness is the key.

Tet represented the trunk of the plant that grew around the chest  containing the body of Osiris; empowered with his strength, it grew into a mighty tree. This tree with the coffin inside it was said to have been made into a column in the palace of the king of Phoenicia. Isis disguised herself to gain entry to the palace and, surrounded with thunder and lightning, split open the column with her wand. Tet is thus a symbol of strength not of only Osiris (although in ritual,

it came to represent his backbone), but also of Isis, who by her power and courage was able to release the body of Osiris from imprisonment.

This hieroglyph says that it is a time to display your strength and determination in order to release whatever is binding you or keeping you from fulfilment. This may involve breaking free from a restrictive situation or a possessive person, insisting on your rights at work, cutting through restrictive practices, or forging a new path on your own terms.

Liberation is the key.

The Heart To the Ancient Egyptians, the heart was the source of good and

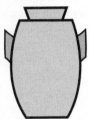

evil intentions, which were just as significant as good and evil thoughts. As the seat of life, the heart required special protection after death, and its sign is the urn in which the heart was preserved separately from the body. In the afterlife, each heart was weighed on scales in the halls of the dead against the symbolic feather of Ma'at. If the scales balanced, the heart was judged to be free from sin.

This hieroglyph represents principles and ideals and the need to define to others and maybe even to yourself what your priorities are. It is also about weighing up options and taking the one that is right for your essential self to thrive, and not what may appear to others to be the most profitable or advantageous to them. You should not accept unjust treatment or the erosion of your values.

Self-knowledge is the key.

The Eye of Horus is a symbol of inspiration representing the white or Sun

(Ra) eye, the full potency of the sun at its height at the Summer Solstice (although the Ancient Egyptians did not actually celebrate this festival). It was from this eye that Hathor drew power for her magic mirror, which saw into the future on one side and on the other reflected the seeker in his or her true light (see also page 171).

This hieroglyph relates to self-esteem and self-confidence, and says that you should not undervalue yourself or judge yourself by the standards of others, who may lack your vision. If you do not value your own worth, neither will others. Trust your clairvoyant powers to see beyond the immediate and the surface issues. Seek the inspirational, off-the-top-of-your-head solution, perhaps using mirror divination as a trigger.

Self-love is the key.

Menat is the symbol of nourishment, reproduction and fertility, both human and of the land, represented by the annual flooding of the Nile. According to myth, this was caused by the tears of Isis, and the rich silt left when the waters receded was her gift to the people. Anuket was the goddess from whose womb the Nile waters flowed, and she was the bringer of abundance, who filled the grain houses and cared for the poor. Menat talks therefore of abundance, of giving and of increase. It is a time when you have much to give to others and to your personal creative life; you will be able to bring ideas into actuality and generate enthusiasm in others for your plans. The more you give, the more you will receive, perhaps not immediately but in the near future. Love and family matters are particularly auspicious.

Fertility is the key.

The Vulture represents the protection and power of Isis, the Divine Mother. Isis demonstrated the power of maternal protection when she cared for Horus in the marshes, guarding him against his evil uncle, who would have destroyed him. Her outstretched wings also shielded Osiris and the Pharoahs. Nekhebet was the Egyptian Vulture Goddess who was said to give her maternal milk to the Pharoahs. The symbol of the vulture is the hieroglyph for mother.

You may need to protect those close to you who are vulnerable from spite, malice or lack of confidence. But do not forget yourself. Avoid anyone who criticises you, for they are prompted by envy. If necessary, you may need to reveal that gentle though you are, you have talons which you will use in defence of your loved ones and yourself.

Protectiveness is the key.

The Ladder In Ancient Egypt, the ladder represented the means by which the deceased could gain access to the heavens. Osiris used a ladder created by Ra to ascend into the heavens. This is, however, the realm of the Sky Mother Nut, Isis's own mother who is sometimes identified with her, and both are depicted covered in stars. Isis veiled is Queen of Heaven.

The ladder represents the transition from the material world to a higher level of awareness, and you too can be a woman covered with stars. Aim high both in terms of ambition and in connecting with your

evolved self. Listen to your higher self or to angelic or devic wisdom that you may receive during meditation or in quiet times of contemplation, especially in the open air on a plain or hilltop You may need to walk alone at these times and seek the inner stillness that enables you to rise above the mundane. Listen to your dreams, and especially if the material world is unfulfilling, remember that the divine spark of Isis is within us all, by whatever goddess name we call her. She and the other Egyptian goddesses are wise guides and can lead you to happiness of a different kind.

Be still is the key.

MOON MAGIC AND YOUR LIFE

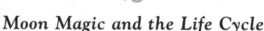

Moon Magic and the Life Cycle

MOON MAGIC WAS one of the earliest forms of female ritual and was rooted in the realisation that the moon reflected, and to early humans seemed to control, the female menstrual cycle. In its apparent birth each month, followed by growth, decline, death and rebirth, the moon also mirrored the three main stages of womanhood: first the slender maiden, then the full-bellied mother, and finally the wise woman/crone. The moon woman/human correlations are still significant in places where artificial lighting is not used and women menstruate on the dark of the moon, the period when the moon is not visible in the sky. The same women ovulate at the time of the full moon, hence its traditional association with love and passion.

Traditionally in many cultures, women who wanted to become pregnant would sleep under the rays of the moon from its waxing until it was full to encourage conception. In some indigenous cultures, women withdraw to a moon lodge, a special hut or tepee, at the dark of the moon. Here, they rest and contemplate while the men and older women care for the home and children.

Although we may have lost such direct connection with lunar energies, they are still of relevance to modern women with their countless demands and myriad choices and opportunities. Like our ancestors, we can use the ebbs and flows of the lunar cycle to harmonise with our own inner fluctuations of energy, rather than swimming against the tide to keep going in a

world that does not recognise the need for rest and withdrawal from non-stop activity and pressure.

Under Useful Addresses (see page 289), I have suggested books that include sections on moon magic. However, you do not need to carry out formal spells; you can rather order your month so that those aspects of your life in which the different phases of the moon are auspicious take precedence.

Tuning Magically Into the Lunar Phases

The cycle from one new moon to the next lasts last for twenty-nine and a half days, but because the moon has an irregular orbit, its rising and setting will vary each day. For this reason, the phases of the moon can vary in length by a day or so each month. The best way to understand the moon is to view it like our ancestors did, by studying it in the sky (it is said that the first calendars were created on bone by women to mark out their menstrual cycles). Use an almanac or a diary that contains moon phases, or consult the weather section of a newspaper to identify the phases to start you off on the right day.

Rituals and Moon Phases

I have divided the moon month into three phases to reflect the three stages of women, maiden, mother and wise woman/crone, all of whom I have written about in different sections of this book.

Waxing Moon

This runs, according to which system you prefer (there are adherents of both), from the time when you first see the crescent in the sky, about two and a half days after the astronomical new moon (that is, when the moon is not visible in the sky). If you wish, you can count the waxing period from the day the new moon is marked in your diary (usually coloured black). You can tell that the moon is waxing if it is increasing in size each night. This continues until the point of the full moon, and the light increases from right to left.

This is the time for new beginnings, and for the gentle growth of long-

term goals that may take months or even a year or more to bring to fruition. Areas of your life into which the waxing moon will bring improvements include health, prosperity, good luck, fertility, friendship, new love and romance, a new or better job, future plans and psychic development. The more the moon increases in size the more powerful its energies become to attract all manner of good things.

The waxing moon is ruled by the virgin goddesses (see page 118).

The Full Moon

Your diary should tell you the exact time the full moon rises in your area. If you are using an almanac geared for a different time, allow for zone variations. Almanacs published in the UK often use Greenwich Mean Time, so allow for summertime variations.

This is the most powerful moment of the month, although the day and night of the full moon and a day on either side also benefit from much of its power. The time of the full moon is ideal for releasing the power accumulated in a spell or an orgasm, or more mundanely for sending an important email or making a special phone call. It is also good for divination for major decisions. Scrying in water in which the full moon is reflected will cast up significant images. The time between its rising and setting is also very potent, and can do wonders for lovemaking that has become routine.

The time of the full moon is good for a sudden boost of power or courage, for psychic protection, for healing acute medical conditions, for attracting a large sum of money that is needed urgently, for the first consummation of love or for making a permanent emotional commitment, for fidelity spells, especially if a relationship is looking shaky, and for justice, ambition and promotion. Because the sun and moon are astrologically in opposition, this is also a time for change, whether in career, location or through travel.

The full moon is ruled by the mother goddesses (see page 10).

The Waning Moon

From the time of the full moon, the energies are waning and the light decreases from right to left. This is the time for banishing and for decreasing influences. The more the moon decreases, the more its potency decreases. The pull that keeps anything negative or destructive in your life is therefore also diminishing. You can use the waning moon like an emptying bath, to

wash away all the bad things into the cosmos or the Earth, to be restored and reformed into positivity.

The time of the waning moon is effective for removing pain and sickness and obstacles to success and happiness. It is also potent for lessening negative influences, addictions, compulsions, negative thoughts, grief, guilt, anxiety, the envy and malice of others and destructive anger that is best let go of. It can be used for gently ending relationships and stages in which there are regrets but also still good will.

The waning moon is ruled by the crone goddesses (see page 125).

Working With the Moon

If you want to harmonise your moon energies at any time of the month, light silver candles the colour of the moon, wear silver jewellery, and burn myrrh or jasmine incense, the fragrances of the moon.

Waxing Energies

- On the crescent moon, charge moonstones with power by placing them in a ceramic or silver dish and making three smoke circles around it with a lighted moon incense stick. Mother-of-pearl, snow and milky quartz, and rutilated quartz are also crystals of the moon and can help to focus its energies.

- Next, pass the dish three times through a moon candle flame.

- You can leave the moonstones to absorb energies from the waxing moonlight of the evenings from the time of the crescent moon to that of the full moon. Although it only takes a day or two for the moonstones to become powerful, if you leave ones that you do not need immediately for the full waxing cycle, they will retain their moon charge for the rest of the lunar month.

- Place one of the moon-charged stones under your pillow if you feel restless or anxious, or to increase fertility if you are trying for a baby.

§ The moonstones are also very good for driving away children's night terrors, and for regularising both your physical and your psychic inner cycle of ebbs and flows.

§ In the daytime, keep a moonstone in a tiny silver purse as a talisman to help you connect with your intuition. To increase prosperity, you can add a silver coin that you turned over three times at the time of the crescent moon.

§ Alternatively, plant the silver coin and moonstone in a pot with moon herbs. These include burdock, which deters negativity, enhances passion and sexuality, and heals loss or betrayal in love; also try lemon balm for healing, love, success and enhanced psychic awareness. Buy the lunar-ruled aloe vera plant, which is a bringer of luck and prosperity, and is also very protective in the home. Plant the herbs on the day before the full moon for maximum growth.

§ Wash the crystals and keep them wrapped in black silk for the last three days of the old moon cycle and the first two days of the new moon to rest them. Recharge them beginning at the time of the next crescent moon.

Full Moon Energies

§ Find a small branch from a moon tree, willow, alder, rowan, mountain ash, mango or banana tree, or any tree that grows near water.

§ At the precise time of the full moon (or as near to it as possible), light a large silver candle and pass a tiny silver charm through the flame to represent what it is you wish to bring to fruition. Hang the charm on the branch (you can hang more than one charm on the branch if you wish to make more than one wish).

§ Make your wish, centred around what the charm represents, for example a silver key for a new home, a heart for a lover reluctant to commit himself or herself, or a teddy bear for a baby.

  • Place the branch where the moon can shine on it.

  • Encircle the branch with pure white flowers from plants such as the jasmine, mimosa, dog rose, gardenia, night-scented stock, poppy or wallflower. If you are unable to obtain these moon flowers, use any pure white flowers.

  • Blow out the candle, sending the silver wishes into the cosmos.

  • Leave the charms on the tree in the light of the full moon, and in the morning wrap them in white silk. Keep them until the next full moon.

  • Place the branch in water and each day add a little moon water (see below).

  • If you are feeling afraid or exhausted at the time of the full moon, go out into the moonlight and breathe in the light and exhale darkness.

  • Leave a silver-coloured or crystal bowl of pure spring water in the full moonlight. You can keep this moon water in a silver-coloured flask and add some to your bathwater, sip it during the waking cycle if you are anxious or stressed, and use it to water any special plants.

Waning Moon Energies

The Archangel Gabriel is associated with the moon; this is a very gentle, compassionate archangel who can help you to let go of things that may be painful, or to deal with shattering illusions or broken dreams. Although angels are usually regarded as androgynous, Gabriel is one in whom the feminine side is well developed.

  • If you are feeling vulnerable or under attack, you may initially find Gabriel easier to work with than the crone goddesses, but you can equally carry out the ritual using the energies of wise Hecate or one of the other crones.

§ To banish a sorrow or a fear, or to reduce the power of an obsession or addiction, go to still water, for example a lake or pond, at dusk, Gabriel's time, and face west.

§ Very gently take a flower of the moon (or any other white flower), and one by one pluck the petals, speaking of your sorrows or your fears, silently if you are not alone.

§ Drop each petal separately into the water and finally set the stalk afloat, saying softly: 'Go in peace.'

§ During the waning period of the moon, try to make a quiet time every day even for a few minutes. Light a silver candle and burn one of the oils of the moon, chamomile, lotus, poppy or wintergreen.

§ Let daydreams and visions come and fade and when you are ready, blow out the candle, sending healing light to any who need it (not forgetting yourself).

WOMEN AND MYSTICISM

MYSTICISM CAN BE defined as an overwhelming sense of being in complete unity or oneness with a deity or the cosmos. Although the state in which mystical experiences occur to an individual may be reached through years of contemplation, study and aestheticism, the single moment of enlightenment or series of visions is invariably spontaneous. Mystical experiences have occurred in all times and in people of different religions, usually within the framework of the existing belief system of the mystic.

In this section I have concentrated on a group of mediaeval and Renaissance women mystics who went against the convention of dependent, compliant women living in the shadow of men. They told the world of their experiences, fired by the certainty that God had spoken directly to them so that they needed to fear no earthly authority. Their freedom of speech and action generally followed the initial verification of their visions by a male cleric.

The women mystics (with the exception of Margery Kempe) benefited by being in religious orders, or in secluded home environments that allowed them to study and contemplate over long periods free from child rearing and domestic responsibilities. But they were not at all remote women, and acted as reformers and social conscience in a world in which women were largely invisible.

Women Mystics and Suffering

A common feature in the lives of the women mystics is suffering, either physical or self-inflicted, as a way of identifying with the agonies of Christ. For example, Hildegard von Bingen, the twelfth-century mystic, suffered from severe migraines and her visions were triggered by these attacks.

According to the findings of a conference of doctors, including psychiatrists, held in San Gimignano, Tuscany in October 1996, the fourteenth-century St Catherine of Siena, the sixteenth-century St Teresa of Avila and, it is hypothesised, many other women saints suffered from anorexia nervosa. It was suggested that anorexics saw in the mystical path a means of expressing blocked inner emotions. Hunger made the mystic enter an altered state of consciousness more easily.

It was reported at the conference that St Catherine began to refuse to eat food at the early age of fifteen. She had, according to contemporary accounts, stated that she was not eating 'in order to correct the vice of gluttony'. Professor Mario Reda, Head of the Institute of Psychiatry at the University of Siena, cited Catherine's dominant mother, who had been pregnant twenty-five times and had pressurised Catherine to eat to become curvaceous in order to attract a prosperous husband. When Buonaventura, one of Catherine's sisters, had died giving birth, Catherine's mother had tried to force the fifteen-year-old Catherine to marry her wealthy brother-in-law in order to ensure the financial well-being of the family. Although her mother lived to be a hundred, on her death Catherine nonetheless demanded that God restore her mother to life because Catherine had already done the requisite suffering for both of them.

Women mystics would often give their food to the poor, and in severe cases of fasting, like that of St Catherine, refused virtually all nourishment except the eucharist. Both St Catherine and the twelfth-century English mystic Christina of Markyate experienced visions immediately after receiving the communion wafer and wine.

Power of the Women Mystics

Although a number of the mediaeval women mystics devoted their lives to prayer and fasting in the hope of experiencing enlightenment, the fourteenth-century mystic Lady Juliana of Norwich did not begin a contemplative life until after she began having visions. She experienced fifteen visions following a serious illness at the age of thirty, from which she had not been expected to recover. Thereafter, she became an anchoress of the Church, devoting the rest of her life to contemplation of the meaning of her enlightenment, and counselling many who came to her for advice. Anchorites of both sexes would shut themselves off from the world inside a small room, usually built adjacent to the church so that they could follow the services; a small window in the room acted as their link to the rest of humanity. In some cases, a burial service was held when they entered the room because they vowed never to leave it except in death.

In her work *Revelations of Divine Love*, Juliana described seeing God holding a tiny thing in his hand, like a small, brown nut, which seemed so fragile and insignificant that she wondered why it did not crumble before her eyes. She was told that it represented the entire created universe, and that 'God made it, God loves it, God keeps it'. Her most memorable expression of the certainty of God's love is the phrase 'and all shall be well, and all manner of things shall be well', which has endured down the centuries and has been quoted many times, for example in T.S. Eliot's *Four Quartets*. Juliana of Norwich was one of the earliest feminist theologians within the established Church, calling Jesus Mother. She saw superimposed over the image of the crucifix a woman suffering labour pains, a very different view from the conventional vilification of Eve in traditional teaching (see Eve, page 274).

In contrast, the twelfth-century Hildegard von Bingen reached her visionary states after years of contemplation, although from the age of three she (in common with many children) had psychic experiences. Hildegard was only eight years old when she entered a Benedictine monastery run according to Celtic principles. She was called the Sybil, or Prophetess of the Rhine, and was sent for training to an anchoress. At the age of thirty-eight, she was elected head of the convent within the anchorage, and in 1141 she had the vision that changed her life: 'And it came to pass when I was forty-two years and seven months old, that the heavens were opened and a blinding light of exceptional brilliance flowed through my entire brain. And so it kindled my whole heart and breast like a flame, not burning but warming.'

Hildegard spent the next fifteen years recording her visions and their significance and producing major works of theology. She also corresponded with kings, nobles, senior churchmen and even the Pope, advising and admonishing them. She wrote nine books and many songs and poems, including a play set to music called the *Ordo Virtutum*, about the struggles of a human soul to find the right path. Her legacy to the New Age has been her writings on the healing properties of plants, and about animals, trees and stones, as well as her music, which has proved inspirational for meditation.

Hildegard regarded the natural world as God's creation, permeated with divine beauty and energy that was entrusted to the care of humankind, and she is therefore the mother of Green spirituality. In common with other female mystics, her writings are full of erotic imagery; this perhaps expressed her own passionate nature, which had been suppressed in a life of chastity. Hildegard was the first writer to describe a female orgasm.

'*When a woman is making love with a man, a sense of heat in her brain, which brings with it sensual delight, communicates the taste of that delight during the act and summons forth the emission of the man's seed. And when the seed has fallen into its place, that vehement heat descending from her brain draws the seed to itself and holds it, and soon the woman's sexual organs contract, and all the parts that are ready to open up during the time of menstruation now close, in the same way as a strong man can hold something enclosed in his fist.*'

St Catherine of Siena, who lived in the fourteenth century, decided to remain a virgin after having a vision of Christ when she was only seven, in which Christ asked for her heart. In spite of, or perhaps because of, pressure from her mother to conform, Catherine began a life of solitude in a room in her father's house when she was fifteen. However, as a result of a mystical experience in which she became the bride of Christ, Catherine abandoned the contemplative life and began to work with the sick, caring especially for those whose illnesses were so disfiguring or debilitating that no one else would tend to them. She also took an active part in politics, corresponding with the princes of Italy, and persuaded Pope Gregory XI to return to Rome from Avignon, where he had set up his See.

The sixteenth-century St Teresa de Avila also displayed religious intensity from an early age. At the age of seven, she tried to run away to the Holy Land to become a martyr. As a nun, Teresa followed an extreme form of aestheticism, rather than pursuing the gentler path of learning as a way of attaining enlightenment. She believed that monks and nuns should return to a life of austerity, rather than living in comfort and devoting their lives to intellectual pursuits that involved no real sacrifice or effort. Initiates under her regime went barefoot or wore sandals instead of shoes, and so became known as 'Discalced (unshod) Carmelites', or Carmelites of the Strict Observance. In one of her many writings, St Teresa described how 'while at prayer in the church before entering the convent life . . . I all but went into rapture and saw Christ Who seemed to be receiving me with great love, placing a crown on my head and thanking me for what I had done for his mother'.

Perhaps partly as a result of her extreme fasting, Teresa experienced frequent 'raptures', akin to out-of-body experiences, in which 'the Lord catches up the soul . . . and carries it right out of itself . . . and begins to show it features of the Kingdom He has prepared for it'. Teresa would sometimes actually levitate and have to be held down by the other sisters in the order. She was, unlike the earlier mystics, pressurised by the Church to produce writings that extolled the virtues of the aesthetic life, but nonetheless she was a powerful, joyous woman who would in the midst of her raptures exclaim, 'Now Lord, put me down,' as though scolding a mischievous boy.

A Very Ordinary Mystic

Margery Kempe was a housewife and mother who is nonetheless reputed to have been one of the most profound mystics of all time. She was born in about 1373 in Bishop's Lynn, near Norfolk, England, and 'talked as easily to God as to my neighbours'.

Margery took many pilgrimages to shrines abroad, where she was known for her loud wailing as she was overcome with emotion by her visions at the holy places. Although she was illiterate, she had a photographic memory and her writings tell of the everyday world in which she lived as well as of her profound spiritual insights. In common with other mystics, she was frequently ill with psychosomatic conditions, but nonetheless was mother to fourteen children. In later life, she refused to have sex with her husband

as she had dedicated herself to God, but she continued in the marriage and he seems to have followed her from town to town as she fled to escape frequent persecution. For although she gained powerful friends on her travels, Margery did not enjoy the protection of the Church. However, during the Great Fire of Lynn in 1421, during which the town was threatened with destruction, the priests issued a challenge to the effect that if she was indeed blessed by God she could save the town. Three days later, a blizzard quenched the fire and Margery was declared a miracle worker.

Peak Experiences

Women's mystical experiences are different in quality and intensity from those of men. Whereas men tend to 'see' visions as pictures separate from their physical beings, for women an experience involves all the senses, including sound, scent, touch and taste. Women become part of a vision, flowing and merging into it.

The twentieth-century US psychologist Abraham Maslow defined mysticism in terms of 'peak-experiences', to encompass the whole spectrum of mystical states of consciousness, secular as well as religious. He believed that people who had not experienced these states or who repressed them could learn to develop the necessary mind-set to follow this empowering route to personal fulfilment and integration.

We have all had those wonderful moments when time stands still, described by T.S. Eliot as 'sudden in a shaft of sunlight'.

The following experiences have come from my own research into spontaneous moments out of time: on a sunny seashore, looking at rippling water; touching the soft cheek of a baby and being rewarded with a smile; making love with the right person at the right time in the right place and merging as one flesh and spirit; hearing a particularly melodious choir in a great cathedral; seeing the dawn rise over a stone circle at Midsummer and knowing that you are one with those who, over the millennia, have also witnessed the dance of the sun; running or riding a horse at full speed along sand or through the desert; rolling in snow and tasting the melting flakes falling from the sky; and swimming underwater among shoals of fish. Almost all of these are spontaneous moments of intense pleasure or insight occurring in the natural world and involving more than one of the senses.

- Although spontaneous peak experiences are often full of movement, the easiest way to induce mystical awareness is in stillness, for example when sitting by a sunlit pool and allowing your mind to enter the depths, listening to a fountain and feeling the water on your face so that you are part of the fountain, or hearing a forest come alive in the wind and dancing in your heart both with the leaves and as them. Go into a museum in the early morning, one where you are allowed to hold Roman pottery or touch the statues. Allow yourself to become one with the ancient world. Lie on the grass or on a sun-bed in the darkness and look up at the stars, focusing on one bright point and letting the others merge and dance so that the Milky Way flows like a river of star milk.

- When the peak experiences occur, allow the outer boundaries between yourself and others to melt and merge with the waves or the bird call.

- Rather than analysing or trying to hold on to the feeling, flow with it, be engulfed by it. *Being, not doing, is the key.*

- Another method is to gaze into a crystal or crystal sphere, for once not asking a question or even seeking impressions as you hold the living energies between your fingertips, perhaps illuminated by candle or sunlight. Become the crystal.

- As you learn to blend more and more with the moments of peak experience, so your awareness will increase and you will see unprompted visions even in city streets and unlovely places; you will enter the heart of the cosmos, of which your own heart is a miniature.

WOMEN AND THE RUNES
Magic and Divination of the Vikings and Anglo Saxons

༄

What are Runes?

RUNES ARE ANGULAR symbols marked for divination on small, round stones, wooden discs or staves. Runic letters can also be found as inscriptions on huge stones marking victories or tombs wherever the Viking and Anglo-Saxon peoples invaded or settled. Like the Ancient Egyptian hieroglyphs (see page 180), as well as representing a letter, each rune was a symbol of power, which could be released by writing, chanting or even forming the shape of the rune with the body in ritual or meditation. When runic forms were combined in patterns as bind runes, they were said to create magical talismans of power or protection.

Divinatory runes were made in sets of sixteen to thirty-six, depending on the particular region in which they were used. They were cast by people in the Scandinavian world as far north as Iceland, among the Anglo-Saxons on the plains of Western Europe, and in the lands that the Germanic peoples conquered, including Northumberland in the north-east of England.

Early runic symbols, many of which were sacred signs associated with the Mother Goddess Nerthus, have been discovered on Late Bronze Age ancient rock carvings in Sweden. Nerthus is the Scandinavian Earth Mother, and fertility ceremonies in her honour have been recorded to as far back as 2,000 years ago, although her worship is said to be much older. Long after Nerthus had been replaced by Odin and his consort Frigga, her veneration continued, particularly among people who worked the land.

Women and the Runes

Runic divination was practised by wise women, or *volvas*, and also by ordinary women who carried out runic rituals and divination in their homesteads. Both *volvas* and the wives, sisters and mothers of men about to leave for purposes of conquest or trade, or to herd the aurochs, or wild cattle, chanted magical incantations as they carved the runes or created bind rune amulets. Women were respected for their prophetic powers throughout Scandinavia and the Anglo-Saxon lands, and no expedition, whether it be

concerned with trade or with battle, took place without first casting the runes.

In the thirteenth century, the author of the Viking saga of Erik the Red described one of the rune mistresses/*volvas*:

> '*She wore a cloak set with stones along the hem. Around her neck and covering her head she wore a hood lined with white cat skins. In one hand she carried a staff with a knob on the end and from her belt, holding together her long dress, hung a charm pouch.*'

Rune Mother

Edda, another form of the ancient Earth Mother, was goddess of all divinatory arts, and it was after her that the great sagas of the Viking and Icelandic worlds were named. Any form of divination would begin by asking for her wisdom and protection.

Women and the Magical Arts

A number of magical arts were practised by women. *Seior* was a word used for witchcraft, which was usually practised by senior women in the clan who lived apart or perhaps with a sister. She would obtain knowledge by channelling spirits. By contrast, the *spá-kona*, or *volva*, would tap into the *orlog*, the web of fate (see also page 137), and use runes as one means of discovering the future paths of individuals or of the whole clan. There are also accounts of *sei*, witches who carved wooden runes for spell-casting; like the *volvas*, many of them were reputed to be powerful rune mistresses.

Rune Divination

I have listed on pages 202–4 some very basic meanings of the twenty-nine Anglo-Saxon runes, one of the most comprehensive sets, and then suggested bind runes that you could create for different purposes. There are a number of good rune books available, and I have listed some that are particularly female-friendly under Further Reading (see page 286). Because you can make your own runes so easily, rune divination is a very personalised and effective form of divination.

- When making your rune set, draw or paint the symbols on round, flat discs of wood, or on stones or crystals the size of a large coin. Red was the traditional colour used for marking runes.

- If you are using stones, choose them on a hilltop or near flowing water if possible; as you make each rune, chant its meaning.

- Place the runes in a circle, beginning with Feoh at the 12 o'clock position. Spread smoke over the circle with a sage, cedar or pine smudge stick or a sweetgrass rope, or with dried herbs burned in a shallow bowl and wafted with a feather. Alternatively, you can use a pine, cedar or sage incense stick.

- With the smoke, waft the protective runic symbols Thorn and Ing (see below) over the centre of the circle, chanting: 'Protect and keep safe, guard and guide, Edda, Nerthus, Frigga, Mothers all.'

- Repeat this ritual every week or so to keep the runes cleansed and charged with power.

- Place the twenty-nine marked discs in a drawstring bag made of a natural fabric.

- Whenever you have a question or need guidance, choose three runes from your bag without looking into it.

- Check the area of your life or strength to which the three runes refer from the list below, then hold each rune in turn in your hand with your eyes closed. Let images or words form. These will suggest positive ways forwards.

§ You can also choose one rune from the bag each morning to obtain an indication of the approach you should take, or of the predominant theme of the day.

The Runes

Feoh (WEALTH) Prosperity, financial affairs, the price that must be paid for change in actual or emotional terms.

Ur (AUROCHS, OR WILD CATTLE) Overcoming obstacles, survival instincts, courage.

Thorn (HAMMER OF THOR, THE GOD OF THUNDER) Protection, challenges, secrecy, conflicts.

Os (A GOD, THE MOUTH OF THE GOD) Inspiration, wisdom, ideals, communication.

Rad (THE WHEEL/RIDING) Travel, change, action, the cycles of life, initiative, impetus.

Cen (TORCH) The inner voice, inspiration, the inner flame, help in difficulty.

Gyfu (GIFT) Generosity, all matters relating to exchanges, including contracts, love, marriage, and sexual union.

Wyn (JOY) Personal happiness, success, recognition of your worth by others and yourself.

Haegl (HAIL) Disruption by natural events and uncontrolled forces, sudden change.

Nyd (NEED) Needs that can be met by action or positive reaction to external events, self-reliance, the desire for achievement, passion.

Is (ICE) Blockage, a period of inactivity that can be turned to advantage, waiting for the right moment.

Ger (YEAR, HARVEST) The results of earlier efforts realised, life cycles that can be fruitful, repetition of old mistakes.

Eoh (YEW) Endings leading to new beginnings, permanence, fidelity, wisdom in the later years, tradition.

Peorth (GAMBLING CUP) Fate, what is known or revealed, the essential self, taking a chance.

Eohl (EEL-GRASS OR ELK) The higher self, spiritual matters, psychic development, the need to take care in a matter of importance, making difficult but necessary decisions.

Sigil (SUN) Success, ambition (especially in career), energy, expansion, unfulfilled potential, talents, unexpected opportunities that should be seized.

Tyr (POLE OR LODE STAR) Justice, altruism, self-sacrifice, following dreams, the keeping of faith through difficult times.

Beorc (BIRCH TREE/MOTHER GODDESS) Renewal, healing, physical or spiritual regeneration, fertility, nature and the environment.

Eh (HORSE) Loyalty, harmony between people or the inner or outer worlds, partnerships and friendships, moving house or changing career.

Man (MANKIND) Wisdom, maturity, acceptance of yourself and others, hidden strengths and talents that can be utilised in a current situation, issues of ageing and mortality, seeing our lives as part of a wider pattern.

Lagu (LAKE/WATER) Birth or beginnings, emotions, following the flow of events, unconscious wisdom, intuition.

Ing (CORN GOD) Protection, fertility, withdrawl in order to grow strong, a time of waiting, allowing events to take their course.

Odal (HOMESTEAD) Home, domestic matters, friendship, the family and family finances, stability, responsibility, security.

Daeg (DAWN) Sudden clarity after doubt or confusion, enlightenment, light at the end of the tunnel, optimism, a chance to wipe the slate clean.

Ac (OAK TREE) Independence, power, authority, traditional wisdom and learning.

Aesc (ASH TREE, WORLD OR COSMIC TREE) Spiritual potential, strength, determination, resistance to opposition, endurance, health, healing.

Yr (BOW) Symbol of inner resources, transformation and rebuilding, clear focus on goals, learning new skills.

Iar (BEAVER) Adaptability, versatility, maximum effort, the ability to integrate all aspects of life and self.

Ear (DUST) An awareness that some avenue of life may no longer be fruitful, but also integration; a return to the original state of optimism, now tempered by understanding.

Making Bind Runes

Bind runes made by combining the shapes of two or three (or sometimes more) separate runes create energies greater than those of the individual runes. They can offer powerful protection or empowerment if worn or carried in a tiny purse.

You can make a bind rune either for general health or protection, or for a specific need, for example an imminent journey about which you are worried. When the need for its power and protection are past, bury the bind rune, cast it into flowing water, or if it is made of wood, burn it, at the same time thanking the Earth Mothers for their kindness. As you make your bind

rune, chant the purpose of its creation and smudge it before use and thereafter every week if it is used as an ongoing amulet.

You can draw or paint bind runes on crystals, or etch them on to circular discs of wood, stone or metal. The runic symbols can be drawn upside down or horizontally or superimposed on to one another, to create your own unique focus of energy. If you like, drill a hole in the bind-rune amulet and wear it on a cord. I have suggested below some combinations of amulets that have worked for me.

- For protection against actual or psychic attack, good for travelling alone

  Thorn and **Ur** can be combined to produce

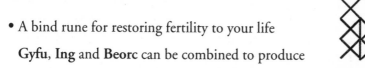

- A bind rune for restoring fertility to your life

  Gyfu, **Ing** and **Beorc** can be combined to produce

- A bind rune for protection against all forms of financial loss and poverty, or to bring prosperity and material security

  Feoh, **Gyfu** and **Wyn** can be combined to produce

- A bind rune to protect against illness and maintain or restore health and harmony

  Eh, **Aesc** and **Ur** can be combined to produce

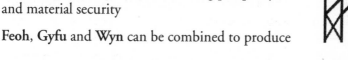

- For protecting the home and family from external attack and internal quarrels, and for bringing happiness and security in the home

  Odal, **Beorc** and **Ger** can be combined to produce

- For strengthening your identity against all earthly malevolence, and for psychic attack from whatever source

  Ac, **Peorth** and **Cen** can be combined to create

TAROT
Mirror of the Soul

T HE TAROT IS the most visual of all the divinatory systems, a gallery of seventy-eight images that tap into a universal system of wisdom that we instinctively understand. It is possible to read the Tarot without any formal knowledge of card meanings because its images are those we see nightly in our dreams, or know from the myths and fairy tales of childhood. Yet because the cards also relate to issues that are relevant to people in all times and places, such as love, relationships, finding a place in the world, power, guilt, fear and joy, they are still relevant to the lives of modern women. Women especially find the Tarot easy to interpret since they are able to adapt the significance of each card to the unique situation of the questioner, rather than trying to fit the situation to the card meaning as many male Tarot readers do.

What is the Tarot?

The first twenty-two cards are called the Major Arcana (Arcana means 'hidden secrets'). They are based on what Jung called the archetypes, the idealised forms of human states: the Mother, the Father, the Divine Child, the Trickster who is necessary to trigger change and self-awareness, the Virgin, the Hero, the Lovers/the Sacred Marriage, the Holy Woman or Man, the Recluse, the Willing Sacrifice, the cosmic forces, the Sun, Moon, and Stars, and principles such as justice, moderation and endurance. According to Dion Fortune, the twentieth-century occultist, if a person meditates upon a symbol with which certain ideas have been associated over the years by a number of people, he or she will obtain access to those ideas through psychic connection with the symbol, in this case in the form of the individual Tarot card.

Some women use only the Major Arcana cards in divinatory readings, and they can be valuable indicators of life changes and are especially valuable for core issues or questions of spiritual concern. I have listed books on the Tarot under Further Reading (see page 285); these offer a good introduction to more formal Tarot reading. The cards can vary slightly in order and name depending on the type of pack. In the descriptions below, where

a card meaning is perhaps a little complex or obscure, I have included greater detail on the basic meaning.

Origins and Symbolism of the Tarot

Tarot cards were a mediaeval creation, although the images and themes are much older. Recent research suggests that they are Italian in origin, dating from about 1470. Because the images are so universal, there are many packs drawing on cultures ranging from the Celtic and Viking, to the Oriental and Native North American; all of them, however, contain the same ideas.

Reading the Tarot Cards

Below I have provided meanings for the first twenty-two Major cards and described their relationships with women's lives. You can use these as a guide to obtain core meanings of the cards if you are unfamiliar with the art. But even the most experienced readers are primarily led by the images and the intuitive insights they invoke. In my own work, I have found that Tarot readings given by beginners are often very accurate precisely because they have no preconceptions.

- ﹩ Find the twenty-two Major Arcana cards, those individual pictures that are numbered 0 to 21 or 1 to 22, depending on the pack. They do not have a suit name and number such as 10 of Pentacles or 5 of Swords. The Kings, Queens and so on belong to the Minor Arcana cards, and you need not use them.

- ﹩ As you shuffle, concentrate on a specific question or an important issue in your life.

- ﹩ Take three cards from anywhere in the pack, which should be held face down, and lay them in a row from left to right in front of you, still face down.

- ﹩ Turn over the cards one at a time in the order you dealt them, and for each write down or record on a tape recorder any impressions that you get. You may find yourself telling the story of the card, or

describing the emotions it invokes in you, or you may identify with one particular character or aspect of the scene.

๑ If you read all three cards in this way, you will find a theme emerging that may offer insight about or a strategy for moving forwards.

๑ You can also select a single card every morning from the face-down shuffled pack. This may suggest the strengths that will be of particular help on the day ahead, or in the way you should approach the day.

The Fool

The Fool is the most exciting, though potentially most challenging, card in the pack: when this card appears, anything is possible. It may point to a new stage that is a step into the unknown and will involve trusting your intuition at every stage, rather than relying on logic or listening to the advice of others. Welcome change and new opportunities, however unlikely or initially unpromising, and for once let the future worry about itself.

The Magician

The Magician is the initiator of change and the creative spark that inspires original but effective action. It is Grandmother Spider Woman weaving and making connections, so you need to rely on inspiration and ingenuity rather than on careful planning. It is a card that says you should use any means to put your plans, great or small, into practice in the immediate future, even if the circumstances and time are less than ideal. Have confidence in your ability to succeed on your own terms.

The High Priestess, or Popess

The High Priestess is the card of the separate self, the archetypal Divine Virgin who needs no man or god to give purpose to her existence or to make her complete. Therefore even if you are happily married or in a permanent relationship, you may need to explore what would fulfil you and make you,

rather than others, happy. Your psychic and spiritual sides are as vital as your worldly commitments, so make time to connect with the natural, slower cyclical female rhythms (more on this in the Moon card description).

The Empress

This is the card of the archetypal Mother, and whether you are a mother or not, you should express your creativity in tangible ways. Now is the time to work on the practicalities of the Magician's schemes and by your efforts sow the seeds that will be harvested in a few months from now. Family, friends and even work colleagues may need your advice and sympathy, or you may find yourself being propelled into counselling work, whether psychotherapeutic, in alternative health or using divination and clairvoyance. Remember to care for yourself as you do for others.

The Emperor

The Emperor is the card of earthly dominion, the ultimate animus or power card. For women, it represents assertiveness, ambition and the courage to stand against the second-rate treatment of yourself and your loved ones, and to protect vulnerable colleagues or friends. The Emperor has many positive roles, from complaining about shoddy service in stores or restaurants, to taking on a paternalistic bureaucracy (more on this in the Justice card description). But do not allow any external Emperor, whether it be your mother, partner, employer or an official, to diminish your self-esteem or try to make your decisions for you.

The Hierophant

The Hierophant, another symbol of animus power, represents tradition of all kinds and accumulated spiritual wisdom. His wisdom is that of conventional and learned insight, gained through application. He is the brake on pure inspiration, demanding that you muster your facts and figures, so that you can make an informed choice. Above all, you may need to listen to your higher self or evolved spiritual nature, the wisest guide of all, and look at any issue in terms of your long-term happiness.

The Lovers

This is the card of duality and of relationships, especially in love and matters of identity. In any pack, this card represents the issues of choice in relationships of all kinds, not just romantic or sexual ones. Usually, the card charts the progress of specific relationships, especially in areas where there are questions of separate identity within the relationship. It may also indicate a need to make choices regarding family, friends and work relationships, using your head as well as your heart, especially if you are being pulled in different directions.

The Chariot

The Chariot is the card of travel, change and ultimately triumph. It is therefore an exciting and challenging card to appear in any spread. It talks of the need for courage and for balancing different needs, and demands creativity, as the rider strives to harness opposing powers and needs to maintain the impetus to succeed. It is, however, primarily a card of questing, whether this involves searching for a personal Holy Grail, or pushing further apart the boundaries of possibility. However, its energies can seem threatening to those who would like us to remain predictable and static.

Strength

Strength can be either card 8 or card 11, depending on how your pack is numbered. In this card, which is also sometimes called Force or Fortitude, a woman is closing or opening the mouth of a lion. The card suggests persistence rather than aggression in long-standing matters, whether these are obstacles to progress, or opportunities slow in materialising. Dramatic actions or walking away from less than ideal circumstances will lose what is of worth in a situation that can be saved and brought to fruition.

You should not, however, give way to intimidation, whether this takes the form of emotional blackmail, threats from officialdom, or an overgrown playground bully at work or home.

The Hermit

The Hermit is the silent wanderer, standing apart from the world. Yet she or he is an integral part of us, representing our wise inner voice, which can

become overwhelmed by the demands and conflicting opinions of others. The Hermit advises stepping back from any conflict, especially if you are acting as a peacemaker, and perhaps temporarily moving away from the world and looking inwards to the world of dreams and visions. If you can listen to your own inner wisdom, you will instinctively know the right words to say and the right course to follow.

The Wheel of Fortune

The Wheel of Fortune varies in different packs. Modern women have far more choices than their grandmothers and great-grandmothers did. However, even the best-organised life can be changed overnight by an unplanned event which, whether it is exciting or frightening, means a radical reassessment of what seemed a settled path. You may not have enough power to choose your next step, but there is always some room for manoeuvre, even in the seemingly most inflexible situations, and even the smallest positive reaction may be crucial to your future well-being. If a new opportunity has unexpectedly come your way, seize it.

Justice

Traditionally, the Justice card is associated with litigation and official matters, and it may appear in a reading when formal steps are being taken. But in practice it usually refers to principles and ideals that are of importance at the time of the reading. If the status quo or individuals are being unfair, then unexpressed and justifiable anger and resentment can too easily be turned inwards or directed against the wrong person. It is not a time to compromise, but to fight for what is important to you, however little support you may have – for you know that you are right.

The Hanged Man

The Hanged Man is in many ways the most profound card in the pack, linked with the voluntary sacrifice of the old King or Corn God so that the new order can begin and fertility continue. This card usually appears when you have reached a crossroads and have to decide whether to give up security, certainty, or a destructive habit, or make an extra effort or give additional input either at work or spiritually, or in a relationship that offers no immediate gain. Three or six months down the road, or perhaps even

longer, you will realise that you made the right choice and will enjoy the benefits.

Death

Death is the card of natural change, and never predicts bodily death. Rather it is a powerful symbol of regeneration, of the transformation of a situation or stage that has outlived its usefulness or run its natural course. There may be a need to close a particular door, whether this be an actual door or lingering regrets about the past, and to move on to the next phase. The card can also refer to ways of responding that are no longer effective (and perhaps never were) to a situation or person that may be holding you back from achieving your full potential.

Temperance

On the surface, Temperance seems to be going against everything modern women have fought for. But Temperance speaks not of passivity, but of harmony and maintaining balance between different aspects of your life, especially your spirituality, in a fast-moving world. Temperance is a card relevant to accepting life as it is and people as they are. It means not trying to be all things to all people. You cannot be held responsible for the happiness or success of others, especially those who revel in crises and refuse to help themselves. Your own peace of mind and inner tranquillity should be your priority, and sometimes that means walking away from adult toddler tantrums with which others may seek to keep you off balance.

The Devil

Like the Death card, the Devil card is a repository of stored energy that can be channelled through the release of positive fears and feelings as a positive, focused impetus for change. We all experience negative emotions, but women are still brought up to be nice and to keep smiling whatever the provocation, and so can end up repressing a great deal of negativity. You met this in the Justice card, but the Devil is about accepting that we are not angels, that we do get angry, resentful or just plain unreasonable, and that psychic PMT is part and parcel of the human soul. Demand from others the consideration you give to them, and remember that 'No' and 'I do mind' can be among the most liberating expressions in the cosmos.

The Tower

The Tower is a card of liberation from restriction, not destruction. It is not, therefore, auguring future disaster, but reflecting an inner awareness that in some area of your life, restrictions or a sense of feeling stifled are clearing and suddenly there are new options or perspectives. Perhaps what might have initially been regarded as a setback has given or will give you an opportunity to rebuild an area of your life in a positive, more fruitful way, using your experience and wisdom to arrange the pieces, perhaps for the first time, in the way you want.

The Star

The Star is an image that is of importance both as the inner star of illumination and as the guiding star towards the fulfilment of tangible dreams. For this is the good fairy card that says you can make those dreams come true, whether you are eighteen or eighty-five, by taking the first steps now, however small. Believe in yourself and do not worry if others say that you do not have the talents, the resources or the staying power to attain your goal. Older women especially may find that adult children, as well as partners, are remarkably resistant to change in those on whom they rely – and who they fear may move the focus of their world to self-fulfilment.

The Moon

The Moon is the woman's Tarot card per se, and reflects the importance of dreams, of lunar intuitive insights, and of emotions even in today's fact-orientated world. Right now, the inner world, the imagination and the instinctive inner voice are the best guides to action. This may be a time when your intuition is at odds with the perceived facts or opinions of others, but do not be pressurised into ignoring your feelings. Listen to your heart, and if a course of action or opportunity feels right go with that option. You may find it helpful to develop your psychic abilities in a more structured way.

The Sun

The Sun is the symbol of conscious power, clarity and drive, and with this card anything is possible. This is the card of returning light that at any time

of the year represents pure energy, optimism, joy and success in the world's terms. It speaks of a return to health or the spontaneous development of healing powers. Money-making ventures are favourable, as are any business ventures. It would be hard to find a negative aspect to this card, and if it appears with the Star card, then you really can fulfil any dream or ambition.

Judgement

Judgement is the card of reconciliation and spiritual renewal, a card of resolving dilemmas and shedding burdens you need no longer carry. You should leave behind regrets and past guilt, and ignore fears for the future that may never materialise.

If you can be reconciled with anyone from whom you are estranged, make a final effort and if this fails, walk free. Your harshest judge on any matter is yourself, but if you can shed the need for approval, especially the voices from the past that may linger in your head, then you can be free to assess each situation on its merit and not be ruled by the emotional pressures of people who may have an interest in fuelling your fires of guilt.

The World

The World is primarily a card of movement and going forwards, whether this involves actual travel or being open to new perspectives and ideas. Or it may refer to a sense of rightness, implying that your life is on course and that the pieces are falling into shape. Now is the time to expand your horizons, whether it be in small ways or involving major life changes, for success is assured in any venture. Whether you go on holiday to a place you always wanted to visit, move house or refurbish your present home, create a wildlife garden on the neat lawn and scandalise the neighbours but delight the butterflies, or relocate in career or in perspective, the world is yours if you open the door and do not look back.

WITCHCRAFT

The Survival of Magic from the Darkness to the Light

'*All witchcraft comes from carnal lust which is in women insatiable. Wherefore, for the sake of fulfilling their lusts they consort even with devils.*

Blessed be the Highest who has so far preserved the male sex from so great a crime: for since He was willing to be born and to suffer for us therefore He has granted to men this privilege.

There was a defect in the formation of the first woman, since she was formed from a bent rib, that is, a rib of the breast – she is an imperfect anima, she always deceives.'

TAKEN FROM THE *Malleus Maleficarum* (the Hammer of the Witches (above)), a book published in 1486 and written by two Dominican Inquisitors, Heinrich Kramer and James Sprenger.

The *Malleus Maleficarum* became the handbook of Inquisitors throughout Europe and Scandinavia and gave justification to more than two centuries of torture and execution of often innocent women between the fifteenth and early eighteenth centuries. The authors of the book accused witches of 'inclining the minds of men to inordinate passion'. True witchcraft, however, has very little to do either with the rantings of the Inquisition or with the modern hype about black magic.

Witchcraft is in reality one of the oldest religions in the world, perhaps originating about 25,000 years ago in Palaeolithic times, when clay animals may have been ritually killed in order to bring about the successful outcome of the hunt by sympathetic or attracting magic. Although the Palaeolithic shamanic figure dancing on the wall of a cave at Les Trois Frères in the French Pyrenees represents a man in animal skins, women probably held much of the magical power in early civilisations. We know this both from anthropological remains and from the practices of indigenous societies that have kept their ancient traditions alive, or at least within memory.

Women were able to give birth to new life, apparently by mystical impregnation (the role of the father in conception would remain uncertain for thousands of years). They were thus seen to possess the same powers as

215

the Earth and Moon Mothers, and menstrual blood was especially sacred. Early mother figurines painted with red ochre have been discovered during excavations, and skeletons in early burial mounds were also smeared with red and set in a foetal position to await rebirth.

Offerings of the finest of the hunt were made to the Mistress of the Herds and Fish, another aspect of the Goddess. Animal bones would be buried so that the animals, like humankind, would enjoy rebirth from the Earth Mother's womb. Indigenous hunter gatherers, such as the Inuits of North America and Canada and the Lapps in the far north of Scandinavia, still practice this ritual.

Witchcraft and Christianity

After the establishment of the Christian religion, the worship of the old deities and the old ways was officially banned and the nature festivals supplanted by religious ones, although Pope Gregory, who sent St Augustine to England in AD 597, acknowledged that it was better to try to graft the new Christian festivals on to the existing Solstice and Equinox celebrations. For centuries, the old and new religions coexisted, although ordinary people gradually transferred their allegiance from the Mother Goddess to the Virgin Mary and the female saints (see Virgin Mary, page 257). In the fields, though, during the seasonal festivals, people would still dance and make love to bring fertility to cattle and corn; they would leap high over fires on staves, staffs and broomsticks to show how high the corn would grow. In remote places, even priests would join in these celebrations, during which the Madonna and female saints such as St Bridget of Kildare were invoked as the female fertility power (see Saints, page 246).

The village wise women – the herbalist, counsellors, seers, and midwives – were the acknowledged centres of the community, handing down their crafts from mother to daughter; in addition, every family had its own secret recipes for herbal remedies that it would also pass down through the generations. Neither priest nor squire had problems with these wise women because they acted as the cohesive force of traditional society. False accusations were few because under the ancient laws, which were repealed in the fifteenth century, the accuser would himself or herself face punishment if the accused was acquitted.

Later, from the fifteenth century onwards, political issues brought about the persecution of witches, who were mainly women. The emphasis on the

sin of Eve and the inferiority of women had existed since the time of St Paul, but with the rise of an organised male medical profession, women healers became a threat, not least because their skills ensured less painful childbirth. This was, according to the fifteenth-century Fundamentalist Church Fathers, contrary to the curse of God that the daughters of Eve should bear children in sorrow (see Eve, page 274).

Midwives were a prime target for the new persecutions, being accused of sacrificing babies to the Devil, an accusation that was seemingly confirmed by 'evidence' gathered by the authors of the *Malleus Maleficarum*. Given the high rate of mortality, a mother grieving for her dead baby might easily blame the midwife once she was labelled an agent of evil by the Church. For there is no doubt that midwives did help women who wished to miscarry if another birth would be dangerous or would reduce the family to starvation level, and that they allowed severely disabled babies to die at birth. They also taught rudimentary birth control, using herbs and pessaries – giving women at least some control over their own fertility, a privilege that they would not enjoy again for hundreds of years.

With the beginning of the appropriation of common land and the enclosure of the smallholdings that almost all peasants possessed around their homes, especially in Europe, accusations of witchcraft that carried the penalty of the seizure of land provided an easy and legitimate way of removing a peasant reluctant to give up his or her land rights. For if the wife was condemned as a witch, the whole family would be implicated and disgraced. The majority of men accused of witchcraft were the husbands, sons or fathers of accused women. In the case of an elderly, childless widow or middle-aged spinster who perhaps had inherited land from her father, or a younger widow who refused to remarry, there would usually be no one to speak on her behalf (see the Bathory case, page 87). High magicians, who were almost always male and who included popes and royalty, usually escaped censure. The female-focused folk religion of the countryside was an easier target. The seasonal gatherings often held at the time of the full moon were now translated into wild tales of female covens meeting during the full moon and copulating with the Devil. Men very conveniently forgot their own leading roles and unbridled sexuality at these celebrations.

As times became more troubled, diverting the anger of dispossessed peasants against one of their own community became an effective form of social control. In extreme cases, whole villages might be wiped out for harbouring witches and the land appropriated by the local landowner. In the hysteria

that ensued, even the wise woman's cat, which was kept to reduce the risk of infection from vermin in her home, was often hanged or burned with her as a demonic familiar.

The true Satanic practitioners were not the wise women who used white magic and healing interchangeably. They tended to be dispossessed or dissatisfied priests or academics who knew the intricacies of the Latin liturgy and could thus recite it backwards, and who had access to churches at night and to the sacrament to despoil.

In December 1484, the Bull of Pope Innocent VII was published, appointing Heinrich Kramer and Jakob Sprenger as Inquisitors against witchcraft and heresy. These two clerics described in lurid detail in the *Malleus Maleficarum* the tortures that could morally be used to obtain confessions from suspected witches. They stated that it was better to kill an innocent person who would be rewarded in Heaven by God than to allow a guilty person to remain unpunished. This book became the best-seller of its time, and was quoted to justify three centuries of atrocities practised against witches in Europe and Scandinavia.

The Inquisitors stripped accused women and carried out intimate body searches, supposedly to find witch marks that might be as innocent as a mole or a discolouration of the skin. They also burned or tore off women's breasts, and penetrated their genitalia with sharp instruments. The more sexually aroused these celibate priests/Inquisitors became, the more they would punish the 'temptress' for using 'witchcraft' to get them to break their vows. Many Inquisitors were very cruel to even young victims, who would confess in the hope of having their interrogation brought to an end. Most confessions that were extracted under torture and published were remarkably consistent in their content.

Young children were regarded as a legitimate source for intimidation because they could incriminate their mothers and grandmothers. A child's evidence was in many lands considered enough to condemn and execute a witch. In the colonies of America, during the course of the trials at Salem between 1692 and 1693, a four-year-old child, Dorcas Good, was the youngest victim to be accused of witchcraft and imprisoned. She was released on bail after her mother was hanged, but her younger sibling died in prison. Dorcas was driven insane by her experience.

Burning Times

No one really knows how many people were put to death for witchcraft. The worst period for witch burnings and hangings in Europe was between the mid-fifteenth and early eighteenth centuries. The number of people found guilty and executed as witches during this period is generally accepted to be about a quarter of a million, although many more people were lynched or hanged by mobs eager to blame bad harvests or dying cattle on a scapegoat.

About three-quarters of those killed as witches in Europe and Scandinavia were women, who were mainly older and from the lower classes. But anyone who was different, eccentric, senile or physically deformed could be accused. With the death of so many experienced healers and wise women, much knowledge was lost forever. For a time, infant mortality grew as male physicians increasingly took over the roles of the deposed midwives, and more women were forced to give birth in unsanitary conditions without the help that they could not afford.

Even fairies became associated with witchcraft. The Bean Tighe, a fairy housekeeper popular in the mythology of Ireland and Scotland, was said to reside with the village wise woman and assist her with chores. During the worst of the witchcraft hysteria, if an old women had an immaculate house it was claimed that she had fairy help – and so by implication consorted with the Devil.

Witchcraft and the Modern World

Although the last execution for witchcraft in England was that of Alice Molland at Exeter in 1712, it was not until 1951 that the Witchcraft Act of 1736 was repealed. While denying that witchcraft existed, this Act had harshly punished those who, it said, pretended to be witches. It was replaced by the Fraudulent Mediums Act.

Those who continued to practise the old ways through the centuries of persecution usually belonged to families that could be trusted not to betray the secrets. Family covens would pass the traditions down through the matriarchal line, and those who could read often inherited the Books of Shadows (named thus partly because of the necessary secrecy involved with them). Gerald Gardner, the father of Wicca, claimed connections with one

of the hereditary covens in the New Forest, having been initiated just before World War II by a witch called Dorothy Clutterbuck.

By the late twentieth century, the US Supreme Court had recognised witchcraft as a valid religion in the US, and it was even accepted by the US army. Other countries, however, including the UK, are not so tolerant. Even where there is no official persecution, in many lands there is still misunderstanding and prejudice, particularly in small communities. In the UK, for example, Wiccan mothers who practise openly are still sometimes regarded with suspicion and even hostility by some health professionals. Lilian, a white witch and healer who once lived in Berkshire, England, recalls how one woman passing her home would always cross herself and walk on the other side of the street, while her children were ostracised by families afraid of being bewitched.

Today, there are still far more female than male witches and it is the Goddess and her representative, the High Priestess, who are the main focus for ritual, channelling her power through the God/consort as the High Priest. The Goddess is generally recognised as the prime mover of existence, who brought forth from herself in the first virgin birth the animus or male principle.

Male witches are usually quite comfortable with the concept of a Divine Feminine. Although there are some traditions, such the Dianic cult (which draws on the precedent ancient witches of Italy who worshipped Diana from about 500 BC), that are strongly feminist, witchcraft manages to be one of the most male-friendly religions in the modern world.

Women, Spirit and Healing

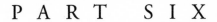

*Spreading light in the
daily world*

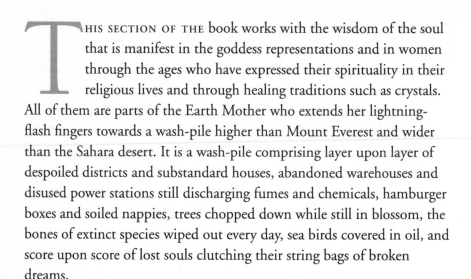

THIS SECTION OF THE book works with the wisdom of the soul that is manifest in the goddess representations and in women through the ages who have expressed their spirituality in their religious lives and through healing traditions such as crystals. All of them are parts of the Earth Mother who extends her lightning-flash fingers towards a wash-pile higher than Mount Everest and wider than the Sahara desert. It is a wash-pile comprising layer upon layer of despoiled districts and substandard houses, abandoned warehouses and disused power stations still discharging fumes and chemicals, hamburger boxes and soiled nappies, trees chopped down while still in blossom, the bones of extinct species wiped out every day, sea birds covered in oil, and score upon score of lost souls clutching their string bags of broken dreams.

Healing Goddesses

Here you will find Brighid the Healer Goddess with her anvil and her herd of cattle, dancing the Wheel of the Seasons. Or is it her successor, St Bridget of Kildare, who sent away with a cuffed ear any village boy or bishop who came to her sanctuary, where for more than a thousand years women tended her sacred flame?

Here also are the shamanic women herding reindeer before them and softly shaking their rattles over the centuries to guide lost souls home. Native American Medicine Women surrounded by rainbow auras are revealing that the land is not dead as they pick herbs that glow yellow, red and blue and drop them into huge, bubbling cauldrons. Into these the goddesses who have donned aprons and tied back their golden tresses are casting anything that cannot be fixed or scrubbed clean, to be transformed, restored and renewed in a new, more perfect form.

Here too is Grandmother Spider Woman, who weaves Dreamcatchers from sunbeams with her gnarled fingers as the babies clap their hands with delight; she is fashioning new limbs for the clay figures of humanity now chipped or distorted out of shape. As she works, she cradles her creations while the sun breathes new life into them. Now she changes

into the ethereal White Buffalo Calf Woman, before whom even the mightiest chiefs must bow as she instructs them in the sacred laws. But in another second she rolls over and is transformed into a tiny buffalo calf that romps with the children and yet is a symbol of hope and promise that all nations will one day be reconciled in peace.

Suddenly the cosmic wash-pile does not look so big and healing the planet and the skies, the sea and the people seems possible and quite attainable, even in this lifetime.

Ways of Healing

As well as working through the healing methods and ideas in this section, you might like to explore other methods of healing, for example aromatherapy, Reiki or spiritual healing. You can work with healing oils and herbs or perhaps sign up for a course on crystals or shamanism. You may want to make a garden or window-box of healing herbs, create a place where wild birds can feed safely, join a society to save an endangered species, or help in the transformation of abandoned industrial land into a wildlife garden in the centre of the city.

For as we learn to heal other people, animals and places either alone or with others, our own healing takes place quite spontaneously. In this way, we continue to evolve spiritually and magically. It may take a lifetime or two to get our angels' wings or to become truly wise, but already we are in the Second Grade of evolution.

There are many wise women teachers who we can call upon in our private meditation. You may seek the compassionate and gentle Virgin Mary, or the Black Madonna, who may be Isis, Mary Magdalene or the woman in the war-torn streets who has looked into the heart of hatred and yet still believes in the innate goodness of humankind. You can call on your own wise grandmother, aunt or mother for comfort and understanding as you did when you were still a child. Or you may look in the mirror and see in your own reflection the wise inner deva or goddess who is part of those ten thousand goddesses and will always be with you as your guiding star.

THE BLACK MADONNA
The Earth Mother in the Christian Tradition

'Darkness precedes light and she is mother.'

THE BLACK MADONNA is the alter ego of the Virgin Mary. She is Queen of the Earth as Mary is Queen in Heaven, and fertile and sensual as Mary is icon of the Immaculate Conception and Incorruptibility. The Black Madonna is the virgin who belongs to no man or deity; she is Mother Nature and all life emanated from her. In contrast, Mary received the seed of God in the form of the Holy Spirit (see Virgin Mary, page 257 and Sophia, page 145).

Black Madonnas are found all over Europe, and especially in France. The most famous images are at Chartres in France, Czestochowa in Poland and Montserrat in Spain.

Some figures portray the Madonna in pregnant form rather than holding a baby, representing her as the fertile mother of the Earth. This symbol of the Goddess with the swollen belly dates back to Palaeolithic times. The fecund Madonna in the Notre Dame de Mende Cathedral at Lozere in France, brought back from the Holy Land by the Crusaders in 1253, is made of walnut or apple wood, both of which are fertility trees.

The shrines of Black Madonnas are sometimes inscribed with the words from the Song of Songs referring to the Queen of Sheba, whose wisdom was greater than that of Solomon, 'I am black but beautiful'. Like the Black Madonna, Sheba was linked to wise Sophia.

The Black Madonna as a Christianised Mother Goddess

For centuries in Europe, the Black Madonnas provided a bridge between the old and the new ways. The Mediterranean region in particular was culturally influenced by Egypt and North Africa through the Moorish conquest, as well as being geographically close to Africa and the Middle

East. Black Madonnas are most frequently associated with the Ancient Egyptian Mother Goddess Isis (see page 176), who is depicted with the infant Horus on her lap and is the original mother and child icon. Other sources of her identity may be Cybele, Artemis or Diana of Ephesus, all black goddesses who were still worshipped in France and on the Mediterranean coast from Antibes to Barcelona during the later centuries of the Roman Empire. During the third century AD, Cybele was the supreme deity of the town of Lyon, which was the capital of a vast area of south-eastern France. Isis gave her name to Paris (par Isis). The black goddess Ceres, Roman goddess of agricultural fertility, is yet another fertility icon associated with the Black Madonna.

Black Madonna statues were often modelled on older statues that had been lost or destroyed. The majority were created in the Middle Ages, when there was still a strong undercurrent of the old ways. This secret paganism was given impetus by Madonna-like Isis images brought back by the Crusaders from the Middle East; other statues survive from the Moorish occupation of Spain, which did not end until the late fifteenth century.

Even as late as the seventeenth century, Black Madonna statues were frequently discovered hidden in trees in France and Spain. These statues may have been representations of the pagan goddesses who were still worshipped in groves, particularly the woodland Goddess of the Hunt Artemis in her black Eastern form, who was also known as Diana of the Wood, or the Golden Bough. Legends grew up which suggest that the statues had magical powers which called the chosen finders to hiding places that were sometimes deep in undergrowth. At Heas in the Hautes-Pyrenees region of France in the sixteenth century, shepherds were led to a wooden statue of the Madonna by two doves, symbols of the Goddess in her form of Sophia. It was believed that this statue magically survived the destruction of its church by an avalanche in 1915. Many other statues were believed to have been similarly preserved by magic. Indeed, as Ean Begg, who has researched the subject extensively, says: 'Again and again in the stories of the Black Virgin, a statue is found in a forest or a bush or discovered when ploughing animals refuse to pass a certain spot. The statue is taken to the parish church, only to return miraculously by night to her own place, where a chapel is then built in her honour. Almost invariably her cult is associated with natural phenomena, especially healing waters or striking geographical features'. (See Further Reading for details of Ean's recent work, page 285.)

Black Madonnas are also associated with and found close to caves, which are symbols of the womb of the Earth Mother; right through Christian

times, images of the Black Madonna were kept in crypts or in subterranean parts of churches or cathedrals, usually near sacred springs or wells. In this respect, the Black Madonna links with the winter aspect of the Corn Goddess Demeter, whose daughter Persephone remained in the Underworld for several months, thus causing winter on Earth. Both mother and daughter were connected with the ancient mystery religions, the rites of which were practised in subterranean places.

Mary Magdalene and the Black Madonna

Mary Magdalene, who was said to have become the wife of Christ and the mother of his son, is believed by some to be the true Black Madonna, especially in parts of France. It is known that the Merovingians in France worshipped Cybele as Diana of the nine fires. In AD 679, Dagobert II, who became St Meroginy, established the cult of 'the one which today receives the name of Our Lady and who is our Eternal Isis'. This designation was incorporated into the identification of the Black Madonna as Mary Magdalene. Through her, the Merovingians claimed to be the rightful kings of France, with descent from Christ's son by Mary Magdalene, the infant in her arms in the Black Madonna statues.

According to the folklore and mythology of Provence, Mary Magdalene migrated with her son from the Middle East to Saintes Maries de-la-Mer, a small village on the French Mediterranean, thirteen years after the Crucifixion. She reportedly spent the last thirty years of her life in seclusion at the cave of St Baume in the French Alps. Although the literature in the monastery that currently exists at St Baume contains this story, it has never entered mainstream Christian doctrine.

Black Madonna statues are also found in places associated with the Grail pilgrimages. The Grail guardians were female and the original Grail cup was the Celtic Cauldron of Regeneration that symbolised the womb of the Earth Mother (see Grail Women, page 59 and Cauldron Goddesses, page 237). Mary Magdalene is in one tradition believed to be the original owner of the Grail cup, in which she collected the blood of Christ after the Crucifixion, and which she then took with her to France.

Magical and Healing Powers of the Black Madonna

Great powers of healing are associated with Black Madonna statues. One explanation for this is that the statues conduct the powerful Earth energies associated with ley lines on which many Madonna sites are found. Ley lines are invisible psychic energy tracks beneath the Earth, and people have built their temples and shrines along them since ancient times. The original Black Madonna of Chartres, France stood in a grotto underneath the mediaeval cathedral next to a healing well. Chartres Cathedral is said to be the most perfect example of Christian sacred geometry and, like many sacred buildings, has a ley line running through it. There has been a shrine to the Mother Goddess at the cathedral since Druidic times, although the Celts did not erect statues as such. Chartres Cathedral is aligned so that the altar and nave are lit by the midsummer sun and has a complex labyrinth set in the floor of the nave (see Labyrinths, page 281). Although the statue was destroyed during the French Revolution in the 1790s, there are many accounts of its healing powers, which perhaps derived from the concentration of Earth powers in the statue of an Earth Mother.

Many cases of healing have been attributed to the Black Madonna of Montserrat, and the statue is also reputed to be able to awaken healing powers in those who touch it. Shirley, who lives on the Isle of Wight, told me about her experience at the cathedral:

'I lost my husband in the crush and found myself before the most wonderful, powerful figure of the Black Madonna. A wrinkled old peasant woman who seemed to know me said in English, "Put your hand on the orb." As I touched the orb that the statue was holding, I felt a strong electric charge tingling through my hand.

'My husband dismissed my experience as static electricity, but it was like nothing I had felt before, a wonderful, pulsating warmth and energy. Soon afterwards, I discovered that I had healing power in my hands, which would become warm and tingling, the same sensation I had received from the statue.

'My friend who was with us on holiday had terrible pain in her arm. Automatically, I found myself rubbing it for her in regular strokes as though I was being guided as to what to do, and I could feel the tingling warmth leaving my fingertips and she could feel it too. The

arm was better almost at once and from then the healing seemed to be always with me. The experience made such a strong impression on me and the black and gold statue contained such power that it changed my life. Even the small Black Madonna image I brought home seems to exude the same energy.'

As a result of her experience, Shirley now cares for and heals elderly people who can no longer live in their own homes.

CRYSTALS AND HEALING

WOMEN THROUGH THE ages have used crystals for healing, although the wise women of old did not have the highly polished stones we have today, which are shipped from many parts of the world and tumbled to remove every imperfection. Theirs were stones with crystal glinting through grey or brown rock, found on local shores, hillsides or riverbanks.

A special healing gem or crystal sphere that may have been brought back by a sailor or traveller generations before would be lovingly wrapped in silk and handed down from mother to daughter. It would be brought out when a family member needed healing. The sick person would hold the crystal or it would be rubbed on a small child or baby; in a transfer of energies, the stone would take away the disease or pain and give its own life essence in return. The crystal would then be washed under running water to remove the impurities, and then returned to its silk wrapping.

Viking women collected amber and rock crystals from the beaches for their domestic healing magic. Although in Iceland Christian law forbade 'curing stones' as well as crystal amulets, they nonetheless continued to be used as part of the folk wisdom until comparatively recently. When I was in Sweden last spring, I went with some Swedish healer friends to the beach where they still gather quartz and amber like their ancestors did more than a thousand years earlier.

Many of the modern healing associations with specific crystals are remarkably consistent with those of different ages, whether the crystal lore is derived from the Orient or from Native North American tradition. For example, the Celts boiled clear crystal quartz in water; they then drank the crystal water over nine days to increase their energy levels and to cleanse their systems. Blue lace agate water, or that made from other pale blue

crystals, was used by the Ancient Greeks to relieve sore throats and also to help speakers to express words that came from the heart. In Babylonia and Ancient Egypt, bloodstones were believed to ease childbirth and stop bleeding. All of these remedies are still part of working crystal lore.

If you give a child a bag of crystals, he or she will automatically select the appropriate crystal for a given ailment, for example an amethyst to soothe a migraine or an orange-banded agate for a stomach pain. This would indicate that crystal wisdom is innate to us all. However, as adults women seem to find it easier than men to trust their intuition to select the right crystal, and to channel their own innate healing powers through the chosen crystal. Women spontaneously merge spiritually with crystal energies.

Ways of Healing with Crystals

You can either choose from the list of crystals given below or first read more extensively about different stones and their healing properties in one of the books suggested under Further Reading (see page 285). It is probably best to start by buying a number of inexpensive small crystals that *feel* right when you pick them up from the mineral trays. As you meditate with the stones, use them as amulets or hold them to answer questions in divination (see Crystal Divination, page 163), you will find that one or two are particularly effective in relieving your own ills and sorrows and those of your family. A gifted healer I know uses what seems a disappointingly dull grey stone that momentarily reflects rainbow light as she works. Bear in mind also that even small stones can become very powerful if regularly used for healing. Once you have identified your special healing stones, keep them separately in a bag or wrapped in white silk when you are not using them.

Contact Healing

You will need three crystals for different purposes for contact healing. I have suggested ones that seem to work well for a number of healers, but you can substitute others of a similar colour. You may choose different crystals for specific problems (see page 233).

Crystal quartz

This clear white stone is best for unblocking stagnant energies and for infusing energy, light and positive feelings into a person who is ill or sad. Clear quartz will trigger the body's immune system and innate regenerative powers. It can also help a person who is exhausted or being drained emotionally. This crystal is for fast results and can be used as a substitute for any other crystal.

Citrine

A pure, sparkling, yellow sun crystal is naturally warming and is gentler than crystal quartz. Melting pain and tension, it encourages the gentle flow of warming energies that will create a sense of well-being and rebalance the body. Citrine unfolds its energies more gradually that crystal quartz.

Rose quartz or amethyst

Pink or purple transparent crystals are soothing, especially for children. They will remove pain or tension, replacing them with calm and the slow infusion of healing energies.

You will need crystals large enough to hold in your hand to direct the energies. I find that using the power hand, the one you write with, works equally well for releasing pain and infusing energies, but do experiment. Other healers may disagree.

Contact healing means that the healing process is carried out with the person being present. Except on a partner or young children, you should hold the crystal a few centimetres away from the body as you work. With children and loved ones you can apply the crystals gently to the skin. The patient can either sit or lie down, whichever is more comfortable. Use an anti-clockwise movement to remove pain and a clockwise one to infuse the body with healing energies.

How Do You Heal?

The healing process can be likened to the way you heal when, for instance, you rub a child's knee better when he or she falls, or soothe a partner's headache or comfort a weeping friend. You *feel* or initially may need to visualise the healing energies as warm liquid beginning in your heart and flowing into your hand and the crystal. This is of course a two-way process, and the powers are also going from the crystal into your heart, and being recirculated via the hand and back through the crystal and into the patient.

❦ The power is often seen as light. This can either be pure white or gold, or the same colour as the crystal you are using. Pass the crystal over the body of the patient in spiralling lines, letting the crystal guide your hand and not the other way around.

❦ Stop to unblock a knot of trapped energy with the crystal as you would a physical tangle of thread, and infuse lifeless areas with energy with circular movements, ending with a circle of light over the crown of the head.

○ You may use one or all three of the crystals in turn, beginning with the rose quartz or amethyst, and moving through to the energising clear quartz.

○ Alternatively if, for example, the patient is complaining of a sore throat, a pale blue crystal could be circled first anti-clockwise, then clockwise over the throat area (see below for healing associations).

❦ Practise with your children and pets (who are remarkably tolerant) until you establish a rhythm of working.

❦ Remember not to hurry healing. Move the crystal over the body very slowly and pause at every stage to let the crystal guide you as to whether to infuse energy or to remove tension.

Absent Healing

In absent healing, you can concentrate on a sick or unhappy person and send healing relief through the focus of a crystal. For absent healing, you need two crystals: a large chunk of uncut amethyst or rose quartz, and either a cloudy, uncut crystal quartz, or a clear crystal sphere. These are relatively inexpensive to buy.

๑ Place the two crystals side by side on a table.

๑ Behind the coloured crystal, light a pink or lilac candle scented with rose or lavender.

๑ Face the direction in which the person lives, visualising him or her in a particular place in a room or garden.

๑ Holding the coloured crystal in both hands, visualise dark rays coming from the patient entering the crystal, and being transformed into circles of crystalline colour and floating like bubbles into the candle, where they are taken back as light. Return the crystal to the table.

๑ From the coloured candle, light a pure white candle perhaps scented with vanilla and place it behind the white crystal.

๑ Pick up the second crystal. Let the light pass through it, forming a prism of rainbow colours that travels to the sick person and enters through the crown of the head and fills the whole body with brilliance. This time visualise a sparkling halo around the head of the patient.

๑ Return the crystal to the table.

๑ Leave the candles to burn through in a safe place in front of the crystals, so that the light from both will continue to filter gently for several hours towards the patient.

While you can send light and love to anyone, it is best to ask permission before removing any energy (even if it is negative energy) from anyone other than a very small child to whom you are closely related in love if not blood.

If you work beyond your immediate circle, you should consider training as a healer (see Useful Addresses, page 289). Many professional healers discovered their gift when healing a family member.

Healing Crystals in Your Everyday World

❧ You can soak crystals in pure spring water for eight hours and then drink the liquid or add it to a bath. The spiritual essence of a crystal will restore your energies or calm, according to its properties.

❧ Keep crystals in a dish of water on your desk at work and splash the water on your wrists and temples to counter tension.

❧ Place crystals directly in your bath water so that you can absorb their gentle spiritual energies as you soak.

❧ Hold a large, uncut piece of crystal, for example rose quartz or pale purple amethyst, in your hand and breathe in the healing light very slowly through your nose, then gently and equally slowly exhale any pain, stress or fear as darkness. This is an excellent method for insomniacs or hyperactive children to try for themselves.

❧ In a special tiny purse or bag, carry a crystal that is related to your current state of health or life, or have a selection of crystal pendants to wear. I have seen some on sale with interchangeable stones.

Ten Female-friendly Stones for Healing and Personal Amulets

Amber

Orange or occasionally brown.

Amber can be up to fifty million years old, and is said to contain the power of many suns. It is good for fertility, and protects the user from

physical, emotional and psychic harm. It also melts tension and stomach anxiety knots, and reduces fear of change, as well as helping its wearer to keep a sense of perspective. Amber is good for detoxification and for protection from over-exposure to computers and other industrial pollutants.

Amethyst

All shades of purple.

Amethyst is excellent for relieving migraines, insomnia, eyestrain, and stress, and for driving away nightmares and helping to fight addictions of all kinds; it is useful in the workplace or at home, and absorbs all forms of negativity and releases healing energies in their place. Kept with other crystals, amethyst will cleanse them. Wash amethyst frequently and rest it wrapped in dark silk.

Apache Tears

Black.

This crystal is named after Native American women who mourned their loved ones and whose tears were said to have become embedded in obsidian that was buried in rock. The crystal brings optimism even in the most difficult circumstances, as well as acceptance of what cannot be changed; it also eases physical pain and mental anguish, especially if there has been injustice or abuse. It is very protective in the workplace if it is placed facing any door or person who is hostile, as it will transform what is negative into positive. It also unblocks energies, particularly in the lower body, and aids healing of all kinds.

Carnelian

Yellow, orange and red, and occasionally brown.

Carnelian strengthens creativity, brings abundance to all aspects of life, repels envy in others, enhances confidence, courage, initiative, and assertiveness, and strengthens identity. It also increases physical energy; aids the healthy functioning of the reproductive system; relieves menstrual cramps and disorders; and encourages healthy circulation of the blood.

A 15th century painting showing Catherine of Alexandria debating with heathen philosophers before Emperor Maxentius.

LEFT: Head of the Celtic goddess Brigit, found in France.

BELOW: A Greek 5th century marble relief showing the birth of Aphrodite.

Stone relief of Persephone and Hecate from 5th century BC.

Mary with the Child Jesus by Raphael.

18th century French painting of the Black Virgin.

Citrine

Sparkling yellow.

Citrine is sometimes called the wish crystal because it translates needs and desires into positive action to make one's dreams come true. It clears energy blockages and brings mental and emotional clarity; reduces anxiety and depression; increases self-esteem; and helps digestive problems, food allergies and food-related illnesses.

Coral

Red, deep pink and orange, and very occasionally black.

Coral is good for childbirth, babies and children. It increases fertility, energises the body and mind, and boosts metabolic functioning and bone and tissue regeneration. Coral in darker shades protects against self-destructive instincts.

Jade

Many shades of green.

Jade is the gentlest of the stones. It is good for arthritis, rheumatism, and kidney and bladder problems, especially water retention; protects against spite and anger in others; enhances self-love, especially if there has been destructive behaviour by others; connects the user with Earth energies and so alleviates anxiety and panic attacks; and offers protection against injury and accidents.

Kunzite

Pink, lilac or purple.

This potent stone is sometimes known as the woman's stone because of its ability to soothe all female disorders. It increases the ability to give and receive love, and is also good for overcoming compulsive behaviour and addictions, reducing mood swings, and opening psychic and spiritual channels for divination and healing. You can keep it in your car, if you have one, for reducing road rage and tensions, or at work for keeping stress at bay. Kunzite is a lovely present for a girl who is entering puberty.

Moonstone, or selenite

Translucent with a white, fawn pink, yellow, or occasionally blue sheen.

Moonstones are believed to absorb the powers of the moon and to become deeper in colour, more translucent and more powerful for healing as the moon waxes and until it is full. The crystal is associated with female cycles, including life cycles as well as monthly ones. It helps hormonal problems, fluid retention, PMT, menstrual and fertility problems, and menopausal symptoms, especially hot flushes; it also keeps away nightmares and encourages clairvoyance and intuition.

Rose quartz

Translucent to clear pink.

Rose quartz is the stone of gentle healing, known as the children's stone because it is so gentle in soothing away childhood ills and sorrows, especially ones that emerge to haunt us years later in adulthood. It is an essential stone for healers, for it will ease any pain or tension, cut or bruise. It promotes family love and friendship, brings peace, self-forgiveness and the mending of quarrels, heals heartbreak from love affairs gone wrong, and overcomes lack of confidence. Cleanse and recharge rose quartz frequently, especially if its colour begins to fade.

Charging and Cleansing Crystals
Before and After Use

If you are in a hurry, you can hold a crystal under running water, having first sprinkled it with a few grains of salt. Leave it to dry naturally, if possible in sunlight. Rose quartz, moonstones and jade prefer moonlight.

Using Smudging

Burn dried sage or cedar herbs by lighting them in a shallow bowl. Pass the crystal nine times anti-clockwise through the smoke to cleanse it, then nine times clockwise to empower it. You can also buy commercially prepared smudge sticks or use incense sticks scented with, for example, cypress, frankincense, myrrh or pine.

Using the Forces of Nature

Put the crystal in a pot of herbs such as lavender, sage or rosemary, which are associated with general healing. Leave it for twenty-four hours before removing it, then, if necessary, wash off any remaining soil with running water.

CAULDRONS OF INSPIRATION
The Healing and Abundance of the Goddess

ɷ

Cauldrons

ARCHAEOLOGISTS IN NORTHERN Europe have discovered a number of cauldrons that would seem to date from pre-Celtic times, the design of which suggests that they may have served ritual functions. Although cauldrons are associated primarily with magic, they are rooted in the world of hearth and home. Many were in fact the iron cooking pots that stood on three legs over the fire or hung from a chain on a black lead cooking range (I had one of these ranges in my early childhood home in the late 1940s in industrial Birmingham). In the folk tradition, cauldrons were more likely to hold a nourishing stew or a herbal brew to cure a cold or a broken heart, than the mythical eye of a newt and wing of a bat.

Cauldron Goddesses

Associated with the womb of the Great Mother, mythological cauldrons of the pre-Christian world were owned or tended by female guardians. Like the more homely versions in later times, the cauldron of legend would contain food that always magically restored itself, a brew endowing wisdom and inspiration or the power to heal even mortal wounds. Invariably, the Goddess cauldrons were stolen from their female guardians by envious male deities and heroes. This caused the loss of their original purpose, which was that their contents should be for everyone, not just for warriors or the deities themselves.

In Celtic lore, the Three Mothers, the Matronae, kept the magic

Cauldron of Regeneration at the bottom of a lake (or the land beneath the waves) until it was appropriated by the Celtic hero God Bran the Blessed, who used it to restore slain warriors. The Matronae were triple Fate and Fertility Goddesses who in Romano-Celtic statues held children or corn and fruit on their knees. They became folk figures in later centuries and Christmas Eve is still known as the Night of the Mothers in parts of Europe (see Seasonal Goddesses for other goddesses associated with Christmas, page 25). Bran was in mediaeval myth himself transformed into Bron, keeper of the Holy Grail cup, the Christianised version of the cauldron, which was guarded by a Grail maiden (see Grail Women, page 59).

Cerridwen and the Cauldron of Regeneration

According to legend, the late-fifth-century Celtic bard Taliesin received his bardic gifts and great knowledge from the Cauldron of Cerridwen through the process of death, transformation and rebirth. Legend relates that in his earlier incarnation he was Gwion, the foster son or servant boy of Cerridwen, the Crone Goddess of Prophecy and keeper of the cauldron in which inspiration and divine knowledge were brewed.

Gwion stole three drops of the brew of wisdom, which was made from the ingredients of every season. The mixture was intended for Cerridwen's son Avagdu to compensate for his ugliness. More favourable versions of the story say that some of the liquid splashed Gwion and he licked his fingers.

Gwion escaped from Cerridwen by changing in turn into a hare, a fish, a bird and a grain of wheat. Cerridwen pursued him as a greyhound, an otter, a hawk and a finally a hen, who ate the grain, so conceiving Gwion as her child. Cerridwen's aim was not to kill Gwion but to reabsorb him. Cerridwen was also called the White Sow Goddess, after the creatures who were said to be notorious for eating their young (see also Woman as Enchantress, page 94).

On May Eve, Gwion was reborn as Taliesin and was cast in a leather bag into the sea, itself a symbol of the womb of the Great Mother. A bard called Elphin found him in the weir of salmon, the fish of wisdom and prophecy and cared for him.

The Pentre Evan Cromlech in Pembrokeshire is a former Druidic sacred site of initiation; in folk tradition it is called the Cauldron of Cerridwen. Initiates would remain at the site in total darkness for several days awaiting rebirth. On the night of the initiation, which might occur at the Spring Equinox, nine virgins would stir and breathe the pure life force into a

cauldron in which a brew of barley, flowers, herbs and sea foam was created. The would-be bards would each drink three drops of the brew to represent Gwion's three drops of inspiration and the rest would be poured away to symbolise the casting off of the former life of the initiate.

Cauldron of Undry, or Annwyn

As well as being a historical poet and seer, Taliesin attracted many stories about his magical origins and nature. According to an early Welsh poem, *Preiddeu Annwyn*, which is often credited to Taliesin himself, he sailed with King Arthur to Annwyn, the Celtic Otherworld, to find the Graal or the Cauldron of Regeneration. This cauldron, which was known as the Undry, provided an endless supply of nourishment, had great healing powers and could restore the dead to life, either to their former existence or in a new life form in the Otherworld. Christian legends tell that Arthur rescued the cauldron from the land of demons and kept it on Mount Snowdon to feed his court and surrounding villages.

The Cauldron of Undry was one of the thirteen Celtic treasures owned by the Father God Dagda. Originally, however, it had been the cauldron of the Great Mother Anu, or Danu. When Arthur found the cauldron, it was filled with pearls and guarded by nine maidens.

Cauldron of Gonlod

Gonlod, or Gunnlod, a beautiful Viking giantess, was the Norse mother of poetry and in early myth was the owner of the Cauldron of Inspiration that the god Odin took by trickery. In other versions of the myth, the cauldron containing the mead of poetry was formed from the blood of wise Kvasir, a sage created from the spittle (that is, the wise words of each one of the gods and goddesses) as the two opposing factions of deities, the Aesir and Vanir, made peace. Kvasir was murdered and two dwarves, Fjalar and Galar, combined his blood containing the wisdom with honey to make the mead; whoever drank this became either a poet or very wise.

According to the same myth, the cauldron was subsequently stolen by Suttung the giant, who made a chamber or cave out of rock and set his daughter, the downgraded Gonlod, to guard what were now three vessels containing the mead. Odin, the Norse Father God, was determined to have the mead for himself, so by disguise and by turning himself into a snake, he obtained access to the subterranean cave. Here, Gonlod sat on her golden

stool hoping for a handsome lover to arrive. Odin, now restored to his godlike state in his mantle of stars, provided three days and nights of bliss. It is recorded by Christian chroniclers of the myth that Odin made an honest woman of Gonlod by taking her as his wife (these chroniclers of course conveniently ignored the fact Odin already had quite a number of wives). In return, he asked only for three drops of the mead, but of course drank all of it. He then turned himself into an eagle, and took the mead back to Asgard, realm of the gods. Occasionally, Odin allowed a little of the mead to fall on favoured mortals, who thus became poets who might record his great deeds.

The son of Gonlod and Odin became the golden-haired Bragi, God of Poetry – for as shown in the myths of other lands, deposed goddesses were useful for producing heirs who became the new hero gods and kings.

The weak, womanly Gonlod thus sacrificed her sacred duty for passion, said the recording monks, who believed it was better for even a bigamist pagan god to be in charge of the poetic mead than the Goddess.

Cauldron in Magic

The cauldron is the one ritual tool that is positively charged by being the centre of domestic life, and it often replaces the altar as a focus for less formal spells. You can adapt any iron pot. There are some splendid ones at garage sales and in cookware shops or even garden centres, and your cauldron need not be large to be effective. Even without casting spells, a cauldron can become the focus of healing and empowering energies if it is kept in a central point in the home, such as a disused hearth.

§ You can fill the cauldron with fresh flowers and herbs of the season.

§ A fire burning in the cauldron was traditionally known as the Balefire, and is considered sacred. You can create your own domestic Balefire by lighting a red candle secured in sand or soil in the centre of the cauldron whenever you need special power or energy.

§ You can also burn fire-element incense sticks arranged in the cauldron in a circle and again secured in sand. Useful types of fire-incense stick include allspice, basil, cinnamon and ginger, which are said to bring courage, passion or money; powers can be invoked if you name the relevant energies as you light them. Wishes written on paper can be burned in the central candle to release their energies into the cosmos.

§ Floating lit candles on a cauldron of water will, after dark, cast images that will reveal answers to questions.

§ Cast flower petals into a cauldron filled with water to get energies flowing; dropping dead leaves on to the surface will banish sorrow, and you can tip the leaves and cauldron water into a flowing source of water after use.

As you use the cauldron for divinatory and ritual work, it will accumulate power; being in your home it will, however, be protected by the security that is inherent in the domestic world.

NATIVE NORTH AMERICAN HEALING WISDOM
The Medicine Women

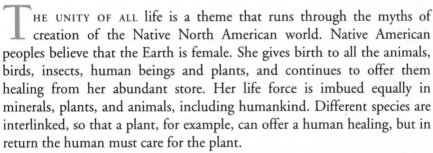

T HE UNITY OF ALL life is a theme that runs through the myths of creation of the Native North American world. Native American peoples believe that the Earth is female. She gives birth to all the animals, birds, insects, human beings and plants, and continues to offer them healing from her abundant store. Her life force is imbued equally in minerals, plants, and animals, including humankind. Different species are interlinked, so that a plant, for example, can offer a human healing, but in return the human must care for the plant.

Healing in this tradition involves maintaining and if necessary restoring the natural balance in the land and people, a harmony that operates on the spiritual as well as on the mental and physical planes. The earthly forms of things are said to reflect their perfect or archetypal forms in the spirit world. Healing and magic are thus one and the same. It is only in the industrialised Westernised world that the two have become separated.

Medicine in the Native North American world means power or energy.

A Medicine Woman is therefore healer, teacher, preacher and weaver of magic. As Jamie Sams, a Native American shaman of Cherokee and Seneca descent, explains: 'When we look at the idea of Medicine, we have to embrace the total person, the body, the heart, the mind, and the spirit. When any of these parts are out of balance, then there is a need for healing.' A person's medicine is that power which is generated by his or her own talents and strengths, used in a positive way to achieve the right path in life, a path that is called the Beauty Way.

Spirits of Healing

The Corn Mother is the manifestation of the abundance of the Earth and represents different stages in the human life cycle and agricultural year. It is she who holds the power of healing. As mentioned in the chapter on Gaia and the creator goddesses, many of the healing goddesses/spirit women who appear among different Native North American nations are forms of Grandmother Spider Woman (see page 11).

Corn Mother of the Native Americans

The Cherokee creation myths tell of Selu and her husband Kanati, who are ruled by Mother Sun. Selu is the Corn Mother from whose body come corn and beans. The Corn Mother's symbol is a perfect ear of corn without a single missing or misshapen kernel. One of these ears of corn is often used as part of a healing medicine bundle, especially if this belongs to a Medicine Woman; it represents fertility, as well as the powers of regeneration.

In Navajo healing, *hatal*, or elaborate songs and chants, are an essential part of the rituals called Ways, which are used both for healing individuals and for specific purposes such as bringing about an abundant harvest.

Pictures are made either in sand, or sometimes on cloth or buckskin using sand, cornmeal, flower pollen, powdered roots, charcoal, stone and bark. These pictures are credited with powerful healing powers. A patient may sit on a picture containing a representation of the Holy Ones and thereby absorb their power. In one version of the ritual, Father Sky and Mother Earth are depicted, so that they can recreate the Earth and thus heal the patient. The place from which the first humans are said to have emerged is symbolised by a small bowl of water buried in the sand or the earth. Once the picture is completed, a line of corn pollen is drawn between Father Sky and Mother Earth to show the path of harmony to be taken by the patient.

White Buffalo Calf Woman, or Wophe, a form of Grandmother Spider Woman, was said to have come to the Lakota nation at a time when there was a famine. She unfastened her medicine bundle, and gave the women corn and root vegetables and showed them how to make fire to cook them. She gave the men the Buffalo Calf Pipe of Peace, which is the most sacred religious object of the Lakota today.

White Buffalo Calf Woman also taught the women how to heal with smudging by lighting herbs, desert sage, cedar and sweetgrass, which were burned in an abalone shell or a shallow bowl; the smoke was wafted over the body with a feather to cleanse impurities and to restore healing energies. Smudging is becoming increasingly popular in the Western world.

Medicine Women

Medicine Women have always been as prevalent as Medicine Men among the Native American peoples. Even where there is a Medicine Man, it is his wife who is keeper of the herb, plant and tree lore that is central to the healing tradition, and who will prepare the herbs for smudging and create healing potions and salves.

A family might have a strong tradition of Medicine Women who inherit the role, or a woman may be chosen as a gifted child who might be trained by a practising Medicine Woman. But in every case, the calling of the initiate is confirmed in a special dream, which is sometimes induced by fasting or a period of solitude. In the dream, the spirit of an animal, a plant or one of the goddess/spirit women imparts secret healing knowledge that can only be validated by the Medicine Woman of the people.

The Medicine Woman's training is not complete until middle age. For healing wisdom does not involve just a knowledge of healing plants; it is a connection with the living spirits of the trees, the herbs and the wise ancestors. An initiate learns to read the cause of imbalance or missing strength from the aura of a sick or distressed person, and to identify the plant whose aura reflects the missing quality or an antidote. The process therefore involves intuitive and clairvoyant powers, and the ability to contact the Wise Ancestors to call down their healing energies.

Because women were revered as daughters of Grandmother Spider Woman, Medicine Women were once asked to make shields for warriors or those who travelled far away, or to endow the shields with power using special chants.

Modern Native American Medicine Women hold the repository of ancient secrets and act as a powerful cohesive force through difficult times, teaching the wise ways of the ancestors to those of the young who are willing to listen. They have also increasingly handed on their wisdom to other nations, holding moon lodges where women can learn to harmonise with their own cycles, to gather herbs for healing potions and to smudge away imbalances. *Medicine Women*, the most famous book of one American writer, Lynn Andrews, brought the ways of the Amerindian wise women to a wide audience throughout the world.

Healing through the Beauty Way

It was said that White Buffalo Calf Woman came to the Lakota nation walking along a path of light from the horizon, and that she departed along a similar path of light. Radiance like this can be used to give a sudden surge of energy, to restore optimism, and to heal old sorrows and pain. It is an excellent antidote for Seasonal Affective Disorder, in which condition the dark days of winter and lack of sunlight bring bouts of depression.

๑ If you create a path indoors across a room just as dawn is breaking, you can step out through an open door into the morning light. In the evening, you can enter through the door from the sunset into the brilliant pathway that can be made on a carpet or on a wooden or a tiled floor.

๑ You can mark the edges of your personal Beauty Way with small, golden glass nuggets, tiny quartz crystals, beads, or pure white stones that reflect the light.

๑ Use mirrors, lamps or candles in floor or wall holders, and experiment until you have enclosed the whole path in radiance.

๑ Modern fibre-optic lamps are an excellent source of moving light.

๑ Surround the path with ears of corn, whole sweetcorn, golden yams, pumpkins, squash, sweet potatoes, nuts, seeds and ripe yellow apples; all these contain the life force in its most vibrant form.

❧ As you walk along the path, breathe in the golden light and slowly exhale darkness, doubts, fears, pain or chronic illness, or if you wish chant: 'I see the Light, I enter the Light, I am the Light, the Light of all nature and of all creation,' over and over again.

❧ When you have finished your Beauty Walk, you may wish to travel along the path two or three more times, ending at the opposite end from the place where you began.

❧ If you are walking indoors at dusk, end at a source of light, perhaps a large lamp or golden candle.

❧ Stand for a moment, drawing in the radiance, until there is no more darkness to exhale.

❧ Collect all the vegetables, fruits and seeds in a basket. Combine those that need to be cooked, and invite friends or family to share a meal of light.

❧ Use yellow sunflowers or other brilliant yellow blooms as a table decoration, and encircle them with the crystals from the path.

❧ Light candles, or if it is light, use natural light sources to make the table shine.

❧ After the meal, eat the fruits and seeds, absorbing the healing light within your body and spirit.

❧ An alternative technique is to recreate a natural Beauty Way by following a path of sunlight or moonlight. A beach on the days leading up to the full moon will form a pathway of gold and you can wade out into the sea a little way. Stand in the golden water, allowing it to swirl around you – this will activate your inner regenerative powers.

❧ Alternatively, go to formal gardens with paths laid out between flowers, and wait until there is a long, straight path bathed in sunlight with the borders shaded. An urban park or square will serve as a Beauty Way and will energise the whole area.

❧ You will rapidly become expert at finding suitable avenues of light in different settings. Let the gold enter your every pore and flood though you so that your whole body is warmed by the radiance.

SAINTS
The Goddess Transformed

෴

T HE GODDESS NEVER really went away when Christianity became the official religion in many parts of Europe. Women especially continued to pray and make offerings to women. Female saints represented different aspects of the Goddess or localised goddesses, and some of them had legends as colourful as the original deities.

Christianised Triple Goddess

Brighid/St Bridget

With the coming of Christianity, the Celtic Triple Goddess Brighid became the semi-mythical fifth-century St Bridget (see also Fire Goddesses, page 152 and Seasonal Goddesses, page 20). Because Brighid was so popular among ordinary people, she could not be demonised or ignored. One of her legends was even woven around the historical and very stern St Patrick, patron saint of Ireland. It is said that he almost succumbed to her charms when she demanded a kiss and proposed to him – he resisted her temptations and paid her off with a green silk dress.

St Bridget may in fact have been a real woman who was converted by St Patrick. She was said to be the daughter of a Druid who was converted by her on his deathbed as she sat by him, weaving from the rushes on the floor what were in Christian myth the very first Bridget crosses. In fact, the original straw crosses were set on fire and cast into the air at Oimelc, the pagan maiden Brighid's festival, to bring fertility to the land. In the pagan tradition, Brighid's Maiden aspect stood for fertility, as well as for inspiration and poetry for both female and male bards. As Mother, she represented the Goddess of midwifery and healing, while as Crone she was patroness of the hearth fire, smiths and craft workers.

An abbess legend tells that, unusually for a woman, Bridget had control over choosing bishops, and that she would appoint only those who were goldsmiths. The presiding Bishop was so amazed by the pillar of fire that came from her head that he realised that her sacred authority was greater than his own. The convent where the original virgin priestesses became the

nuns tending her sacred fire was at Cill-Daire, later called Kildare, which means Church of the Oak, a distinct link with the Druidesses (Druid means wisdom of the oak).

In her Mother aspect, St Bridget was called Mary of the Gael, the Irish Mary who was the midwife and foster-mother of Christ. This character was said to have put on a crown of candles (a link with the festival of light held on her day) to distract Herod's soldiers so that the Holy Family could escape. She is also credited with a number of miracles in which the nurturing power of the Mother is the theme: it was said that whenever she gave a drink of water to a stranger it would turn to milk, and on one occasion she turned her bath water into beer to satisfy a visiting bishop and his entourage. A hymn attributed to St Bridget herself relates:

'I'd like to have the three Marys
Their fame is so great
I'd like to have people
From every corner of heaven.

I'd like to have a great lake of beer
For the King of Kings
I'd like to watch the family of heaven
Drinking it through all eternity'.

The Goddess Brighid was, especially in her Crone aspect, associated with the serpent, the symbol of feminine wisdom and fertility. In Wales on St Bride's Day (Bride is the Welsh form of Bridget), a prayer was said to the serpent:

'Today is the Day of Bride,
The serpent shall come from the hole,
I will not molest the serpent,
Nor will the serpent molest me.'

There are also legends relating how on St Bridget's (Bride's) Day, her lamb fought and defeated the dragon of the old Hag of Winter Cailleach. Originally, this battle was between winter and spring, but it was transformed into the battle of the Lamb of God against sin (see dragon-slaying saints, page 249). This theme is still played out in mystery plays in parts of Scotland.

Lady of the Wells

St Winefrede

The sacred Goddess wells were frequently Christianised with spectacular miracles designed to ensure that locals would transfer their allegiance from the original well spirit, although the healing properties of these wells and often the human female guardian tradition remained the same (see also Well Goddesses, page 38).

One ancient Welsh healing well of indeterminate origin became a major Christian pilgrimage centre. According to myth, the sixth-century Winefride, a niece of St Beuno, was attacked by a local chief, Caradoc, who tried to rape her. When she resisted, he cut off her head, which rolled down the hill, where it fell into a deep hollow. Instantly, a stream burst from the rock on to which her head had fallen. The ground opened and swallowed her assassin, but Beuno set Winefrede's head back on her shoulders and she became an abbess. The waters of the stream were found to have healing properties, and fifteen centuries later it is still a place of pilgrimage and healing.

Anglo Saxon Saints and the Goddess

Sexburgha: the Christianised Mother Goddess

The most famous Anglo-Saxon saint is Sexburgha, who married Ercombert, King of Kent. Encouraged by her, he destroyed many stone circles, including one that was said to be near her abbey, the Monasterium Sexburgha in Minster on the Isle of Sheppey, Kent. She became abbess in AD 668 after being regent for her son Egbert on the death of the king.

Sexburgha was famed for her healing powers, as were the waters of Sexburgha's Well within the abbey grounds. This had originally been the

ancient pre-Celtic fertility Well of the Triple Goddess, which has accounted for several 'miracle' babies under its revived pagan auspices. Sexburgha ruled a community of seventy-seven nuns, and a number of the older women may have been priestesses of the Triple Goddess well before the opening of the abbey.

The waters of a recently excavated abbess well nearby are said to be especially potent for relieving eye problems. Coins found in this well suggest that it may have been dedicated to Diana Triformis, the triple Diana, during the Roman occupation, demonstrating that wells may have changed their associations with different goddesses even before the coming of Christianity.

Although Sexburgha and her abbey are long gone, the Goddess links have remained. On a column at the present Minster Abbey, which was built on the site of Sexburgha's old abbey and its grounds, there is an image of a goddess with three wheat stalks, a fertility symbol. Minster Abbey is very close to the Well of the Triple Goddess. Moreover, on a triangular stone above the priest's door in the Sexburgha Chapel, the 'S' of the saint's name appears entwined with the Green Man, the image of pagan fertility.

Dragon Slayers

The killing of dragons is usually associated with St George or St Michael. In this respect, it represents the slaying of the Mother Goddess religion, for dragons are closely aligned to serpents (see page 35). None of the women slayers used violence or the sword against the dragons. But what are female saints doing slaying dragons?

The most famous of the dragon slayers is St Martha, patron saint of housewives, cooks and servants, who in the Gospel of St Luke is described as cooking for Jesus and tending to his needs. Her dragon-slaying role occurred after she crossed the Mediterranean to go to France following the Crucifixion, accompanied by Mary Magdalene, Mary Jacobe, the mother of the disciple James, and Mary Salome, daughter of Mary Jacobe, plus a casket containing the remains of Anne, the grandmother of Christ. St. Martha defeated her dragon at Tarascon by sprinkling it with holy water.

St Margaret of Antioch was the daughter of a pagan priest, but she became a Christian. She refused to marry Olybrius, governor of Antioch, because she had dedicated herself as Christ's bride. Olybrius tortured and imprisoned her, and it was while she was in prison that the Devil in the form of a dragon tried to devour her. She killed the dragon by making the sign of

the cross. A third female dragon slayer was St Catherine of Alexandria, the fourth-century saint to whom young virgins prayed for a husband.

To St Catherine and St Margaret, the dragon was the sexuality that threatened their virginity – and perhaps also the symbol of their own sexual desires. For unlike the pagan virgin goddesses and a number of their priestesses, virginity in Christianity meant total chastity. To the motherly St Martha, however, the dragon was a threat to the people she had promised to protect. It was St Martha's gentle dragon-slaying ability, together with her homely virtues, that made her (unlike the virgin slayers) so beloved and reassuring to women throughout the centuries.

SHAMANISM AND WOMEN

S HAMANS ARE THE magician priest and priestess healers in indigenous communities around the world. They are found in India, Australia, Japan, China, Siberia, Mongolia, Africa, North, Central and South America, and among the Bedouins in the Middle East. Women have always played a significant role in shamanism, although as indigenous cultures have increasingly come into contact with the Westernised world, so women shamans are becoming downgraded.

Among the Sami hunting peoples in Lapland and the far north of Norway, women are today having to fight hard to continue their traditional role as reindeer herders. Once women become consigned purely to the domestic sphere, their spiritual position also tends to become marginalised. It is the strength and fierce independence that makes the Sami women shamans such powerful forces in a world where for much of the year they endure the same physical hardships as their male counterparts.

Archaeological evidence indicates that female shamans have probably existed since early times. The Russian archaeolgists D.A. Sergeev and S.A. Arutiunov have recently uncovered a tomb of an elderly woman shaman at a 2,000-year-old Inuit cemetery at Chukotka, on the Russian side of the Bering Strait. The stone, wood, and whalebone tomb held elaborate ritual offerings, and the skeleton of the woman had a wooden mask at its knees. Artefacts related to healing were also buried with it.

In a number of Siberian tribes, male shamans wear women's dress, perhaps suggesting a female origin to the craft. Similarly, in parts of Africa

today, men wear ceremonial masks of women's faces and headdresses, although in practice taking part in shamanic mask dances and ceremonies is now generally denied to African women, perhaps as a result of the paternalistic missionary attitudes.

Mother Goddess and Shamanism

There is evidence that in prehistoric times women shamans may have been seen as representatives of the Mother Goddess, and this connection has survived in a number of shamanic cultures. The Tetun people of the narrow central section of Timor, Indonesia, believe that women represent the sacred world, while men represent the secular. In ancient Korea, it was the prevailing all-female shamanic tradition that made possible the rule of the first queen in her own right. In AD 634, Sondok became the sole ruler of Silla and was especially famed for building the Tower of the Moon and Stars, the first observatory in the Far East. In her time, women shamans regulated state rituals and many others were hereditary family and village priestesses. The latter resolved neighbourhood quarrels, carried out rituals to ensure the fertility of people and the land, healed the minds, bodies and souls of the sick, and foretold the future. Sondok herself was a seer. She was followed by two more queens, and Korean women continued to occupy central roles in politics as they did in shamanism until Confucianism became influential in the fifteenth century. Even today, there are still female as well as male shamans in the region.

Women Shamans as Nature Priestesses

Shamanism is the oldest 'green' spirituality, maintaining balance and harmony in society and the individual. Shamans form a bridge between the essences of fish, birds, animals, rocks, and trees in this world, and the animal and helper spirits in the lower realms and the wise ancestors who, in the shamanic cosmology of many lands, reside in the upper realms with the Great Ones. For this reason, shamanism has become relevant to ecofeminists in the modern world. The American white witch Starhawk, for example, combines ecstatic ritual with seasonal celebrations to bring the natural cycles back into the lives even of city dwellers, and to raise awareness of our interconnectedness and dependency on the Earth.

From early times, women were regarded as the magicians of the tribe because of their ability to bring forth new life like the Earth Mother herself. In Greenland, it is the woman who returns the kidneys of a slaughtered seal to the sea and who, before cooking and eating, performs rituals of thanks and respect to both the animal which gave its life and the Mistress of the Herds.

Many of the deities of the herds and the sea were female, so it is not surprising that those originally chosen to negotiate with them were also women. Bugady Musun was the Siberian Mother Goddess of the Animals, an old but physically very powerful goddess who sometimes assumed the form of an elk. Zonget was a Siberian Mistress of the Herds. She ruled all birds, animals and the people who hunted them. Birds and animals would allow themselves to be trapped if she ordained it, and the shamans had to make sure that she was given offerings and that the creatures were treated with reverence so that the food supplies would continue. Ardwinna was the Celtic Goddess of the Wild Wood. She demanded an offering for every animal she allowed to be hunted, and rode on a wild boar (see also Sedna, page 113).

According to the Siberian Buryat myths, the first shaman was female. These myths say that an eagle was sent by the deities to teach the ways of the gods to men. But because men were unable to understand the eagle's wild cries and gestures, he flew away. The eagle then saw a young woman asleep at the foot of a tree. He made love to her, and their daughter was able to interpret the will of the gods to men. Thus the combination of the sky power of the eagle who sat at the top of the World Tree, which formed the axis of the world, and the female Earth power that was at its roots, founded the shamanic heritage.

One of the roles of the shaman was to maintain, and if necessary to restore, the balance between Father Sky and Mother Earth. In Mongolian shamanism, Mother Earth is called Itugen, and the name for a female shaman is derived from her name. Her daughter Umai is the womb goddess and caretaker of the unborn human souls roosting in the World Tree. Another daughter, Golomto, the Spirit of Fire, sits in the smoke *holis*, or hole, at the centre of the world. She is also present in the sacred centre of the family *kiva*, or yurt, where the smoke rises through the hole in the centre of the tent from the fire. In shamanic ritual, the ascending smoke forms the ladder to the upper world. The domestic world is thus a symbol of the sacred world.

Women and Shamanism

A shaman had to seek a lost soul to restore a patient's health – in traditional cultures, a person had up to four souls representing his or her different aspects, which might be lost in the upper or lower realms, or the Underworld, or even in high trees. In the modern world, we may find it hard to believe in literal soul loss – it has been said that this is because few of us have sat in the wilderness at midnight with only a tiny lamp as we follow the herds. We can, however, relate to symbolic soul loss, which may manifest itself as a cessation of a sense of empathy with those with whom we share our lives, a lack of energy or enthusiasm, an inability to relax or a disharmony with the natural cycles of the body. PMT, painful menstruation, extreme menopausal reactions, migraines, phobias, addictions and allergies may be symptoms of this dispiritedness.

Shamanism provides a powerful form of self-healing, and like the shamans we can travel in our spirit canoe down watercourses that lead deep into the earth or across oceans, ride a horse through the narrow passageways of the Earth womb or across the open plains, don feathered wings, or climb the World Tree to reach the upper world to find the missing part of ourselves. As the twentieth-century poet E.E. Cummings wrote: 'For whatever you lose like a you or a me, it's always yourself you find by the sea.' For women especially, using dance, drumming, rattles and chants to create an altered state of consciousness is a remarkably liberating form of spirituality in a society in which the wild, uninhibited side of the female psyche is still regarded with suspicion.

Creating a Healing Journey

Shamanic Chanting

The easiest stimulus is chanting. As children, we made up songs or hummed melodies, and we still experience the mental and physical release of singing in the bath or while engaging in physical work.

✿ Work with like-minded friends or where you will be undisturbed.

- Either sit or lie where you are comfortably supported, or let your feet move as you chant.

- Visualise golden light emanating from the throat and begin with the lowest note you can comfortably make and then the highest without any undue strain. This is your natural range, and you can experiment with sounds and chants that emanate spontaneously.

- Shamanic chants frequently use a pentatonic scale – five notes instead of the eight in the octave. You can find one example of the pentatonic scale by playing only the black notes on a piano.

- Allow words and sounds to form faster and faster until they are entirely spontaneous, then create a regular rhythm, perhaps of three or four words that can be repeated.

- Use the words to allow your mind to leave everyday concerns and rise on the sound. As you move, see your etheric or spirit body dancing or leaping out of your physical form, which can sink and relax, letting the sounds get gradually quieter and slower until they fade away. Fly free with the birds, swim in the deep blue ocean, travel down tunnels to explore lands of talking animals, personifications of our instinctive wisdom, where you may learn the answers to unspoken questions.

- You may find here a plant, a tree spirit, an animal or a wise woman who will offer healing, but as you explore what is essentially a journey through a waking dreamscape, you will understand what it is that has caused your soul loss.

- You may even see a huge sunbeam, moonbeam, star or rainbow bubbles that float towards you and surround you with light. You will feel this entering your body especially through the crown of your head and your heart, and it will fill your whole body. It is the joyful, vital part of your soul or psychic essence returning – it was not taken by spirits, as the ancients believed, but simply ceased to operate under stress or was overwhelmed by the negativity of others.

Drums

In all these methods, you can return when you want to, or will find that the experience ends spontaneously after a few minutes

♠ You may want to add or substitute a drumbeat for a chant. You can use anything from a child's drum to a drum set you have made yourself. Improvise with different hollowed-out containers, or stretch a piece of leather over a wooden tub. Many ethnic craft shops sell very cheap drums from different parts of the world.

♠ You should aim for a steady 240 drumbeats a minute that correspond to your brain waves. This takes care of the lower vibrations of the ear and is considered the single most effective tool for raising consciousness.

♠ Use hand contact, rather than drumsticks: drum with the thumbs and the sides of the hands until you have a steady rhythm, then increase the rhythm until you can feel it in every part of your body.

♠ You may find that you are swaying as you drum. This is a natural inducement to wriggling out of the physical body.

Rattles

Some shamans use a rattle, and this method addresses the higher vibrations of the ear.

You can buy rattles cheaply from music or craft shops, or make your own using beads, beans or rice inside a sealed container. Best of all is a gourd that can either be clasped between the hands or held by a wooden handle attached with a nail. Traditionally, rice is swished by a winnowing fan; you can alternatively make or buy a traditional rain stick (details on how to make rain sticks are contained in the *Complete Guide to Psychic Development*, see Further Reading, page 285). You can shake the rattle as you chant; as you do so, you will flow out of

your body and dive into the ocean or soar like the eagle whose wing-beat you can hear.

Stepping or Dancing Out of the Body

- Sit or lie in a comfortable place and play a compact disc or tape that features drumming, rattles or shamanic chants. There are many recordings of Native North and South American music, and of African drumbeats. I have listed some music suppliers at the back of the book (see page 290); listen to a selection of recordings and choose those that instinctively feel right.

- Sway backwards and forwards as you listen to the music to create the initial vibration, then continue the movement with your mind's eye.

- Dance yourself free or visualise stepping out of your body as if you were a hermit crab leaving a shell.

- Pull or wriggle yourself free of your physical body with your hands, as you would shed a tight wet-suit, or roll over in your mind's eye and leave it behind.

- As you dance or move, see your feet leaving the ground and continuing to move or dance as you rise into the sky or dive into the ocean. At this point, your physical body will stop moving and sit or lie motionless until you are ready to return from your journey with new knowledge and the truant soul.

VIRGIN MARY
The Perfect Mother

MARY IS THE personalised face of divinity within the Christian faith, and especially the Roman Catholic Church; as such, she has been the touchstone for women throughout the ages. She is portrayed as a gentle, nurturing loving mother with her infant on her knee, or as the sorrowing Mater Dolorosa, Mother of Sorrows, cradling her dead son.

With the coming of Christianity, Mary took over many of the functions of the pagan Mother Goddess in the lives of ordinary people, and assumed her healing role especially at the newly Christianised Lady wells and at wayside shrines, where women had come to ask for fertility or healing for themselves or their families for thousands of years.

Mary's attested apparitions number many thousands spanning almost every country in the globe, even where Christianity is not the dominant religion. The first of these apparitions was recorded in AD 40, even before Mary's death, when she appeared to encourage the dispirited St James the Apostle in Sargossa in north-eastern Spain. But even when she was conveying globally significant and secret messages, as she did at Fatima in Portugal in 1917, she usually appeared to simple peasant children who would not sully her words with official dogma or their own interpretations.

Yet although only mainly children could see Mary, none could doubt her presence. The Portuguese newspaper *O Dia* reported the scene at Fatima on 14 May 1917:

> '*As if like a bolt from the blue, the clouds were wrenched apart, and the sun at its zenith appeared in all its splendour. It began to revolve like the most magnificent fire wheel that could be imagined, taking on all the colours of the rainbow and sending forth multi-coloured flashes of light, producing the most astounding effect.*'

Mary has also come many times to ordinary women in dreams or visions in their homes, or in lonely places as they cried out for their own mothers in childbirth or in grief, or sought her comfort at their own passing. These

visitations are usually not witnessed, but they bring private messages of reassurance and comfort from a mother who herself experienced sorrow and fear. She came, for example, in a dream to young girl I know called Anna whose father was dying. Mary showed Anna a beautiful island where she promised the family would live after Anna's father had recovered, an event that came to pass six years later, when the family was given the opportunity to move to the Channel Islands. Anna recognised the cove and the steps where she had seen the Lady in the dream.

History of the Virgin Mary

There are remarkably few references to Mary, mother of Jesus in the Bible. Knowledge of Mary's own birth and childhood comes from early Christian writings, especially the Nativity of Mary, sometimes called the Protoevangelium of James. Because the Nativity of Mary was written less than sixty years after Mary's death, it is considered to be accurate because memories of her life were still vivid at the time.

Mary the Daughter

It is from the later *Golden Legend* by Jacobus Voragine, which was translated by William Granger Ryan for Princeton University Press in 1993, that details emerge of the early life of Mary. From this we learn, for instance, that Mary's mother Anna taught Mary to sew, embroider and read. Scenes of Mary and her mother are also depicted on the St Anne altarpiece created by Gerard Davis in about 1500–1520, which is now in the Washington Gallery of Art. Yet here, as in the Bible, details of Mary's emotions, or her reactions to the events of her life, are largely absent.

When Mary was three, Anna brought her to the temple to be dedicated as a temple maiden because, as is revealed in the Nativity of Mary, Anna had promised God that she would do this if she was allowed to have a child, although she was apparently barren and past her child-bearing years.

'And the priests took her and placed her on the third step of the altar, and the Lord God put grace upon her and she danced for joy with her feet, and the whole house of Israel loved her'.

NATIVITY OF MARY, 7.3.

'And her parents went home marvelling and praising God, because Mary did not turn back after them'.

NATIVITY OF MARY, 8.1.

Mary remained at the temple for ten years. She took a vow of life-long chastity while in temple service. At the age of thirteen, however, she was sent home by the temple priests to be betrothed to a much older man, Joseph, a Nazarean carpenter. Did she feel secret fear or resentment at being abandoned? Did she try to go to her mother when she was left with strangers at the age of three? We read the story through the eyes of modern psychology, and it is hard to understand such an unquestioning obedience or sense of duty.

Mary the Mother

Mary has been represented in Christian art as the ideal mother. The Renaissance led to the flowering of images depicting the maternal love of Mary for her infant; they include Raphael's *Alba Madonna* (1511), now in the National Gallery of Art in Washington, and Michelangelo's *Pieta*, an exquisite marble statue of Mary holding the crucified Christ carved in 1499 and now in St Peter's Basilica in Rome. According to the New Testament, Mary was a virgin, probably in her early teens, when she conceived Jesus through the intercession of the Holy Spirit. Mary was greeted by the angel Gabriel as 'full of grace, the Lord is with you' (Luke 1:28), a unique biblical phrase indicating, it is said, her freedom from the sin of humankind, which was given to her by the grace of God through her own miraculous conception by Anna.

We know both from the Bible and from the Nativity of Mary that Joseph was also visited by an angel, who reassured him that Mary's son was indeed the child of God. Mary's Magnificat offers the only soliloquy attributed to her in the Bible. In this beautiful hymn of praise, she says:

'*F*or behold from henceforth all generations shall call me blessed for he that is mighty hath done to me great things and Holy is his name.'

LUKE 1:17–9, 20

In the biblical representation of Mary, nothing is revealed of her emotions during the pregnancy, the birth or the visits from shepherds and wise men with precious gifts, apart from the enigmatic words:

'*B*ut Mary kept all these things, and pondered them in her heart.'

LUKE 2:19

This phrase is echoed through Mary's life, for she was in the background throughout Christ's earthly ministry. Her final act of love to her son, recorded in the Bible, is her vigil with him in his death agony. Mary's words or even her tears were again not recorded. All we are told is that as she stood at the foot of the cross:

'*W*hen Jesus saw his mother and the disciple John whom he loved, he said to his mother, "Woman, behold your son." Then he said to John, "Behold your mother."'

JOHN 19:26

Did Mary in fact hold her dead son in her arms, or was this an artistic interpretation of a mother's grief? Did she watch passively through all the long hours? Could any mother? Could any mother turn away?

Mary in the Folk Tradition

As if to compensate for the lack of official knowledge of Mary's everyday world, a rich folk tradition grew up showing the fallible but loving and sometimes angry woman. The English folk song *The Cherry Tree Carol*

suggests that though the angel assured Joseph that he could marry Mary with honour, Joseph was far from happy about Mary's pregnancy:

Then up spoke Virgin Mary so meek and so mild
Saying: 'Pluck me cherries Joseph for I am with child.'
Then Joseph flew in anger in anger so wild,
Saying: 'Let him pluck thee cherries who got thee with child.'

Another folk song, *The Bitter Withy*, would have been sung or heard by English peasant woman who visualised the Virgin Mary as a mother like themselves with their hopes, fears, troubles and unruly children. The willow, or withy tree, was sacred to the ancient Goddess of Death.

It came about on a bright summer's day
Small rain from the sky did fall
And our saviour asked his mother dear
If he might play at ball.

'O yes,' his mother Mary said,
'O yes my little young son.
But don't let me hear any mischief of you
In the time that you are gone.'

So it's up the hill and down the hill
Our sweet saviour ran,
Until he spied three rich young lords
A-playing in the sun.

'Oh we're all Lords and Ladies' Sons.
Born in the highest hall,
You're a poor carpenter's son.
And we won't play at ball.

So he built him a bridge of the beams of the sun
And over the river ran he,
Those three young lords followed after him,
And drowned were all three.

So Mary mild brought home her child,
And laid him across her knee.
And with a bundle of withy twigs,
She gave him lashes three.

In a secular age in which film stars and royalty reveal every detail of their thoughts, feelings and actions, it can seem hard to imagine Mary's quiet acceptance of her destiny which makes the Madonna not an impossible act to follow, but like many mothers, a woman who did her best. Even though Jesus may have been the Son of God, he was also her son.

Mothering Ritual to Bring You Closer to Your Mother

This ritual can be followed whether your mother is living or dead.

§ Take a picture or symbol of your own mother and surround it with flowers sacred to the Virgin Mary, such as the snowdrop, the lily, the rose or any white flowers.

§ Place a circle of pure white candles around the symbol; use as many or as few candles as you wish.

§ As you light each candle, speak or say in your mind the feelings that you would like to communicate to your mother were she present, such as gratitude, confusion, anger, grief, regrets, love, understanding, or perhaps a mixture of all of these.

§ If any of the emotions are sad or negative, take a dying or withered leaf or a tiny twig from a healing ash, a willow, or an olive for peace for each burden you wish to shed.

⚜ Burn the leaf in one of the candles, naming the sorrow or regret for the final time, then sit quietly in the candle light with only the most positive aspects of your relationship to recall.

⚜ Visualise your mother's face in the candle flame and send her love.

⚜ When the candles are burned through, put the flowers into water and place them where you can see them as you work or relax.

⚜ On the next day, contact your mother and perhaps send her a small bouquet of Mary flowers.

⚜ If your mother is no longer with you, go to a place where you were happy together and relive the joyful times, the jokes and the family legends. You may momentarily sense your mother's presence or detect her favourite fragrance. Alternatively, you may experience a sense of peace and being cared for, which can be equally rewarding.

WOMEN AND VOODOO

VOODOO, OR VODUN, has a very dark reputation, mainly because of the sensational media images of voodoo dolls with pins through the heart, zombies, the living dead who obey the command of their mistresses or masters, and malevolent hags who use footstep magic, in which the soil over which a person has walked is used to poison a victim. Just as witches are portrayed quite erroneously as dancing and fornicating with the Devil and drinking the blood of babies, so the dark side of voodoo, called *petro*, which involves curses and the infamous dolls and zombies, is very much a fringe element.

The negative power of voodoo resides in those who use the fears of its ability to kill by thought power to gain control, especially over vulnerable young people. As with all such corruptions of a religion, it is the secrecy surrounding the beliefs that enables the unscrupulous, who are rarely genuine practitioners, to manipulate the vulnerable through superstition, usually for financial gain. While I was writing this chapter I heard reports of young Nigerian girls who were secretly initiated by violence and threats in

the name of voodoo before being brought to England. This was done to enable a vice ring to control the girls' minds and sell them into prostitution abroad.

True voodoo is one of three similar religions brought to the Americas by the African slaves. It is still practised in Haiti as openly as Catholicism and sometimes in tandem with it. Voodoo grew up in the French-speaking colonies; in the Spanish colonies the new religion was called Santeria and in Portuguese Brazil Candomblé.

Many of the slaves came from what is now Dahomey in West Africa. In their ceremonies, worshippers would seek to be possessed by an orisha, much as some trance mediums allow their bodies and minds to be temporarily taken over by spirit helpers. Orishas are elemental spirits/ deities, formed of or closely identified with the elements of fire, earth, water or air, and the moon and stars. They are thus very potent but also volatile, and so must be appeased with prayers and offerings.

Women in Voodoo

Women play an important part in the voodoo religion, perhaps because of the strong matriarchal traditions of West Africa, where the power of any household was said to reside within the female breasts. They were also the ones to make a home in new lands under very difficult circumstances, and they kept the wisdom of the homelands alive in myth and in spiritual songs.

When the slaves were taken to the French, Spanish and Portuguese colonies, they were forbidden to follow their old religion. Instead of being destroyed, however, their beliefs became secret and mingled with the Catholic faith. The saints became identified with the orishas. For example, St Barbara, who is known as the keeper of lightning, became synonymous with Chango, the God of Thunder. St Barbara acquired this title because her father, who betrayed her, was struck down by a divine lightning bolt.

Voodoo

The name voodoo derives from the word *vodu*, meaning spirit or deity in the Fon language of Dahomey. The central aspect of voodoo is healing. Healers employ herbs and faith healing (with the help of Ioa and other spirits), and today incorporate Western medicine into voodoo. The priest-

hood contains both men (houngan) and women (mambo), who invoke the spirits at ceremonies during which members of the congregation become possessed by the spirits and go into a trance. A voodoo temple (houmfort) has a central post from which the Ioa descend to 'mount' the worshipper.

Voodoo thrived in New Orleans, with its unique blend of French, Spanish and Indian cultures. Today, it is estimated that up to fifteen per cent of the city's inhabitants practise voodoo. The famous voodoo queen of New Orleans was Marie Laveu, who was born in the city in 1794 and died in 1881. Her tomb in St Louis Cemetery Number One is covered with rosaries, flowers, coins and other offerings. A ritual for obtaining favours from the spirit of Marie Laveu involves marking the tomb with three red crosses, closing your eyes and rubbing your foot against the tomb three times while telling Marie what you want.

Marie, a free woman of African, Indian, French and Spanish descent, began as a hairdresser and later worked as a nurse. She then started practising voodoo and held rituals behind St Louis Cathedral, the prominent Catholic church in the French Quarter – and charged for her services. She became so famous and powerful that she acclaimed herself the Pope of Voodoo in the 1830s.

Santeria

Santeria is found in Spanish-speaking former colonies such as Cuba and Puerto Rico. One of its adherents, the Cuban musician Celina Gonzales, gained international fame with her song *Santa Barbara*, a hymn to the god Chango.

Santeria has two priesthoods. The first is open to women and men (the priests are called santeras and santeros respectively), and the second only to men. The male-only priests are called babalawos.

The priests and priestesses of Santeria are accomplished herbalists, and herbs and flowers make up the majority of the ingredients used in their magical rituals. The aim of a spell is to gain the 'ashe', or power, of the saints. Ashe is bestowed on humankind by the Creator God or Goddess, and the orishas transfer it to the congregation. An offering, known as ebbo, is made to the orishas when asking them for ashe to solve a problem. At birth, everyone is under the protection of a certain orisha who becomes a guardian angel, and it is this orisha that one receives when entering the priesthood.

For women in Santeria, the most important orisha is Yemaya. She is the Mother Goddess who guards women and children, and offers protection in pregnancy. She is also goddess of the moon and oceans, queen of all brujas y brujos – male and female sorcerers – and patron saint of sailors. She is identified with the Catholic saint Our Lady of Regla, whose feast day is on 7 September, and also with the Virgin Mary as Stella Maris, Star of the Sea (see Women of the Sea, page 112).

Oshun, youngest of the orishas and one of the most popular, controls the rivers as well as love, sexuality and money matters, the arts and human pleasures. She also rules over marriage. Ever eager to help her followers, she is slow to anger – but once angered she is the hardest orisha to appease and the most dangerous. When she cries this is a sure sign that she will grant whatever is asked of her. She is linked to the Catholic saint Our Lady of La Caridad del Cobre, whose feast day is on 8 September.

Divination is very important in Santeria and its sister religions, and the traditional African forms have been augmented with Western ones, such as astrology, the Tarot and palmistry.

Candomblé

The women slaves in Brazil took over the formerly all-male priestly duties when the men had to work in the fields. Their role as mistresses to white Portuguese masters also elevated their status, and they preserved their faith by claiming that the freedom to worship their gods helped to maintain their sexual skill and prowess.

The first Candomblé centre was set up in 1830 in the Salvador, now capital of Bahia, by three former female slaves called Maes de Santo, the Mothers of the Saints. They trained other women, the Daughters of the Saints, and even today their descendants perform political as well as spiritual duties in Candomble.

Afro-Brazilian traditions stress the importance of healing the spirit. The moment of greatest spiritual healing occurs when a person becomes one with his or her orisha during initiation. The followers of Candomblé call on exus, primal forces of all nature who act as divine tricksters and messengers to the gods.

Every year on 1 January, one of the biggest Candomblé celebrations, in honour of Iemanjá, the Sea Goddess, is held at beaches across the country (see also page 112). More than a million devotees dressed in white wade

into the ocean at dusk. Priestesses light candles, then purify and ordain new priestesses. As the sun sets, worshippers decorate a small wooden boat with candles, flowers, and figurines of the saints. At midnight the boat is launched. If it sinks, Iemanjá has accepted her children's offering and promised to help them for another year.

Hoodoo

Hoodoo, a form of folk magic that is very popular in the US today, draws upon the African tradition but has also incorporated Native North American and European magic. It applies many of the traditional practices of the African world, for example purifying the home by washing floors with salt, pepper and water at dawn, and the use of various roots and herbs for good fortune. Although Hoodoo has, in recent years, adopted elaborate incenses, powders, oils and candles (a scarlet candle representing two entwined lovers is, for example, burned to bring passion), much of its lore is based on the earlier tradition of using very simple ingredients available even to the poorest people. This perhaps partly accounts for its popularity.

The Mojo Bag

The mojo bag has spread in popularity even beyond Hoodoo, and is, like the Native American medicine bundles, used by people interested in New Age concepts who seek a traditional focus of power. The term mojo probably comes from a corruption either of the European word magic, or more likely of the West African word *mojuba*, which means a prayer of praise. The original African medicine bags were used by diviners, many of whom were women, and these bags contained animal bones and shells. People in many lands still create divinatory mojo bags, which now often contain crystals or marked stones (see also Crystal and Rune Divination, pages 163 and 201).

Mojo bags are small bags containing an odd number of symbols from 1 to 13; these symbols are associated with particular energies. They are generally made of red flannel, but can be in different colours

or even leather. For example, green can be used for money, white for a new baby, scarlet for love, and pale blue for domestic harmony. Mojo bags containing herbs, natural substances and man-made symbols are created for almost every purpose. For example, the root of the orchid that is popularly called Lucky Hand Root is placed in a bag to bring luck to gamblers.

- A protective mojo bag might contain herbs such as angelica root, salt and pepper, and perhaps an animal or bird bone.

- A prosperity bag could contain a silver dollar or other silver coin, plus basil or dried kelp, wrapped in a green currency note. High John the Conqueror root, lodestones and sugar also bring money.

- A love mojo bag would include a silver heart, lavender and a lock of the lover's hair.

- A fidelity bag might contain a pair of lodestones, ivy, yarrow, bay and a gold ring.

- A bag to remove bad luck or break the hold of a possessive lover could hold broken chains and rings, salt and rosemary.

- A fertility bag might contain an ear of corn, a tiny silver knife, an empty blue-bird eggshell and a doll.

A few drops of liquid are traditionally sprinkled on the bag after it has been filled to empower it. This may be either a specially bought Hoodoo oil or alcohol. Whisky attracts money, barley wine fertility. In the past, sexual fluids were used for passion, and urine for protection.

Mojo bags are carried around the neck on a cord, in a pocket or slung around the hips. They are always kept out of sight. Those protecting homes or work premises are kept near the door, again out of sight, for it is believed that if a mojo bag is touched by someone other than the user, it loses its power and good fortune.

FERTILITY SYMBOLS
Palaeolithic Times to Twentieth-century Africa

I DID NOT REALLY understand the power of fertility figurines and amulets until I visited the newly opened African rooms at the British Museum in London. Here I discovered that in the pots and carvings of a civilisation that has not lost connection with its early roots, the clay and wood, themselves born of the Earth, can, by being fashioned into images of fecundity, act as a powerful channel for transmitting the fertility of the Earth into human lives.

Early Fertility Figurines

What has survived as evidence from early preliterate societies in ancient Europe are female stone figurines that perhaps celebrated and also stimulated (by a process of sympathetic magic) fertility in a woman and the animals on which tribes depended for food. It is very likely that countless other Mother Goddess images made from less durable clay, wood and bone were created that have been lost over the millennia. As is the practice in some African societies today, such figurines may have been given as dolls to young girls, which were adorned with symbols of fecundity when they reached puberty, and they were perhaps held by women in childbirth as they called out to the Great Mother.

It is speculated that the early hunter-gatherer societies worshipped the Earth Mother as the giver of all life and fertility, and that menstruation, pregnancy and childbirth were thus likewise regarded as sacred. The *Venus of Willendorf*, the earliest fertility figurine, dates from around 24,000–22,000 BC and is made of limestone. She is just under four and a half inches high, with full, voluptuous breasts, buttocks and thighs, a deliberately emphasised genital area and a swollen stomach. As is the case with similar figures (more than a hundred and thirty have been found in total) she has no face, and rows of plaited hair are wrapped around her head.

A particular characteristic of Palaeolithic Mother Goddess figurines is the lack of feet. It may have been that such images were private icons that could be held in the hand by women as a fertility token and also during labour. Alternatively, they may have served as a focus for fertility rites for the

herds as well as for humans, and were perhaps placed in the Mother Earth herself by the pointed end, and carried from place to place as the tribes followed the herds.

As civilisations evolved, so the importance of fertility was linked to the continuation of the blood line. This became increasingly significant since both titles and property required an unbroken link of descent in order to prevent wars when a leader died. This need filtered down to even those who had the humblest dwellings or tools to pass on to a new generation.

Fertility Symbols in Ancient Egypt

In Ancient Egypt, the Nile was important because it gave fertility to the land when it flooded. Nile creatures such as the fish, the hippopotamus and the crocodile were considered deities of human fertility. Heket, the Frog Goddess, assisted in childbirth, as did Tauret, Taueret or Tawaret, the hippopotamus-headed Goddess, who ruled over conception and pregnancy and was invoked for safe and easy birth. Images of these goddesses were carved on amulets, and their statues were given offerings by women at domestic as well as at temple altars. Mummified parts of the crocodile and frog were prized by women as fertility icons, while the thigh bone of the hippopotamus was a male potency symbol.

Clay, wooden or stone images of nude women with the pubic triangle clearly marked were offered to Hathor, the Ancient Egyptian Goddess of Wisdom and Music, who was closely connected with sexuality and fertility. These offerings were made as requests for children or in thanks for safe births. Statues of the Egyptian Goddess Isis holding the infant Horus celebrated woman as the mother and were powerful fertility icons (see also The Black Madonna, page 224).

Celtic Fertility Symbols

The Celts had fertility figurines that survived into the Middle Ages and beyond. Sheelagh-na-gig is an abstract Celtic figure of a hag-like, female form, probably the Crone form of Brighid the Triple Goddess. She is depicted squatting, and holds her vulva open as though she is about to give birth. As late as the sixteenth century, her image appeared on carvings in churches in Ireland and in parts of England, sometimes over the entrance,

which symbolised the entry into the womb of the Mother. One example of this can be found at Killinaboy in Ireland, a church that is now ruined. Sheelagh-a-na-gigs are also found in Ireland on stone crosses, especially those that are situated at crossroads and on moorlands. Small Sheelagh statues may have been used by mothers who were in labour, and some Wiccan mothers today use a Sheelagh figure for this purpose.

Fertility images of the Celtic and pre-Celtic Triple Goddess were also cast into sacred wells by women who wished to become pregnant. The Triple Goddess well in Minster, Kent was excavated in 1990–1991 by Brian Slade, President of the Sheppey Archaeological Society, and his team. Ian, one of the archaeologists at the site, was up to his waist in well water when he found a small metal figurine. Brian identified it as a three-headed pregnant woman, with no legs, squatting as though about to give birth, and dated it to possibly pre-Celtic times. Experts later confirmed the accuracy of this identification.

It is speculated that the metal figurine represented an early form of the Triple Goddess Brighid. It may have been thrown into the well by a rich, childless woman, or else it could have been an original mould for wax fertility images, which had perhaps been dropped into the water by accident. This theory is strengthened by the discovery of fragments of beeswax in the well which, when pieced together, made up a Triple Goddess image. Such swollen-bellied figurines may have been powerful pleas from distant ages for a child from the Mother of all life.

Nine months to the day after Ian, the archaeologist, had found the image, his wife gave birth to a daughter after years of late miscarriages for which doctors could find no cause or cure. Five other 'miracle' babies have been born to parents who were experiencing fertility or pregnancy difficulties and have handled the figurine.

Fertility Icons in the African Tradition

Many African peoples believe that women are closely linked with the natural world, which is regarded as the source of creation, warmth and light, while men are linked with the worlds of laws, weaponry, destruction, death and coldness. As the source of life, woman is thus sacred.

Women make the vast majority of domestic pots in Africa. These pots have great magical significance as representations and containers of the life-giving powers of the potter, and through her of the Great Mother (see also

Cauldron Goddesses, page 237). Pregnant women do not make pots because they already have demands on their fertility; only men or post-menopausal women can decorate pots with animals or human figures because it is thought that if a fertile woman did this, it would compromise her creative power.

Pottery is regarded as one of the most ancient crafts and may have given birth to metalworking if the techniques for this were discovered during the firing process. In the sub-Saharan region, the wives of smiths are generally potters.

In West Africa, the senior female potter in a village is generally also the midwife; she is usually married to the blacksmith, who will combine this role with that of undertaker. Because of the powers over life and death held by this couple, the clay pots and images created by them are regarded as containing great supernatural power. For this reason, disease may be trapped in the jars the woman makes. Among other African peoples too, an older female potter will be the village healer. She will smear an afflicted part of a sick person with clay, and then create a pot from this that the patient will keep in his or her hut until recovery.

For me, perhaps the most fascinating ritual vessel is one that I saw in the British Museum. It dates from the early twentieth century and came from the Bauchi people in Nigeria. It is shaped in the design of female genitalia. A young man would sleep with it beside his bed, make offerings in it at the harvest for good fortune, drink from it only if his best friend used it as well, and finally be buried with it.

Among the Bemba women of Zambia, *mbusa*, or ritual pots, were given to girls in puberty; each of these pots contained lessons about female life in its shape. For example, a clay mortar and pestle, symbolising the union of an ideal couple, would be presented to a girl with ritual singing and chanting at the time when she began courting. At weddings, new pots would be made for the bride, while at funerals pots would be broken to symbolise the severing of life. Other vessels would contain offerings linking the everyday and spirit worlds, and would provide a safe location for the spirits of the dead. Sometimes a ground-up pot belonging to a deceased person would be incorporated into a new pot.

Even the ornately decorated vessels made by men or older women would frequently contain a female fertility image. For example, at the museum I saw a heavily ornamented pot in the shape of a pregnant woman, again created during the twentieth century, from the Edo people of Benin in Nigeria. It had been placed on a woman's shrine to the God Oloukun and kept filled with river water to attract fertility.

Woodcarving is almost an entirely male occupation throughout Africa, although it may also be practised by post-menopausal women. However, woodcarvings also express the power of the female. Among the Yoruba people, a kneeling or seated female or a woman nursing a baby may be carved on house posts to acknowledge that the power of the household and life resides in the breasts of the child-bearing female.

Most of the emblems of the Luba royal family, who live in the area of the Democratic Republic of the Congo, also incorporate the female form, for they regard women as custodians of royal secrets, and acknowledge the dependency of men on female fertility.

Making a Clay Fertility Jar

This can be a vessel for representing not only physical fertility, but also any venture or area of your life in which you may need inspiration and creativity.

᪥ Take a large ball of clay and fashion a pot either on a wheel, or by using clay coils to create the shape and then smoothing them down.

᪥ If possible, work in sunlight. Otherwise light yellow candles and surround yourself with yellow flowers, fruits and vegetables.

᪥ As you work, visualise the golden light entering the clay. You can, if you wish, recite a mantra over and over again, for example: 'Earth give birth, make of worth, this vessel of fertility.'

᪥ When you have finished, leave the pot to dry in the sun or have it fired in a kiln at a pottery.

᪥ Alternatively, buy a large ceramic pot and paint it with designs of spirals, suns and moons, snakes, fruits and flowers, again reciting a mantra as you work.

᪥ When the pot is finished, sprinkle it with nine grains of sea salt, pass around it nine circles of smoke from a frankincense or sandalwood incense stick, and nine circles of fire from a yellow candle. Finally, anoint it with nine drops of olive oil, saying: 'Mother of fertility, mother of life, bring warmth, bring inspiration and abundance, for growth, for maturation and fruition of this my venture.'

    ❧ In your pot, place symbols of fertility, such as a few grains, nuts, olives or seeds.

    ❧ Each day, add fresh fertility symbols to the pot, repeating your mantra and naming a special project that you wish to bring to fulfilment.

    ❧ On the seventh day, bury the contents of the pot in soil and begin again. Continue this until your venture has taken seed.

EVE

Impure Lover and Mother or Freedom Fighter?

I am Eve, great Adam's wife,
Tis I that robbed my children of Heaven,
By rights I should have gone upon the Cross.
There would be no ice in any place,
There would be no hell; there would be no sorrow,
There would be no fear, if it were not for me.

FROM THE LAMENT OF EVE, AN ANCIENT IRISH POEM TRANSLATED BY
WALTER DE LA MARE (1873–1956).

The view of Eve that was propagated from the time of St Paul onwards was that she and her female descendants were the causes of all sorrow and sin. Lilith, Adam's first wife, was regarded as even more evil, because she committed the ultimate crime of refusing to submit sexually to her husband (see Lilith, page 64). She was blamed for every male infidelity through Christian times and beyond.

Eve and the Mother Goddess

Eve's name means 'she who gives life', and even Adam referred to her as Mother of All. After the Fall, however, according to Genesis 40:1, 'Much labour was created for every man, and a heavy yoke is upon the sons of Adam from the day they come forth from their mother's womb till the day they return to the mother of all.'

Although according to ancient myth Adam was created from menstrual blood and clay, by the time of the Genesis 2 account dating from around 900 BC, God makes Eve out of the rib of Adam. In this version, therefore, the Mother did not give birth to Adam her son/consort in the manner recorded in myth for millennia before, but she was herself extracted from his rib by the Father God. As in the case of the Greek Zeus who produced Athena from his head, this was an usurpation of the natural female birth processes.

Interestingly, even the symbol of the rib has a precedent in earlier goddess worship. Ninhursag, the Sumerian Mother God, healed the rib of Enki, Father God of the Sweet Waters and later the patriarch, through the creation of Nin-ti (*ti* means both rib and life), and Nin-ti created infant's bones from their mothers' ribs as they grew within the womb.

Punishment for Seeking Knowledge

In the Garden of Eden, Adam and Eve could eat freely of the Tree of Life (itself a Mother Goddess symbol in many early cultures), but not of the Tree of Knowledge or Wisdom. Because Eve tempted Adam to eat the forbidden fruit, herself listening to the serpent (who is sometimes associated with Lilith), Adam and all his descendants lost their immortality. The Mother Goddess who took the deceased into her womb and gave them rebirth was therefore now replaced by death with no hope of rebirth. According to Paul and the Church Fathers, this dreadful curse was transmitted when men had sex with Eve's daughters, who by their weaker nature shared the ongoing blame for tempting men.

Of course, all this was not spelled out in Genesis but grew over the centuries as women were generally downgraded. The Greek philosopher Aristotle (384–322 BC) invented the theory that the generative process owed its origins to the semen of the male, and that the female was a mere

hatchery. Moreover, he wrote that the creation of a female child was due to a flaw in nature and in the egg.

St Paul (AD 3–68) was a great advocate of celibacy and some say that he himself chose to be castrated to rid himself of the repressed sexuality that burned in him. In 1 Corinthians 7:29 he declares: 'Blessed are they who have wives as if they had none, for they shall inherit God', and in 2 Corinthians 6:16 he states: 'Blessed are they who have kept the flesh pure, for they shall become a temple of God.' St Paul advocated marriage as an antidote to uncontrolled sexuality, and often quoted the sentiment that it was better to marry than to burn.

This doctrine of original sin and the culpability of Eve were enshrined by the Church Father St Augustine (AD 354–430), who referred to Eve as the Devil's gateway: 'For we were all in that one man who fell into sin through the woman who was made from him.' Eve was also punished by God with a twin curse: 'In sorrow thou shalt bring forth children and thy desire shall be unto thy husband and he shall rule over thee.'

Second Eve

Mary was the Second Eve, who was free from sin because of her own immaculate conception by her mother Anna and because of her obedience to God in her role as perfect mother and wife (see also Virgin Mary, page 257). The Second Eve and Christ, the Second Adam, did not, however, restore the promise of rebirth for all. Eternal life was only for the faithful who worshipped the one prescribed God, a means by which people were for centuries kept within the parameters of the knowledge ordained as desirable for the populace by the Church Fathers. Women too, were for centuries still under the rule of their fathers, their husbands, the Church Fathers and every other male authority figure – including, if a woman was widowed, her eldest son.

Magic of Childbirth

The curse of painful childbirth was not lifted with the coming of the Second Eve. Moreover, the execution of many wise women and midwives during the Burning Times between the fifteenth and seventeenth centuries meant the end of the herbal pain relief given by midwives to women in

labour, as well as of effective methods of contraception (see also Witchcraft, page 215).

The female power inherent in the birthing process remained a problem for the Church and for male society in general. Indeed, in many societies throughout the world the new mother was so endowed with supernatural power that she could, it was believed, threaten the safety of those around her, especially her husband if he came too close. In Greenland until fairly recent times, women who were in labour or who had just had a baby were credited with the ability to control a storm and calm it. They had only to go out of doors into the wind, fill their mouths with air and come back into the house and blow it out again. Various rituals were created to minimise the apparent dangers posed by women who were undergoing the birthing process.

In Tahiti, a woman who had given birth was secluded for two or three weeks in a hut on sacred ground. During the time of her seclusion, she was not allowed to touch provisions and had to be fed. If the father touched the child during this period, he was subject to the same quarantine.

Romany women were regarded as *mochard*, or unclean, both when giving birth and for a period afterwards. Women who were in labour would leave the living wagon or tent so that it would not be defiled by the birth. It is recorded that until thirty or forty years ago, some New Forest gypsy women used to go alone to a particular holly tree in a sheltered spot along Godshill Ridge to give birth. More frequently, however, a special tent was set aside for women who were in labour and men were banished from the scene. The gypsy mother had her own set of crockery and did not prepare food for several weeks before and after the birth of her child. The mother and child might remain in the tent for up to two months, after which everything the woman had used during the birth was burned.

Churching of Women

The Christian Church had very similar if more formalised rituals that were inherited from Judaism. The first biblical reference to the purification of women, which has shaped both Jewish and Christian ritual, is found in Leviticus 12, where a woman who gives birth to a son is counted as ritually unclean for forty days and for twice as long after the birth of a female child. After this period of purification, the mother must go to the temple and bring the required offerings to the priest as an atonement.

Luke, Chapter 2 relates how on the fortieth day after Jesus's birth, the Virgin Mary brought him into the temple and was purified. In accordance with Jewish practice, five shekels were offered to God to buy back a first-born son.

The rite of purification of a mother after childbirth did not officially find its way into prayer books of the Western Church until about the eleventh century. The mother waited for the priest kneeling at the church porch, her head covered in a white cloth. The priest would arrive with two servers carrying candles and holy water and lead her into the church, where she was cleansed with holy water. This tradition was changed in the 1552 prayer book: the concept of cleansing the mother was removed and the ritual given its modern name of The Thanksgiving of Women after Childbirth, commonly called the Churchynge of Women. The puritans abandoned this ritual altogether during the Interregnum, much to the indignation of many mothers, who felt that the ceremony offered recognition of their role as mothers and marked their safe delivery from childbirth. Many mothers arranged secret ceremonies thereafter.

The churching ceremony recommenced after the Restoration of Charles II in 1660, but it was never again as popular as it had been. Only women in wedlock might be churched. Unmarried mothers had to repent of their sins openly in church on a Sunday before they were allowed to participate in the ceremony.

In modern times, the Churching of Women has been transformed into a celebration of the birth and recognises the wider context of the family, although the older ceremony still appears near the backs of prayer books. For example, the 1979 American Prayer Book contains a rite called A Thanksgiving for the Birth or Adoption of a Child. Here the joy of new life is celebrated and is welcomed into the individual family and the family of the Church. In modern Australia too, there are such ceremonies as the Thanksgiving for the Gift of a Child, which are held by the Uniting Church.

LABYRINTHS
Walking the Sacred Spiral

&

THE LABYRINTH IS based on the spiral, one of the most ancient Mother Goddess symbols. It is a universal symbol of transformation, created to represent the search by humankind for its core of divinity. The basic labyrinth motif has been discovered on a figure in the Ukraine that may date back to 15,000 BC or even earlier, and it is possible that labyrinths have always been connected with the worship of the Earth Mother, whose womb they represent.

The most famous labyrinth is connected with a possible fertility cult on Minoan Crete. According to Greek myth set down hundreds of years after the fall of the Minoan civilisation, the labyrinth held the mythical Minotaur, who had the head of a bull and the body of a man. In the myth, the Minotaur was created when the Sea God Poseidon enchanted Pasiphaë, Queen of Crete, so that she would mate with the snow-white bull. Poseidon had sent the bull to her husband King Minos, and Minos had angered Poseidon by refusing to sacrifice the animal.

The bull symbol is, however, far more ancient than these myths suggest. It dates back to early Neolithic images of the Earth Mother giving birth to the bull/Horned God figure who was her son/consort.

Greek Myth and Ariadne the Goddess

Greek myth relates how the Minotaur was imprisoned in a labyrinth in the palace of Knossos on the island of Crete. The Cretans ruled the seas, and each year demanded tribute from Athens of six young men and six maidens, who were sacrificed to the Minotaur. The Greek hero Theseus volunteered to go with those to be sacrificed in the hope of killing the monster. The Weaver of Fate Goddess Ariadne has in this myth become the daughter of King Minos, rather than his goddess. She naturally fell in love with the hero and gave him thread to unreel as he went into the labyrinth. When he had slain the monster, Theseus followed the thread back to find his way out.

In 1900, the British archaeologist Arthur Evans unearthed a large, complex palace at Knossos on Crete. In it was found evidence of a possible

bull-worshipping cult, and murals depict the fantastic activities of bull dancers. In these murals, young males and females who may have performed with bulls in an arena are shown grabbing bulls by the horns and somersaulting over their backs.

The complexity of the layout of the Knossian palace – a succession of palace buildings had been built on top of each other over the centuries – would perhaps have made possible the construction of a labyrinth beneath the palace. Such a labyrinth may have been connected with bull and goddess worship rather than with imprisoning a monster.

The word labyrinth derives from *labrys*, meaning double-headed axe. The double axe may have been the instrument used to ritually sacrifice a bull. One theory is that immediately before the annual sacrifice, the Cretan High Priest or King, wearing bull horns or a bull mask (and thus resembling the Minotaur) ritually mated with the Goddess Ariadne in the form of her chief priestess or the Queen. According to this theory, he would enter the subterranean labyrinth (representing the womb of the Mother), in the centre of which Ariadne waited. Their yearly consummation of the sacred marriage ensured the fertility of the land and the sea.

Power of Theseus

Minoan culture in Crete may have been a Goddess-worshipping one for two thousand years or more, and Ariadne was perhaps not the helpful virgin but a powerful fertility mother whose oracular priestesses used snakes in their divination (female figurines with coiled snakes around their arms have been found on Crete). Disruptions on Crete in around 1450 BC may have weakened Crete, and according to later Greek myth it fell prey to invaders from the Greek mainland led by Theseus.

As a great navigator, Theseus hardly needed a ball of thread to find his way out of the labyrinth. So what was he seeking from Ariadne? Reassurance as he entered the darkness of the labyrinth, which was outside the sway of even the mighty Poseidon? Recognition of his position as a hero/king through a ritual mating before or immediately after killing the sacred bull? Theseus took Ariadne away with him, it is said willingly, to the world where the Sky Gods held sway. However, he abandoned her on the journey to his

home on the Aegean island of Naxos, perhaps because she refused to recant her goddess worshipping.

Labyrinths: the Path of the Mother Goddess

Just as labyrinths may have had a religious significance for the Minoans, so they can be found as symbols of the Great Mother in cultures as far apart as those of the Hopi Indians of North America and the Scandinavians. The Hopi called the seven-path labyrinth 'mother within the earth'. Hindu midwives used the *yantra*, a labyrinthine geometric shape on which mothers meditated while giving birth. This was believed to help women dilate and to reduce the pain of contractions. In Scandinavia, sailors created and walked through labyrinths marked out with stones or drawn in the earth to raise winds when they were becalmed, or to control storms that made setting out to sea impossible.

More than thirty ancient stone labyrinths have survived in Sweden, some dating from the Bronze Age. The powers believed to be magically held by witches and women who had just given birth could be invoked by men by praying to Nerthus the Earth Mother while walking the sacred spiral. In parts of Sweden and Finland, between the Spring Equinox and Midsummer, games are still held in which a maiden stands in the centre of a labyrinth and youths compete to rescue her. This custom may date back to ancient fertility rites in honour of Nerthus.

In the Middle Ages, labyrinth designs appearing on the floors of large churches and cathedrals symbolised the winding pathway to the inner mysteries. The most famous indoor labyrinth is in Chartres Cathedral. This eleven-circuit design, built around AD 1200, is divided into four quadrants, each with seven sharp turns. It was originally walked for meditation purposes, and also by would-be pilgrims as a substitute for the journey to the Holy Land. Although today there are chairs over parts of the labyrinth, pilgrims still walk the sacred spiral undeterred. Mother Goddess symbolism is also strong at Chartres, which has a former Mother Goddess well nearby; a statue of the Black Madonna stood in the crypt until the 1790s (see page 227).

In modern times, the Reverend Dr Lauren Artress has revived the labyrinthine form at the Grace Cathedral of San Francisco. More than a million people have walked the labyrinth in the grounds of the cathedral. She attributes the rise in popularity of the labyrinth to the realisation that

modern culture has lost touch with the spiritual world – 'the web of creation has been thrown out of balance', she writes.

Using the Labyrinth

Walking or dancing through labyrinths creates an altered state of consciousness akin to a light trance. Moreover, the action is said to activate the inherent magic in this sacred geometric form and in the energies within the Earth. This is the case whether the labyrinth is cut in turf, drawn in soil or sand, created with high earth walls, or marked out with seeds or corn. Crop circles that appear spontaneously in fields have reproduced the spiral form, and some people interpret this as a message from the Earth Mother (see also Gaia, page 16).

You may be lucky enough to have a labyrinth near your home in a church or in a sacred spot. If you have a particularly large garden or yard, or a room with an uncarpeted floor, you can mark out a labyrinth in paint, chalk or with small stones. Some women paint a labyrinth and place a rug or carpet on top, or make one with a long rope that can be fixed at various points to the floor. With patience, you can even make a seven-circuit labyrinth with shrubs or perennial flowers, choosing those that bloom at different times of the year. Alternatively, photocopy, draw or trace a labyrinth design on to paper or card. There are many different designs that can be downloaded from the World Wide Web for inspiration. You can also draw the spiral in earth or sand so that you connect with Mother Earth. On a seashore, you can make a labyrinth just below the high-tide line and let the sea carry it away when you have finished.

When you wish to meditate, trace the pattern of the spirals with your finger, allowing the design to guide your hand around the circuits to the centre. Visualise yourself walking around the spiral, perhaps deep beneath a palace, on a shore or between green hedges, your feet moving rhythmically along the well-trodden path of the ages. Colouring or painting the labyrinth also aids meditative states.

Suggestions for Labyrinth Work

- If possible, work in a sheltered spot just before dawn outdoors, or near an open window indoors. You can illuminate the path dimly with small candles, or with electric torches if it is windy.

- As you walk or dance through the labyrinth, allow the path to guide you inwards from where you stand.

- As you walk inwards, shed any worries, doubts or trivial concerns that cloud your consciousness, so that you feel lighter and less connected with the mundane world.

- Drop seeds or herbs such as dried lavender flowers on the path to symbolise your concerns as you continue to move inwards. You may wish to rewrite the legend so that it is the power of the Goddess within you that is going to the centre to rescue the temporarily lost or overburdened woman that you have become. Welcome the darkness and stillness as a warm, enveloping blanket.

- When you reach the centre, sit quietly with your eyes closed and allow the darkness and silence to restore your inner self. Do not seek answers or contact guides, but let yourself become the darkness.

- Open your eyes. When you feel restored and you can see the dawn breaking, move outwards again, pausing to extinguish the outer candles, for you are now filled with growing inner light.

- Once out of the labyrinth, dance in a spiralling motion to absorb the power from the Earth, and raise your arms high to be filled with the growing light from the sky.

- As with the Beauty Way described in the section on Native North American Medicine Women (see page 244), if you cannot work near the time of the dawn, walk outwards towards a huge golden candle.

- If your life seems especially tangled, knot together threads of natural fibres representing your anger, pain or confusion, saying as you work: 'Tangle the anger, tangle the pain, by these knots make me free again.'

§ When you reach the centre of the labyrinth you can cut through the knots with a silver knife, saying: 'Tangle the anger tangle the pain, I cut the knots and leave the pain.'

§ Leave the knots behind you if you are working on a seashore, and let the sea carry them away along with the used labyrinth. Alternatively, take the knots outside and bury them near the entrance, scattering any remaining seeds on top to bring new life.

You can also use the labyrinth walk with a partner or lover to heal wounds and doubts. Sit together in the centre of the labyrinth holding hands and make love as dawn breaks.

FURTHER READING

General Goddess and Feminist Mythology Titles

Baring, Anne and Cashford, Jules, *The Myth of the Goddess*, Arkana, 1999
Budapest Zsuzsanna, E., *The Grandmother of Time*, Harper, 1989
Budapest, Z., *The Holy Book of Women's Mysteries*, Harper Row, 1990
Condren, Mary, *The Serpent and the Goddess*, Harper and Row, 1989
Downing, Christine, *The Goddess: Mythological Images of the Feminine*, Crossroad
    Publishing, 1984
Ehrenberg, Margaret, *Women in Prehistory*, British Museum Press, 1995
Engelsman, Joan C., *The Feminine Dimension of the Divine*, Westminster Press,
    1989
Gadon, Elinor W., *The Once and Future Goddess*, Aquarian Press, 1990
Gimbutas, Marija, *The Gods and Goddesses of Old Europe*, Thames & Hudson,
    1986
Graves, Robert, *The White Goddess*, Faber and Faber, 1988
Guiley, Rosemary Ellen, *Encyclopedia of Mystical and Paranormal Experience*,
    Grange Books, 1991
Harding, Esther, *Women's Mysteries, Ancient and Modern*, Harper and Row, 1971
Larrington, Carolyne, *The Feminist Companion to Mythology*, Pandora, 1991
Monaghan, Patricia, *The Goddess Companion*, Llewellyn, 1999
Walker, Barbara, *The Encyclopedia of Women's Myths and Secrets*, Pandora, 1983

Alien Abductions

Randles, Jenny, *The Complete Book of Aliens and Abductions*, Piatkus, 2000

Angels and Fairies

Burnham, Sophie, *A Book of Angels*, Ballantine, 1999
Bord, Janet, *Fairies – Real Encounters with Little People*, Michael O'Mara, 1997
Briggs, Katherine, *The Fairies in English Tradition and Literature*, Routledge and
    Kegan Paul, 1967
Daniel, Alma, Wylie, Timothy and Ramer, Andrew, *Ask your Angels*, Piatkus,
    1999

Candle Magic

Buckland, Ray, *Advanced Candle Magic*, Llewellyn, 1996
Eason, Cassandra, *Candle Power*, Blandford, 1999
Larkin, Chris, *The Book of Candle Making: Creating Scent, Beauty & Light*,
    Sterling Publications, 1998

Celtic Spirituality

Anderson, Rosemarie, *Celtic Oracles*, Piatkus, 1999
Bradley, Zimmer Marion, *The Mists of Avalon*, (fiction) Sphere, 1988
Ellis Berresford, Peter, *Celtic Women*, Constable, 1995
Green, Miranda, *Dictionary of Celtic Myth and Legend*, Thames & Hudson, 1992

Crystals, Healing and Divination

Bourgault, Luc, *The American Indian Secrets of Crystal Healing*, Quantum, 1997
Cunningham, Scott, *Encyclopedia of Crystal, Gem and Metal Magic*, Llewellyn, 1991
Eason, Cassandra, *Crystals talk to the Woman Within*, Quantum, 2000

Dark Feminine Power

Begg, Ean, *The Cult of the Black Madonna*, Arkana, 1995
Keane, Patrick, *Yeats, Joyce, Ireland, and the Myth of the Devouring Female*, University of Missouri, 1988
Matthews, Caitlin, *Sophia, Goddess of Wisdom*, Mandala, 1991

Divination and Astrology

Eason, Cassandra, *Complete Guide to Psychic Development*, Piatkus, 1997
Eason, Cassandra, *Pendulum Dowsing*, Piatkus, 2000
Eason, Cassandra, *Runes talk to the Woman Within*, Quantum, 2000
Eason, Cassandra, *Tarot talks to the Woman Within*, Quantum, 2000
Fenton, Sasha, *Predicting the Future*, Piatkus, 1999
Nichols, Sallie, *Jung and Tarot*, Samuel Weiser Inc.,1988

Individual Goddesses and Calendars

Durdin-Robertson, Lawrence, *The Year of the Goddess, a Perpetual Calendar of Festivals*, Aquarian Press, 1991
Kinsley, David R., *Hindu Goddesses*, University of California, 1988

Healing, Aura and Chakras

Brennan, Barbara Ann, *Hands of Light: a Guide to Healing through the Human Energy Field*, Bantam Publishers, 1987
Eason, Cassandra, *Aura Reading*, Piatkus, 2000
Eden, Donna, *Energy Medicine*, Piatkus, 1999

Incenses and Oils

Cunningham, Scott, *Complete Book of Oils, Incenses and Brews*, Llewellyn, 1991
Dunwich, Gerena, *Wicca Garden, a Witch's Guide to Magical and Enchanted Herbs and Plants*, Citadel, 1996

Magic and Ritual

Bowes, Sue, *Woman's Magic*, Piatkus, 2000

Eason, Cassandra, *Complete Guide to Magic and Ritual*, Piatkus, 1999
Eason, Cassandra, *Every Woman a Witch*, Quantum, 1996
Matthews, Caitlin and John, *The Western Way: a Practical Guide to the Western Mystery Tradition*, Arkana, 1994
Fortune, Dion, *Applied Magick*, Samuel Weiser, 2000
Fortune, Dion, *The Goat Foot God*, (fiction) Societies of the Inner Light, 1991
Fortune, Dion, *Moon Magick*, (fiction) Aquarian, 1985
Fortune, Dion, *The Sea Priestess*, (fiction) Samuel Weiser, 2000
Valiente, Doreen, *Natural Magic*, Phoenix Publishing Inc., 1985

Motherhood
Eason, Cassandra, *The Mother Link*, Ulysses Press, 1998
Eason, Cassandra, *Mother Love*, Constable Robinson, 1998
Thurer, Shari L., *The Myths of Motherhood: how Culture Reinvents the Good Mother*, Penguin, 1991

Mysticism
Maxwell, Meg and Tschudin, Verena, *Seeing the Invisible*, Arkana, 1990

Native North American Spirituality
Andrews, Lynn V., *Medicine Woman*, Arkana, 1991
Andrews, Lynn V., *Flight of the Seventh Moon*, Arkana 1992
Moondance, *Wolf Spirit Medicine*, Sterling, 1995

Psychic Protection
Eason, Cassandra, *Psychic Protection Lifts the Spirit*, Quantum, 2000
Fortune, Dion, *Psychic Self-Defence*, Aquarian, 1988

Shamanism
Johnson, Buffie, *Lady of the Beasts, Ancient Images of the Goddess and Her Sacred Animals*, Harper and Row, 1988
Johnson, Kenneth, *North Star Road*, Llewellyn, 1996
Wahoo, Dhyani, *Voices of our Ancestors*, Shambhala, 1987

Witchcraft
Adler, Margot, *Drawing Down the Moon*, Penguin, 1997
Crowley, Vivienne, *Wicca: the Old Religion on the New Age*, Aquarian, 1989
Farrar, Janet and Stewart, *The Witches' Goddess*, Phoenix Publishing, 1995
Guiley, Rosemary Ellen, *Encyclopedia of Witches and Witchcraft*, Facts on File, 1994
Galenorn, Yasmine, *Embracing the Moon*, Llewellyn, 1998
Murray, Margaret, *The God of the Witches*, Oxford University Press, 1992
Starhawk, *Dreaming the Dark*, Beacon Press Books, 1997
Starhawk, *The Spiral Dance*, Harper Row, 1999

Women and Sexuality; the Sacred Marriage

Ashe, Geoffrey, *The Goddess of Love*, Constable, 1984

Qualls-Corbett, Nancy, *The Sacred Prostitute: Eternal Aspect of the Feminine*, Inner City Books, 1988

Wolkstein, D. and Kramer, S.N., *Inanna, Queen of Heaven and Earth*, Harper and Collins, 1981

USEFUL ADDRESSES

Angel and Devic Workshops

UK
Findhorn Foundation,
The Park,
Forres,
Scotland IV36 OTS.

US
Two Angels,
PO Box 669,
Sedona AZ 86339.

AUSTRALIA
Vicki Engeham,
PO Box 1084,
Alice Springs,
Northern Territory 0861.

Celtic Spirituality

Caitlin and John Matthews,
BCM Hallowquest,
London WC1N 3XX.

Druids

UK
The Order of Bards, Ovates and
Druids,
(Also throughout the world. Strong
links with Australia.)
PO Box 1333,
Lewes,
East Sussex,
BN7 1DX.

Earth Energies

UK
British Society of Dowsers,
Sycamore Barn,
Hastingleigh,
Ashford,
Kent TN25 5HW.

US
The American Society of Dowsers,
Dowsers Hall,
Danville,
Vermont 05828-0024.

AUSTRALIA
Dowsers Society of New South Wales,
c/o Mrs. E. Miksevicius,
126 Fiddens Wharf Road,
Killara,
New South Wales 2031.

Southern Tasmania Dowsing
Association,
PO Box 101,
Moonah,
Tasmania,
Australia 7009.

Goddess Organisations

EUROPE
The Goddess Regenerated,
PO Box 73,
Sliema,
Malta.

UK

Fellowship of Isis,
(A worldwide network of Goddess worshippers.)
Lady Olivia Robertson,
Clonegal Castle,
Enniscorthy,
Co. Wexford, Eire.

US

Covenant of the Goddess,
PO Box 1226,
Berkeley CA 94704.

The Goddess Regenerated,
PO Box 269,
Valrico FL 33595.

Herbs and Oils

UK

PROFESSIONAL ORGANISATIONS
The National Institute of Medical Herbalists,
56 Longbrook Street,
Exeter,
Devon EX4 6AH.

The International Society of Professional Aromotherapists,
Hinckley and District Hospital and Health Centre (Head Office),
The Annexe,
Mount Road,
Hinckley,
Leicestershire LE10 1AG.

Information on Herbs

The Herb Society,
PO Box 599,
London SW11 4BW.

AUSTRALIA

PROFESSIONAL ORGANISATIONS
The National Institute of Medical Herbalists,
PO Box 65,
Kingsgrove,
New South Wales 2208.

Meditation, Visualisation and Shamanic Music

UK

Stress Busters,
Beechwood Music,
Littleton House,
Littleton Road,
Ashford,
MiddlesexTW15 1UU.

AUSTRALIA

New World Productions,
PO Box 244 WBO,
Red Hill,
Queensland 4059.

Meditation, Visualisation and Music

US

Raven Recordings,
744 Broad Street,
Room 1815,
Newark,
New Jersey 07102.

Mysticism and Occultism

The Secretariat,
Society of the Inner Light,
38 Steele's Road,
London NW3 4RG
(Correspondence courses.)

Paganism, Wicca and Witchcraft

UK
The Pagan Federation,
BM Box 7097,
London WC1N 3XX.

US
Circle Sanctuary,
(Contacts with 700 pagan groups,
networks, etc.)
PO Box 219,
Mount Horeb WI 53572.

Green Egg,
PO Box 1542,
Ukiah CA 954.

Temple of the Sacred Earth,
Phyllis W. Curott,
PO Box 311,
Princes Street Station,
New York City NY 10012.

The Witches' Voice Inc.,
(A resource organisation with
worldwide links.)
PO Box 4924,
Clearwater,
Florida 33758-4924.

Australia
Novocastrian Pagan Information
Centre,
Laren,
PO Box 129,
Stockton,
New South Wales 2295.

The Pagan Alliance,
(An umbrella movement for pagan
organisations.)
PO Box 823,
Bathurst,
New South Wales 2795.

Shamanism

UK
Shamanka,
(A women's shamanic empowerment
organisation.)
Middle Piccadilly,
Hotwell,
Dorset DT9 5LW.

Faculty of Shamanics,
Kenneth and Beryl Meadows,
PO Box 300,
Potters Bar,
Hertfordshire EN6 4LE.

US
Dance of the Deer Foundation,
Center for Shamanic Studies,
PO Box 699,
Soquel CA 95073.

Foundation of Shamanic Studies,
PO Box 1939,
Mill Valley CA 94942.

Spiritual Healing

UK
British Alliance of Healing
Associations,
Mrs Jo Wallace,
3 Sandy Lane,
Gisleham,
Lowestoft,
Suffolk NR33 8EQ.

National Federation of Spiritual
Healers,
Old Manor Farm Studio,
Church Street,
Sunbury on Thames,
Middlesex TW16 6RG.

US
World of Light,
(Has a list of healers.)
PO Box 425,
Wappingers Falls,
NY 12590.

Australia
Australian Spiritualist Association,
PO Box 248,
Canterbury,
New South Wales 2193.

Canada
National Federation of Spiritual
Healers (Canada),
Toronto, Ontario. Call for
information 284-4798.

Spiritualist Church of Canada,
1835 Laurence Ave East,
Scarborough,
Ontario M1TR 2Y3.

Cassandra Eason's website is at www.Cassandraeason.co.uk

COLOUR PLATE CREDITS

Mamacona, gold figurine, Peru, Inca, 1430–1532 AD, Museum fur Volkerkunde, Berlin. ©
Werner Forman Archive
Medusa, Detail of a floor mosaic, 2nd Century, Archaeological Museum, Tunisia. © AKG
London/Gilles Mermet
Gaia, mosaic from Church of Mirrata, Syria, Maarrat an-Numan Museum, Syria. © AKG,
Berlin/Jean-Louis Nou
The Sycamore goddess Nut pouring a liquid drunk by the bird-like soul of Nespawershefi,
plastered and painted wood, Dynasty XX1, 990–969 BC, Fitzwilliam Museum,
University of Cambridge, UK. © Bridgeman Art Library, London
Two Amazons in combat with a Greek Tarquinia, Museo Archeologico, Florence, Italy. ©
Bridgeman Art Library, London
Snake Goddess, terracotta, painted, Middle Minoan, 17th century BC, Found: Temple
depositories, Knossos, Archaeological Museum, Heraklion. © AKG Berlin/Erich Lessing
Queen Mab from Shelley's Poem by Henry Meynell Rheam (1859–1920), English, The Fine
Art Society, London, UK. © Bridgeman Art Library
Ishtar, ivory plaque, Nimrud, c. 725 BC, Iraq Museum, Baghdad. © Werner Forman Archive,
London
Fairy Morgan, French illumination, 15th century, from *Le livre de Lancelot du lac*, Ms. francais
116, fol. 688 v, Bibliotheque Nationale, Paris. © AKG London
Sirens, Arnold Böcklin (1827–1901), tempera on canvas, 1875, National Gallery, Berlin. ©
AKG London
Kali, Indian miniature, gouache on fabric, 17th century, Chandigarh Museum. © AKG
Berlin/Jean-Louis Nou
Kwakiutl house post, Museum of Anthropology, University of British Columbia, Vancouver. ©
Werner Forman Archive, London
Hathor, ivory, 12th–14th century BC, Found: Megiddo, Israel, Rockefeller Museum. © AKG
London/Erich Lessing
Mayan woman weaving, terracotta, Jaina Island, 600–900 BC, National Museum of
Anthropology, Mexico City. © Werner Forman Archive, London
Vishnu and Lakshmi, miniature, Jodhpur Museum, India. © AKG Berlin/Jean-Louis Nou
Sarasvati, Indian sculpture, 12th century, Pallu, Rajasthan. © AKG London/Irmgard Wagner
Two Witches Riding on a Broomstick, 15th century, French, Bibliotheque Nationale, Paris. ©
AKG London
Alberich curses Wotan and Loge, Franz Stassen, coloured lithograph, 1914. © AKG London
The Fortune-teller, on wood, Lucas van Leyden (1494–1533), Musee du Louvre, Paris. © AKG
London/Erich Lessing
Venus of Willendorf, chalky sandstone statuette painted with red chalk, c. 2,000 BC, Found:
Willendorf, Austria, Natural History Museum, Vienna. © AKG London/.Erich Lessing
Dispute of Saint Catherine of Alexandria, Bicci di Lorenzo (1373–1452), on wood, Museo
Banaini, Fiesole. © AKG Berlin/S. Domingie
Birth of Aphrodite, marble relief, c. 470 BC, Museo Nazionale Romano delle Terme, Rome. ©
AKG London/Erich Lessing
Brigit, Kerguilly en Dineault, bronze, Finistere, France, 1st century AD, Musee de Rennes. ©
Werner Forman Library, London
Persephone and Hecate, stone relief, 5th century BC, Archaeological Museum, Eleusis. © AKG
London/Erich Lessing
Mary with the Child Jesus, Raphael (1483–1520), tempera on canvas (on wood), c. 1502/03,
State Hermitage, St Petersburg. © AKG London
The Black Virgin given by Louis XI, 18th century, French School, Musee Crozatier, Le Puy-en-
Velay, France. © Giraudon/Bridgeman Art Library

INDEX